GREY HAWK

LIFE AND ADVENTURES AMONG THE RED INDIANS

By John Tanner

THE NARRATIVE PRESS
TRUE FIRST-PERSON HISTORICAL ACCOUNTS

This publication is a reproduction of an original edited by James MaCaulay, A.M., M.D., and published by J. B. Lippincott & Co., 715 and 717 Market Street, Philadelphia: 1883

The Narrative Press
P.O. Box 2487, Santa Barbara, California 93120 U.S.A.
Telephone: (800) 315-9005 Web: www.narrativepress.com

ISBN 1-58976-259-2 (Paperback)

CONTENTS

INTRODUCTION.

About fifty years ago there came to New York a man, who wore the dress and spoke the language of the Whites, but in his appearance, habits, ideas, and ways was more like a Red Indian. He was then in the employment of the United States Government as Indian interpreter, at Sault de St. Marie, to which northern outpost he was soon to return.

His had been a life of strange incident and adventure. When yet a boy, he had been carried off from his father's home in Kentucky by a marauding band of Shawnees, from whom he was transferred to the Ojibbeways, by a chief of which tribe he was purchased, and adopted by his wife, in place of a son who had died. At first he had hope of making his escape, but, finding this impossible, he became naturalized among the Indians, sharing their adventures and hardships, and living among them as one of themselves, during thirty years. He thus came to know more of their customs and manners, of their occupations and whole life, than perhaps had ever been known before by any white man.

When at New York he met an American physician, Dr. E. James, the same who had written an account of Major Long's expedition to the Rocky Mountains. To him he gave many details of his past life, which were published in 1830, under the title of "Narrative of John Tanner's thirty years' captivity among the Indians in the interior of North America." His father's name was Tanner, but among the Indians he had been called the Falcon, or Grey Hawk.

The book, as originally published, contained not only the incidents of his life, but also disquisitions and essays upon the natural history, traditions, languages, religion, and the political relations of the various tribes, at that time, to the American Government. Much of this matter is of limited, and some of it of temporary and bygone importance; but it appears to the present editor that the story of Indian life and adventure would prove of permanent interest to youthful readers, both in England and America, and on that account worthy of reproduction. The personal narrative is in the main a reprint from the original work, with the omissions already indicated, and with only such alterations as seemed necessary for the structure of a story which is founded on fact. That the book will afford amusement, and convey instruction, there is no doubt; and the editor hopes it will also serve the higher purpose of interesting many readers in the condition and prospects of a people whose history is full of mysterious romance, and who have in recent times shown themselves capable of civilization, and of becoming good citizens and good Christians.

The position of the Indian race is widely different now from what it was at the time of this story. In the early part of this century the Red men were still numerous and powerful in the States east of the Mississippi. They hunted their game, and built their lodges in regions which are now richly cultivated and densely peopled. Cities, which are to-day the busy marts of commerce, were then remote outposts of civilization. Chicago, for instance, was then only known as a small trading station. Of the fierce and dangerous race, branches of which once spread along the Atlantic and Gulf coasts, not a tribe now remains on its original soil. The sons of the hunters and warriors of other days have learned the arts of peace. They plough the soil, plant corn, build houses, schools and churches; for they are adopting the religion and knowledge, as well as the arts and laws of the white men. Most of them have fixed settlements on lands reserved for them, one of which—"the Indian Territory"—set apart for the tribes removed from the Mississippi States, is a space of nearly 70,000 square miles of fertile country.

It is the same in Canada. Large numbers of the Indians have there also settled down in peaceful and industrial life, in fixed districts, and receiving, as their brethren in the States do, certain gifts and annuities, as compensation for territories ceded by them, or taken from them. A curious illustration of the altered state of life was witnessed not long ago in England, when the hereditary chief of the once formidable Ojibbeway nation, Coming Thunder, as his native designation would be, appeared as the Rev. H. Pahtahquahong Chase, an ordained clergyman, in the diocese of the Bishop of Huron.

Lake Winnipeg, and the Assineboin River, and other places, which are constantly named in this story, are now attracting hosts of emigrants, who have already formed the rising province of Manitoba. The Indians are now seldom seen in the old places, except when they come for peaceful trading, or to receive their annuities at the stations. In the same way the Indians of the American Republic are never seen by the people of the older States, except when occasionally some chiefs or delegates come from afar to Washington, to pay their respects to the Great Father, the President, and to transact some business about their annuities or reserves.

But beyond the ever-advancing lines of settled territories, on the Pacific slopes in the States, and in the remote regions of the Canadian North-West, large numbers of Indians still lead their old independent and nomadic life. On the north of the boundary line these remnants of the ancient race give little trouble, being chiefly engaged in their old pursuits of hunting, fishing, and trading. On American soil they more frequently meet the Whites in fierce conflict, in the vain effort to stem the tide of westward colonization. The white border ruffians too often shoot them down as vermin, and it is therefore no wonder that the old war spirit is not extinct. The main pretext for maintaining even a small standing army by the United States Government is defence against the hostile Indians. The duties of the troops would be lighter if the Red men were more protected from the aggressive violence of the settlers.

Till this protection is more efficient, there is little hope of the nomadic tribes of the far west being soon brought under the influences of peace and civilization.

Chapter I.

***RECOLLECTIONS OF MY EARLY LIFE—CAPTURE
BY SHAWNEE INDIANS—FLIGHT AND PUR-
SUIT—JOURNEY FROM THE MIAMI RIVER TO
SAU-GE-NONG—ILL-TREATMENT BY THE INDI-
ANS—CEREMONIES OF ADOPTION INTO THE
FAMILY OF MY FOSTER PARENTS—MANITO-O-
GHEEZIK, CHIEF OF THE BAND, AND HIS SON
KISH-KAW-KO, MAKE ME WORK LIKE A SLAVE-
BOY.***

The first event of my life of which I have any recollection
is the death of my mother. This happened before I was three
years old. I have no distinct remembrance of her person, but
only of the love with which she loved me, and of the aching
void in my young life when I saw her no more, and heard her
voice no more. That impression of blank grief long remained
with me. I do not remember the name of the place where we
then lived, but have since learned that it was on the Kentucky
River, at a considerable distance from the Ohio. My father,
whose name was John Tanner, had come from Virginia to settle, upon new land, as many were then doing, and he
removed, soon after my mother's death, to a place called Elk
Horn.

Of this settlement at Elk Horn, where we stayed several
years, I have a few distinct recollections. Not far from our
house there was a cavern in the solid rock, which I sometimes
went to with my elder brother. We took two candles; one we
lighted on entering, and went on till it was almost burnt down;

then we lighted the other, and began to return, reaching the mouth of the cavern before it was quite burned out. I have since been told that there are vast underground caves in that part of the country, but I suppose our cavern was one which two boys could visit without danger of losing ourselves. We only thought it a sort of adventure to go through the dark cave with a light in our hand.

A more constant excitement in those early years was what we heard about the Indians. Hostile parties of the Shawnee tribe had occasionally visited the settlement at Elk Horn, driving away cattle and horses, and sometimes killing white people. One night, my uncle, my father's brother, went out with other men to surprise a camp of these Indians, which they knew was in the neighbourhood, and from which they feared an attack. They came upon the camp unobserved, and firing into it, killed one man, the rest escaping, some of them jumping into the river. My uncle brought home the scalp of the slain Indian, and it was hung up, like the skin of vermin, on the outside of one of the log cabins.

In the course of our residence at this place an incident occurred, to the influence of which I attributed many of the disasters of my subsequent life. My father was starting early one morning to go to a distant village, and gave, as it appeared, a strict charge to my two sisters, to send me to school. It was wet and unpleasant weather, and they neglected to attend to my father's charge till the afternoon. It being still rainy, I then insisted on staying at home. When my father returned in the evening, and found that I had been at home all day, he sent me for a bundle of small canes, and flogged me far more severely than I thought the offence merited. I was displeased with my sisters for laying the whole blame upon me, saying I had refused to go; which was true as to the afternoon, but they had neglected to tell me I was to go to school in the forenoon. From that day my father's house was less like home to me, and I often thought and said, "I wish I could go and live among the Indians."

I cannot tell how long we remained at Elk Horn. My father did not find farming there answer his expectation, and he determined to remove. Having arranged his affairs, we set out with our horses and wagons, and the cattle, and the goods we were to take with us. After travelling two days we came to the Ohio River. My father bought three flat-bottomed boats. In one we embarked, having the bedding and other furniture; in the second we put the cattle and horses; and in the third were some negroes, with the remainder of our property. The cattle boat and the family boat were lashed together. We descended the Ohio, and on the morning of the third day came to Cincinnati. Here the cattle boat, which had been leaking badly, sunk in the middle of the river. When my father saw it was in a sinking state, he jumped on board, and cut loose all the cattle, and they swam ashore on the Kentucky side of the river. The people from Cincinnati had by this time come out in boats to assist us, but my father told them that all the cattle and the horses were safe.

In one day we went from Cincinnati to the mouth of the Big Miami River, opposite which we were to settle. Here was some cleared land, and one or two log cabins, but these had been deserted on account of the Indians. My father repaired the cabins, and enclosed them with a strong stockade. It was early in the spring when we arrived at the mouth of the Big Miami, and we were soon engaged in preparing a field to plant corn. I think it was not more than ten days after our arrival, when my father told us in the morning, that, from the restlessness of the horses, there had been Indians near us in the night, and that they were probably lurking about in the woods. He said to me, "John, you must not go out of the house today." After giving strict charge to his wife, my step-mother, to let none of the children go out till his return, he went to the field, with my elder brother and the negroes, to drop corn.

During the forenoon, I became impatient of confinement. Watching an opportunity, when my step-mother was occupied with her baby-child, I escaped unnoticed into the yard; thence through a small door in the large gate of the enclosure into the open field. There was a walnut-tree at some distance from the house, at the side of the field nearest the uncleared woods, where I had been in the habit of going to look for some of last year's nuts. To get to this tree, without being seen by my father and those with him in the field, I had to use some precaution. I remember perfectly well how I could see my father, and how I watched him, as I was skulking towards the tree. He stood in the middle of the field where they were, with his gun in his hand, to watch for Indians, while the others were all dropping the seed corn. As I came near the tree, I thought to myself, "I wish I could see these Indians." Soon I was busy looking for nuts, and finding a good many, I put them into the straw hat which I wore.

Suddenly I heard a crackling noise not far off in the wood behind me. Turning round I saw some Indians, and in an instant, before I could utter a cry if I had so wished, I was seized by both my hands by two Indians, and dragged off between them toward the wood. One of them took my straw hat, emptied the nuts on the ground, and clapped the hat on my head. We were soon far from the house and fields. It all happened so quickly that I was not conscious of anything that passed for some time. I can only remember that of the two who seized me one was an old man and the other a young man. Their names I learned subsequently were Manito-o-gheezik and his son Kish-kaw-ko.

Long afterwards, I heard several particulars relative to my capture, which were of course unknown to me at the time, and which it may be as well now to record. It appears that the wife of Manito had recently lost her youngest son, and was in great grief. She said to her husband that unless he could bring back her son, she could not live. This he took as an intimation that he must bring to her a captive whom she could adopt in the place of her lost boy. Manito then lived at Lake Huron, and, taking with him his son Kish-kaw-ko and two other Indians, he travelled eastward with this sole design. On the upper part of Lake Erie, they had been joined by three other young men, and they proceeded on, now seven in number, to the settlements which were then being newly formed on the Ohio. They had arrived the night previous to my capture at the mouth of the Big Miami, had crossed the Ohio, and concealed themselves within sight of our house. The horses had been disturbed on hearing their stealthy reconnoitring that night. Several times in the course of the next morning old Manito-o-gheezik had the utmost difficulty in restraining the ardour of the young men, especially the three who had joined the party. They became impatient at seeing no opportunity to steal a boy, nor could the others be expected to think of this, as much as the old man and his son did. They were more anxious for plunder, and wished suddenly to attack and fire upon the people who were dropping corn in the field. Only my father had a gun, and several of them had firearms. It must have been about noon when they espied me coming in their direction and stopping at the walnut-tree, which was not far from their place of concealment.

I have also been since told that my father came back from the field not many minutes after I had been taken. My step-mother had not noticed that I was absent, till my father, not seeing me, said, "Where is John?" My brother ran immediately to the walnut-tree, which he knew was my favourite place of resort, and saw the heap of nuts which the Indians had emptied out of my hat. A sudden instinctive feeling, arising from our father's warning words in the morning, led him at once to fear that I had been made captive. Search was instantly made for me, but to no purpose. My father's distress, when he found that I was indeed taken away by Indians, was, I have been told, very great. Perhaps he thought then of his own harshness and comparative want of feeling toward me, although I believe it was due more to roughness of ways, caused by his life of hardship and anxiety, than to lack of real affection. I also now regret that I ever was disobedient or troublesome; but of such feelings I knew nothing at the time I am describing, and to which I must now come back. I had no thoughts then except fear and surprise, which filled my mind as soon as consciousness returned to me; for I had fainted soon after the first rush, and on recovering I was lying on the ground beside a great log, which must have been at a considerable distance from the house.

We were quickly moving again, as my captors no doubt feared pursuit. The old man I did not now see; I was dragged along between Kish-kaw-ko and a very short, thick man. I had probably caused some check to the pace, which he supposed to be resistance on my part, or had done something or other to irritate this man, for he took me a little to one side, and drawing his tomahawk, motioned to me to look up. This I plainly understood, from the expression of his face and his manner, to be a direction for me to look up for the last time, as he was about to kill me. I did as he directed; but do not know whether he was really enraged or only intended to terrify me. Kish-kaw-ko seemed to think he was in earnest, for he seized his arm as the tomahawk was descending, as if he feared he was going to split my head open. Loud and fierce talking ensued between them. Kish-kaw-ko presently raised a shrill yell, which was evidently a signal, for the old man and the four others answered by a similar yell, and came running up. I have since understood that Kish-kaw-ko complained to his father that the short man had made an attempt to kill his little brother, as he called me. The old chief, after reproving him, took me by one hand, and Kis-kaw-ko by the other, and dragged me betwixt them; the man who had threatened me, and who was now an object of terror to me, being kept at some distance.

It is possible that the man had only been provoked by the degree to which I retarded their speed, and so endangered their own lives; for they must have been apprehensive of being overtaken.

More than a mile from my father's house we came to the river Ohio, where they thrust me into a hickorybark canoe, which was concealed under the bushes upon the bank. Into this canoe they all seven leaped, and swiftly crossed the river, landing at the mouth of the Big Miami, and on the south side. Here they abandoned the canoe, and stuck their paddles in the ground, so that they could be seen from the river. At a little distance in the woods they had some blankets and provisions concealed. They offered me some; but I could not eat. They could see my father's house; they pointed it out, looking at me, and speaking and laughing, but I have never known what they said.

After they had eaten and made a short halt, they began to ascend the bank of the Miami, dragging me along as before. They took off my shoes, as they seemed to think I could run better without them. Although I perceived I was closely watched, all hope of escape did not immediately forsake me. While they hurried me along, I endeavoured to take notice of such objects as might serve as waymarks in case of need. A hope entered my mind that I might escape after they should have fallen asleep at night. I had even the presence of mind, when we came to any long grass, or soft ground, to try to leave tracks, in case pursuers passed that way.

When night came they lay down, placing me between the old chief and Kish-kaw-ko, so close together that the one blanket covered all three. I was so fatigued that I fell asleep immediately, and did not wake till sunrise next morning, when the Indians were up and ready to proceed on their journey.

Thus we travelled for about four days; the Indians hurrying me on, and I continuing to hope that I might escape, but still every night so fatigued that as soon as I lay down I was immediately overpowered with sleep. My feet being bare, they were often bruised and wounded, and at length were much swollen. The old man perceiving my lameness, examined my feet, and after removing some thorns and splinters, and putting some cool leaves round at night, gave me in the morning a pair of leather moccasins, which afforded considerable relief. The first day I had scarcely been able to eat, and felt very weak as well as weary; but I had begun to take some of the dried strip venison, which they carried with them, but could not touch the bear's fat, which they relished.

It was, I think, four days after we left the Ohio, that we came to a considerable river, running, as I suppose, into the Miami. This river was wide, and so deep, that I could not wade across it; the old man took me on his shoulders and carried me over; the water was nearly up to his arm-pits. As he was carrying me across, I thought I should never be able to cross this deep river alone, and gave up all hope of immediate escape.

When he put me down on the other side I ran up the bank, and a short distance into the wood, when a turkey rose and flew up at only a few steps before me. The nest she had left contained a number of eggs, which I put into the bosom of my shirt, and returned with them towards the river. When the Indians saw what I had got, they laughed, and took the eggs from me. Then kindling a fire they put them in a small kettle to boil. I was then hungry, and sat watching and waiting for a portion of food which I could enjoy. Suddenly the old chief came running as fast as he could from the direction of the ford where we had crossed; he caught up the kettle, threw the eggs and the water on the fire, at the same time saying something, in a hurried and low tone, to the young men. I inferred that he was afraid of the smoke of the fire being seen if there was a hue and cry after me. I knew my people would not soon give up the pursuit, and have since understood that they did not. My father and the others being mounted on horses, they would have probably overtaken the Indians, although they ran so swiftly, but had lost the tracks when we crossed the river.

The old chief may possibly have espied some of them on the opposite side. The Indians hastily gathered up the eggs, and dispersed themselves in the woods, two of them still urging me forward to the utmost of my strength.

It was a day or two after this that we met a party of between twenty and thirty Indians, on their way towards the settlements. The old chief had much to say to them. Subsequently I learned that they were a war party of Shawnees; that from our party they received information of the whites who were in pursuit of us about the fords of the Miami River; that they went thither; and that, having fallen in with them, a severe skirmish took place, in which many were wounded, and some killed on both sides.

Our journey through the forest was tedious and painful. It might have been ten days after we met the war party, when we arrived at the Maumee River. The Indians now scattered about the woods examining the trees, yelling and answering each other. They soon selected a hickory-tree, which was cut down, and the bark stripped off to make a canoe. In this canoe we all embarked, and descended till we came to a large Shawnee village, at the mouth of a river, which enters the Maumee.

As we were landing, great numbers of Shawnees came about us. There was much talking, part of which was no doubt about me. One young woman, as soon as she saw me, ran up, with a loud cry, and struck me on the head. Some of her friends had been killed by the whites. Others of the Shawnees looked fiercely, as if disposed to kill me, but Kis-kaw-ko and the old man interposed and prevented them. I could see that I was often the subject of conversation and arguing. The old chief knew a few words of English, which he occasionally used, to direct me to fetch water, make a fire, or perform other tasks which he required of me.

We remained two days at this Shawnee village, and then proceeded on our journey in the canoe. Not very far from the village we came to a trading-house, where were three or four half-breed men, who could speak English. They spoke to me, and told me, after a good deal of talking, that they wished to have purchased me from the Indians, so as to restore me to my friends, for which they probably expected a reward. But the old man would not consent to part with me, so the traders told me I must be content to go with the Indians, and to become the old man's son, in the place of one he had lost; promising at the same time that after ten days they would come to his village, which they knew and visited, and try to get me released. They treated me kindly while they stayed, and gave me plenty to eat, which the Indians had neglected to do. When I found that I was compelled to leave this place along with the Indians, I began to cry for the first time since I had been taken. I consoled myself, however, with their promise that they would after ten days come for me.

Soon after leaving this trading-house, we came to the lake. We did not stop to encamp; but soon after dark the Indians raised a yell, which was answered from where there were some lights on shore, and presently a canoe came off, in which three of our party left us. I have little recollection of anything that passed from this time till we arrived at Detroit. At first we paddled up in the middle of the stream till we came opposite the centre of the town; then we ran in near the shore, where I saw a white woman, with whom the Indians held a little conversation, but I could not understand what was said. I also saw several white men standing and talking on shore, and heard them talk, but could not understand a word. It is likely that they were speaking French. After exchanging a few words with the woman, the Indians pushed off, and ran up a good distance from the town.

It was about the middle of the day when we landed in the woods, and drew up the canoe. They presently found a large hollow log, open at one end, into which they put their blankets, their kettle, and some other articles. They then made signs for me to crawl into it, after which they rolled some other logs so as to close up and conceal the end at which I had entered. I heard them talk for some time on the outside, then all was still, and remained so for some time. If I had not long since relinquished all hope of making my escape, I soon found it would be in vain to attempt to release myself from my present confinement. After remaining some hours in this situation, I heard them return, and they began to remove the logs with which they had confined me in the hollowed tree. On coming out, I could perceive, although it was very late in the night, or probably near morning, that they had brought three horses. On one of these they placed me, on the others their baggage; and sometimes one, sometimes another of the Indians riding, we travelled rapidly, and in about three days reached Sau-ge-nong, the village to which old Manito-o-gheezik belonged. This village, or settlement, consisted of several scattered houses or huts. Two of the Indians left us soon after we entered it, Kish-kaw-ko and his father only remaining. Instead of proceeding directly to their home, they left their horses, and borrowed a canoe, in which we at last arrived at the old man's house. This was a hut or cabin built of logs.

As soon as we landed, Manito's wife came down to us to the shore, and after he had said a few words to her, she commenced crying, at the same time hugging and kissing me, and thus she led me to the house.

Next day they took me to the place where the old woman's son had been buried. The grave was enclosed with a rude stockade, and on each side of it was a smooth open place. Here they all seated themselves,—the family and relations of Manito-o-gheezik on the one side, and strangers on the other. They had not long been thus assembled, when my party began to dance, dragging me with them about the grave. The dance was energetic and lively, after the manner of the scalp dance, which I afterwards saw. From time to time, as they danced, they presented me with something of the articles they had brought; but as I came round in the dancing to the party on the opposite side of the grave, whatever they had given was snatched from me. Thus they continued for a long time, until the presents were exhausted, and they themselves wearied, as I was, when they returned home.

It must have been early in the spring when we arrived at Sau-ge-nong, for I can remember that at this time the leaves were small, and the Indians were about planting their corn. They managed to make me assist them in their work, partly by signs, and partly by the few words of English which old Manito-o-gheezik could speak. After planting, they all left the village and went out to hunt, to obtain meat, of which they cut up and dried the largest part. When they came to their hunting-grounds, they chose a place where many deer resorted, and here they began to build a long screen like a fence, made of green boughs and small trees. When they had built part of it, they showed me how to remove the leaves and twigs from the side of the fence, to which the Indians were to come to shoot the deer. In this labour I was sometimes assisted by the squaws and children, but at other times I was left alone. It had become warmer weather now, and it happened one day that having been left alone, being tired and thirsty, I left my work, and, lying down, I fell asleep. I cannot tell how long I slept; but when I began to awake, I thought I heard some one crying a great way off. Then I tried to raise my head, but could not. Being now more awake, I saw my Indian mother and sister standing by me, and they were crying bitterly. I soon perceived that I had been badly hurt in my head, which was swollen and gave great pain. It appears that while I was lying asleep, Manito came, and on seeing me, in his passion, gave me a terrible blow with his tomahawk, by which I was stunned. He thought probably that I was dead, for he took me up and threw me into the bushes; but my head was only cut, and the force of the blow had made me insensible. When the old man went back to the camp, he had said to his wife, "Old woman, the boy I brought to you is lazy and good for nothing; I have killed him, and you will find him in the bushes near the fence." The old woman and her daughter having found me, discovered still some signs of life; and having brought water to wash my head, they had stood over me for a long time, pitying me and crying in their grief. After a time, I was able, with their help, to get back to the huts, and in a few days I was enough recovered to be again set to work at the screen. I was now more careful not to fall asleep, and I endeavoured to work to the best of my knowledge and strength in whatever they gave me directions to do. Notwithstanding my efforts to please them, I was treated with great harshness by the old man and by two sons, younger brothers of Kish-kaw-ko.

When we returned from hunting, I carried on my back a large pack of the dried venison all the way to the village; but though sometimes almost starved, I dared not touch a morsel of it. My Indian mother, who really had some compassion for me, would sometimes secretly hide some food for me, and give it to me after the old man had gone out. Later in the summer, whenever the weather was favourable, the young men were engaged in spearing fish, and they took me to steer the canoe. As I did not know how to do this well at the first, they would often turn upon me, strike me, or knock me down with the pole of the spear. By one or other of them I was beaten almost every day. Whether they were vexed at their mother having taken the fancy to adopt another son, and so have another mouth to feed, or some other feeling of jealousy or dislike caused it, I was treated very badly. Some of the Indians, not of our family, would sometimes seem to pity me, and when they could, without being observed by the old chief, they would give me food and take notice of me, as the women did when we were at home.

In the fall or autumn, after the corn was gathered in, and placed in the caches or pits where they hide it for the winter, they went to hunt on the Sau-ge-nong River. Here, as had always been when I went out with them, I was often distressed with hunger. In the woods I saw them picking up and eating some nuts, which I found very good to one so hungry, and which I knew afterwards to be beech-nuts.

We were still engaged in hunting when winter came on, and snow began to fall. I was compelled to follow the hunters, and made sometimes to drag to the lodge a whole deer, if they found that I could at all move it All this expedition I had to toil beyond my strength, with poorly supplied food, and cruelly harsh treatment. Towards the end of winter we removed towards the sugar grounds, to be ready for tapping the sweet juice of the maple when it begins to rise in the trees.

Chapter II.

*KISH-KAW-KO AND OTHERS GO ON A RAID
AGAINST THE WHITES—ON THEIR RETURN
REPORT THAT ALL MY FAMILY WERE KILLED—I
LOSE ALL HOPE OF ESCAPE—AFTER A YEAR AND
A HALF MY CAPTORS GO TO ATTEND A COUNCIL
HELD AT MACKINAC—THEY MEET THERE A
KINS-WOMAN, NET-NO-KWA, HEAD OF THE
OTTAWWAW TRIBES—SHE OFFERS TO PUR-
CHASE ME—THE BARGAIN COMPLETED—
TREATED AS A SON BY NET-NO-KWA AND HER
HUSBAND—ENTRUSTED WITH A PISTOL AND
SHOOT PIGEONS—TAUGHT HOW TO TRAP MAR-
TENS—CAMPING IN THE FOREST—GO WITH
SOME MUSKEGO INDIANS TO LAKE SUPERIOR—
THENCE TO THE LAKE OF THE WOODS AND
LAKE WINNIPEG.*

At this time, Kish-kaw-ko, along with four other young Indians, resolved to go on a war expedition. The old man, as soon as the sugar was finished, and they returned to their village, with other Indians, also made preparations to start. Having now been a year among them I could understand a little of their language. The old man, when he was about to start, said to me, "Now I am going to kill your father and brother, and all your relations." All the time they were away my thoughts were troubled and anxious. The first to return was Kish-kaw-ko. He was ill, from a bad wound. He said he had been with his party to the Ohio River; that they had, after watching for some time concealed on the bank, fired upon a small boat going down the stream, and had killed one man, the rest jumping into the river. In pursuing them Kish-kaw-ko had wounded himself in the thigh with his own spear, and had to be helped by his companions to get back to their home. They brought with them the scalp of the man they had killed in the boat.

The old chief returned a few days afterwards. He brought with him an old white hat, which I knew, from a mark in the crown inside, to be that of my brother.

He said he had killed all my father's family, and the negroes, and the horses, and had brought my brother's hat that I might see he spoke the truth. I now believed that my friends had all been cut off, and was on that account the less anxious to return. This, I think, was the purpose of the old man, who was thereby relieved from the fear of my leaving them, for I had now become more useful to him as a drudge in all sorts of work.

But only a small part of his story was true. Long after, when I had left my life among the Indians, I went to see Kish-kaw-ko, who was in prison at Detroit, and I asked him, "Is it true that your father has killed all my relations?" He told me it was not true; that Manito-o-gheezik, the year after I was taken, returned to the woods near our house, about the same season; that, as on the preceding year, he had watched my father and his people planting corn, from morning to noon; that then they all went into the house except my brother (who was then nineteen years of age). He remained in the field ploughing with a span of horses, having the lines about his neck, when the Indians rushed upon him. The horses, terrified, started to run. My brother was entangled in the lines and thrown down, when the Indians seized him. The horses they killed, and carried my brother away into the woods. They crossed the Ohio before night, and had proceeded a good distance in their way up the Miami. At night they bound my brother to a tree, securely as they thought. His hands and arms were tied behind him, and there were cords round his neck and breast, but having managed to bite through some of the cords, he got a knife that was in his pocket, with which he cut himself loose. He immediately ran towards the Ohio, at which he arrived, and which he swam across, and reached my father's house at sunrise in the morning. The Indians were roused by the noise he made at first getting away, and pursued him into the woods, but in the darkness of the night were not able to overtake him. His hat had been left in the camp, and this they brought to make me believe that they had killed him.

All this I learned long after. In the belief that my father and his people were dead, I remained another year with the Indians under Manito-o-gheezik, gradually having less and less hope of escape, although I did not forget what the traders on the Mauinee had said about coming to fetch me. I wished they would remember their promise. It was a life of much misery. Often the men got drunk and sought to kill me. At such times I ran and hid myself in the woods, and dared not return till the drunken bout was over. They got the rum from other Indians, who had obtained it in bartering with the traders. During these two years the suffering at times from actual hunger was terrible. Though strangers, not of the family, sometimes gave me food, I had never enough to eat If it had not been for the old woman—"the Otter woman" as they called her, the Otter being her *totem*, or mark—and her daughter I must have perished of hunger. Kish-kaw-ko, the eldest son, was only a slight degree less savage and cruel than the father and the two younger brothers, who continually maltreated me. Only once while I was at Sau-ge-nong did I ever see white men. Then a small boat passed, and the Indians took me out to it in a canoe, threatening to kill me if I said anything, but rightly supposing that my wretched appearance might excite the compassion of the traders or whatever white men they might be in the boat. They threw to me some bread, apples, and other things, all which, except one apple, the Indians took from me.

I had been a little more than two years at Sau-ge-nong when a great council was called by the British agents at Mackinac. This council was attended by the Sioux, the Winnebagoes, and many remote tribes of Indians, as well as by the Ojibbeways, Ottawwaws, and others nearer the place of council. Manito-o-gheezik went, and on his return I soon learned that he had there met his kinswoman, Net-no-kwa, who, notwithstanding her sex, was regarded as the principal chief of all the Ottawwaws. This woman had lost her son, of about my age, by death; and having heard of me from sonic of our people, she wished to purchase me to supply her son's place. Whether this is common, or whether she was struck with the fancy on hearing that it had been done by "the Otter woman," the wife of Manito, her kinsman, I do not know. When my Indian mother, the Otter woman, heard the proposal she was angry, and vehemently protested. I heard her say, "My son was dead and has been restored to me; I cannot lose him again." She really had come to regard me with motherly affection, and she would have treated me with more marked kindness had she not known that this would have led her husband and the sons to deal more harshly with me, if not to kill me. But all her remonstrances proved unavailing when the great Net-no-kwa arrived at our village with some of her people, and bringing a large keg of whisky, tobacco, blankets, and other valuable articles. She was thoroughly acquainted with the dispositions and wants of those with whom she had come to negociate. After plenty of drinking and smoking, and making presents, the objections to my removal were overcome, and the men prevented the Otter woman from making further protest. So the bargain was completed, while more drink was following, and I was transferred to Net-no-kwa.

This woman, although more advanced in years, was of a more pleasing aspect than my former Indian mother. She took me by the hand, after she had completed the negociations with my last possessors, and led me to her own lodge, which stood near. Here I was soon aware that I would be treated with more indulgence than I had been during the two years of servile drudgery I had passed. She gave me plenty of food, good clothes, and told me to play with her own sons. We did not remain long at Sau-ge-nong. She would not stop at Mackinac, perhaps fearing that questions might be asked by the white agents there, but ran along during the night to Point St. Ignace, where she hired some Indians to take charge of me; and then she herself returned to Mackinac, with one or two attendants, as she had some business still to transact there. This being finished she came back to Point St. Ignace, and continuing our journey we arrived in a few days at a place called Shab-a-wy-wy-a-gun. The corn was ripe when we reached this place, and having waited till it was gathered we proceeded three days up the river towards where they intended to pass the winter. We then left our canoes, and travelling over land camped three times before we came to the place where we set up our lodges or wigwams for the winter.

The husband of Net-no-kwa was an Ojibbeway of Red River, called Taw-ga-we-ninne, or the Hunter. He was many years younger than Net-no-kwa, and had dismissed a former wife on being married to her. He was kind to me from the first, and treated me as one of the family, always calling me his son when speaking to me. Indeed, he was himself only of secondary importance in the family, as everything belonged to Net-no-kwa, and she had the direction in all affairs of any moment. She imposed on me my tasks after arrival. She made me cut wood, bring home game, and perform other services not commonly required of boys of my age; but the training turned out to be useful to me, and as I was kindly treated and had plenty of food, my position was greatly better and I was far more contented than I had been in my former home. I sometimes was struck by her, as were her own sons, if they displeased her, but I never was so severely and frequently beaten as I had been before.

Early in the spring Net-no-kwa and her husband, with their family, started to go to Mackinac. They left me, as they had done before, at Point St. Ignace, as they would not run the risk of losing me by suffering me to be seen at Mackinac. On our return, after we had gone about twenty-five or thirty miles from Point St. Ignace, we were detained by contrary winds at a place running out into the lake. Here we encamped with some other Indians and a party of traders. Pigeons were very numerous in the woods, and the boys of my age and the traders were busy shooting them. I had never killed any game, and indeed had never in my life discharged a gun. Taw-ga-we-ninne had a large horseman's pistol, and being emboldened by his indulgent manner toward me, I requested permission to go and try to kill some pigeons with the pistol. My request was seconded by Net-no-kwa, who said, "It is time for our son to begin to learn to be a hunter." Accordingly my father, as I called Taw-ga-we-ninne, loaded the pistol and gave it to me saying. "Go, my son, and if you kill anything with this you shall immediately have a gun and learn to hunt."

Since I have been a man I have been often placed in difficult situations; but my anxiety for success was never greater than in this, my first essay as a hunter. I had not gone far from the camp before I met with pigeons, and some of them alighted in the bushes very near me. I cocked my pistol, and raised it to my face, bringing the breech almost in contact with my nose. Having brought the sight to bear upon the pigeon, I pulled the trigger, and was in the next instant sensible of a humming noise, like that of a stone sent swiftly through the air. I found the pistol at some paces behind me, and the pigeon under the tree on which he had been sitting. I ran home, carrying my pigeon in triumph, but my face was much bruised and covered with blood. The wounded face was soon healed; my pistol was exchanged for a fowling-piece; I was accoutred with a powder-horn, and furnished with shot, and allowed to go out after birds. One of the young Indians went with me, to observe my manner of shooting. I killed three more pigeons in the course of the afternoon, and did not discharge my gun once without killing. Henceforth I began to be treated with more consideration, and was allowed to hunt often, that I might become expert.

Great part of the summer and autumn passed before we returned to our own village, and when we arrived we found the Indians suffering from a severe visitation of the measles. Net-no-kwa being unwilling to expose herself and the family, passed through the village, and encamped on the river above. But, notwithstanding her precaution, we soon began to fall sick. Of ten persons belonging to our family, including two young wives of Taw-ga-we-ninne, only Net-no-kwa and myself escaped being attacked. Several of them were very ill, and the old woman and myself found it as much as we could do to take care of them. In the village many died, but all of our family recovered. As the cold weather came on, they began to get better, and then we went to our wintering ground, at the same place where we had spent the former winter.

Here I was set to make marten traps, as the other hunters did. The first day I went out early, and spent the whole day, returning late at night, having made only three traps. In the same time a good hunter would have made twenty or twenty-five. Next morning I visited my traps, and found only one marten. Thus I continued for some days, but my want of skill and of success exposed me to the ridicule of the young men. At length my father began to pity me, and he said: "My son, I must go and help you to make traps." So he went out and spent a day in making a large number of traps, which he gave me, and then I was able to take as many martens as the others. As I became more and more expert in hunting and trapping, I was no longer required to do the same kind of work as the women did about the lodge.

In the following spring, Net-no-kwa, as usual, went to Mackinac. She always carried a flag on her canoe, and I was told that .whenever she came to Mackinac, she was saluted by a gun from the fort. I was now thirteen years of age. Before we left the village, I heard Net-no-kwa talk of going to Red River, to the relations of her husband. Many of the Ottawwaws, when they heard of this, determined to go with her. Among others was Wah-ka-zee, a chief of the village at War-gun-uk-ke-zee, or as the French called the place, L'Arbre Croche, after a crooked pine-tree long standing there. In all there were six canoes. Instead of leaving me, as on former occasions, at Point St. Ignace, they landed with me in the night, among the cedars, not far from Mackinac; the old woman then taking me into the town, to the house of a French trader, with whom she had sufficient influence to secure my concealment. Here I stayed, not being allowed to go out, but well treated in other respects. When ready to resume the journey they were detained by head winds, at a point since made a missionary station. Here a sad event occurred. The Indians having been drinking, my father was wounded by a young man and died of the injury then received. He felt he was dying, and made me sit down with the other children and talked much with us. He said, "My children I must leave you. I am sorry I must leave you so poor." He said nothing about the young Indian who had struck him with the stone, as others would have done. He probably knew he had given provocation, and he was too just a man to seek revenge, or to involve his family in the troubles which such a course would have brought on them. The young man remained with us, notwithstanding that Net-no-kwa told him it might be unsafe for him to go to Red River, where her late husband's relations were numerous and powerful, and might avenge his death.

When we came to the Sault St. Marie, we put all our baggage on board the trader's vessel, which was about to sail to the upper end of Lake Superior, and went on ourselves in the canoes. The winds were light, which enabled us to run faster than the vessel, and we arrived several days before it at the Portage. When she came at last, she anchored out a little distance from the shore. After about eight or ten days we commenced crossing the Grand Portage. My father lingered till we had passed two of the carrying-places, and when we arrived at the third, called the Moose carrying-place, he said:

"I must die here; I cannot go further." So Net-no-kwa determined to stop here, and the remainder of the party went on. After they started there remained only the old woman and one of the younger wives, the elder son, the second, and myself, the youngest of the family.

Camp and canoe in the forest

It was about the middle of summer, for the small berries were ripe, when we stopped here, on the borders of Moose Lake, which is of cool and clear water like Lake Superior. It is small and round, and a canoe can be easily seen across the widest part of it. There were only two of the party able to do much, myself being so young and without any experience as a hunter, so that we began to have fears that, being thus left, we might soon be in want of food. We had brought with us one of the nets used about Mackinac, and setting this, the first night we caught about eighty trout and other fish. After remaining here some time, we found beavers, of which we killed six; also some otters and musk rats. We had brought with us some corn, so that with the fish we caught, and the game we killed, we lived comfortably. But at the approach of winter, the old woman told us she could not remain longer, as the winter would be long and cold, and no people, either whites or Indians, near us. Ke-wa-tiu, the second son, had been ailing for some time, and became so weak that in returning to the Portage, we were compelled to move very slowly. When we arrived, the waters were beginning to freeze. He lived five or six weeks, and died before the middle of winter. The old woman buried him by the side of her husband, near the Grand Portage, and hung up one of her flags at his grave.

We now, as the weather became severe, began to grow poor, Wa-me-gon-a-biew, the elder brother, and myself being unable to kill as much game as we wanted. He was about seventeen years of age, and I thirteen, and game was not plentiful. As the weather became more and more cold, we removed from the trading-house, and set up our lodge in the woods, that we might get wood more easily. Here my brother and myself had to exert ourselves to the utmost, to avoid starving. We used to hunt two or three days' distance from home, and often returned with but little meat. We had, on one of our hunting paths, a camp built of cedar boughs, in which we had kindled fire so often that it became very dry, and at last caught fire while we were lying in it. The wood was so dry that it burnt rapidly, but fortunately we escaped with little injury. As we were returning, and still at a great distance from home, we attempted to cross a river, which was so rapid, as it turned out, as never to freeze very sound. Although the weather was so cold that we could every now and then hear the trees crackling with the frost, we broke through the ice in crossing. Owing to our hands being benumbed, it was very difficult to extricate ourselves from our snow shoes, and we were no sooner out of the water than our moccasins and leggings were frozen stiff. My brother was soon disheartened, and the numbing effect of the cold made him say he was willing to die. I tried to encourage him, but had not much more energy in so great a danger. We got to the shore, but we were unable to raise a fire, and we thought we must perish of cold. I kept moving, however, and helped him to lie down in a place where there was shelter. I found some dry rotten wood, and by rubbing was at last able to get a light and to kindle a fire. We got our clothes and moccasins dried, and became more comfortable, though very hungry. At the earliest dawn we left our camping place, and proceeded towards home. At no great distance we met our mother, who had felt anxious, and brought some food in case we were in want. She must have had a presentiment of the danger, for she had started the evening before and had walked all night, meeting us not far from the place where the accident happened.

We remained for some time in a suffering and almost starving condition, when a Muskego or Swamp Indian, called the Smoker, came to the trading-house, and learning that we were badly off, invited us to go home with him to his country, saying he would hunt for us, and bring us back in the spring. We went with him two long days' journey to the west, and came to a place called Burnt Wood River, where his lodge was. While we remained with him we wanted nothing. Such is the custom of the Indians, when not at war, and when remote from the trading whites; but the Ottawwaws and other tribes near the settlements have lost these hospitable customs, and have learned to be like most of the whites, and to give only to those who can barter or pay.

We had been for a short time at the Portage, when another man of the same tribe of Muskegoes invited us to go with him to a large island in Lake Superior, where, he said, there were plenty of caribou and of sturgeon; and where, he had no doubt, he could provide all that would be necessary for our support. We went with him, and having started in the very early morning, we reached the island before night, although a light wind ahead retarded the speed of the canoe. In the low rocky headlands of the island we found abundance of gulls' eggs. We took, with spears, two or three sturgeons soon after our arrival, so that our want of food was satisfied. Next day Wa-ge-mah-wul, a relative of Net-no-kwa, went to hunt, and returned in the evening having killed two caribou. On the island where we were there was a lake with beaver, otter, and other game, so that there was no lack of food.

Here we met with relations of Wa-ge-mah-wul, in eight canoes, and with them, ten canoes altogether, we started to return to the Portage. When we were setting out, and had got about two hundred yards into the lake, the chief, in a loud voice, addressed a prayer to the Great Spirit, entreating him to give us a good lake to cross. "Thou hast made this lake," he said, "and thou hast made us thy children; cause the water to be smooth that we may pass over in safety." He then threw a small quantity of tobacco into the water, his example being followed in each canoe. He then began a song or chant, but I do not know the meaning. I thought probably it was a religious song. Although I had forgotten my mother tongue, and had few ideas of the religious teaching of the whites, I felt the address and conduct of the chief to be very solemn and impressive. On that great lake or inland sea, in frail bark canoes, they could not but feel their helplessness and dependence. I have often since remembered that scene, and have thought that the feeling of these untaught Indians might put to shame many who have had greater advantages of knowledge and training.

By this time I had been so long among the Indians, that I was becoming at home among them, and learning their ways. Believing the story that had been brought as to the death of my father and all my relations, and being destitute of any property, I thought to myself that I must be exposed to extreme poverty, even if I made a successful attempt to escape from my present way of life. I saw among the Indians that those who were too weak or too young to find food for themselves were always supplied by others. I had no other choice at the time but to remain among them, although always retaining an intention, at some future time, to return and live among the whites.

We were now again at the Portage, whence we had twice removed on the hospitable invitation of the Muskegoes. It was necessary to determine what to do. When our mother had at length made up her mind to continue on to the Red River, according to her original plan before the disasters occurred which I have narrated, she heard from one of the traders that her son-in-law, husband of one of her daughters, had been killed. He was among the party who proceeded from Moose Lake, at the time we had to stop there with Ke-wa-tiu, who fell ill after the death and burial of his father. The traders brought the widow as far as Rainy Lake, whence she had sent word to her mother to come and join her. This was an additional inducement to move on toward Red River, and we determined to proceed without delay.

Our canoe had been lent to the traders, and was sent on the route toward Red River to bring packs, as they were about to despatch more canoes. Net-no-kwa requested that they would distribute us, one or two to each canoe, so that we might go on till we should meet our own canoe. After a few days we met the French traders with our canoe, which at first they were disposed not to give up, but Net-no-kwa demanded it with such authority that they gave way. I have never met with any Indian, either man or woman, who had greater influence than Net-no-kwa. She always had her way, and could accomplish what she desired, cither with the traders or the Indians. Probably it was because of the high character she bore, never attempting to do anything or demand anything that was not right and just.

At Rainy Lake we found the widow, the old woman's daughter, in the care of some Indians, but very poor. Net-no-kwa conferred long with her; talking of our past losses and troubles; of the death of her husband and son, and now of her son-in-law; and how all this bore upon our situation. She knew, she said, that her two sons who remained were young, but they were now becoming able to do something; and that since she had come so far, for the purpose of hunting beavers at Red River, she was not willing to turn back. My brother and myself, although deeply interested in these consultations, were not allowed or expected to have any voice in the matter.

It being determined that we should go to Red River, we continued on to the Lake of the Woods; called by others the Lake of the Sand Hills, a more suitable name, for there is very little wood about it. Here we were in some danger from the high wind, so that with difficulty we could prevent the canoe being swamped by the water dashed into it, and which I helped to bale out with a large kettle.

In the fall of the year we arrived at the Lake of Dirty Water, as the Indians call it, Lake Winnipeg of the whites. I am sorry to say that here Net-no-kwa, apparently over-whelmed with grief and anxiety, and brooding over her losses, began to drink, which was unusual with her, and became quite helpless. We lifted her into the canoe, deter-mined to cross to the other side of the lake. The traders tried to dissuade us, as the wind was rising, but we would not lis-ten, and pushed off, also raising our sail. Before long the wind blew and the waves rose, and we were in real peril. The old woman was roused by the tumult, and becoming aware of the situation, she applied herself with wonderful energy to the use of her paddle, encouraging the others, and directing my brother how to steer. We noticed that she at times addressed cries and prayers to the Great Spirit, whether from fear only, or from any sense of her fault, I cannot tell. After much exer-tion we got to shore at a rocky place, in utter darkness, a place where in daylight it seemed marvellous how we got safely to land.

We remained here encamped most of the next day, which was calm and fair, drying our baggage, and towards evening embarked again, and ran for the mouth of Red River. We did not enter the mouth of the river till late at night, and perceiv-ing a lodge we landed, and laid ourselves down without kin-dling a fire, or making any noise to disturb the people, as we did not know who they were. In the morning they came and waked us, and we found them to be the family of one of the brothers of Taw-ga-we-ninne, Net-no-kwa's late husband, and the very people we had come to seek.

Chapter III.

AMONG OJIBBEWAY AND OTTAWWAW TRIBES AT RED RIVER—GO UP THE ASSINEBOIN RIVER TO HUNTING GROUND—FIRST SIGHT AND CHASE OF BUFFALOES—BEAVER TRAPPING—I KILL MY FIRST BEAR—NET-NO-KWA'S DREAM—AT A TRADING-HOUSE—WITH PE-SHAW-BA, AN OTTAWWAW CHIEF—KILL MY FIRST STURGEON—PERILS AND ADVENTURES IN A CANOE VOYAGE—A WILD GOOSE CHASE—KILL MY FIRST BUFFALO—BEAVER SHOOTING ON THE ICE—NARROW ESCAPE FROM DROWNING—LEAVING TRAPS AND PELTRIES IN CACHE AT RAINY LAKE.

After a few days, we started to go up the Red River, and in two days came to the mouth of the Assineboin, where we found great numbers of the Ojibbeways and Ottawwaws encamped. As soon as we arrived, the chiefs met, to take our case into consideration, and to agree on some method of providing for us. "These our relations," said one of the chiefs, "have come to us from a distant country. These two boys are not able to provide for them, and we must not suffer them to be in want among us." Then one man offered to hunt for us; and they agreed, also, since we had started to come for the purpose of hunting beaver, and as our hunters had died on the journey, that each should give us some part of what they should kill.

We then all started together to go up the Assineboin River, and the first night we camped in the midst of a place where were buffaloes. In the morning I was allowed to go out with some of the hunters. We killed one of four buffaloes which we saw. We continued to ascend the river for about ten days, killing many bears as we travelled along. The fat of the bear is preserved for use. The Assineboin River is broad, shallow, and tortuous; and the water turbid, like that of the Red River. But the bottom is more sandy than that of Red River, which is mostly mud at bottom.

Buffalo hunting

The place to which we went on the Assineboin is about seventy miles distant from the mouth by land, but much more by water from the great crookedness of the stream. The banks on both sides are covered with poplar and white oak and other trees, which grow to a considerable size. The prairies, however, are not far distant, and sometimes reach down to the immediate neighbourhood of the river. It is a country where there could be rich and fertile settlements.

We stopped at a place called Prairie or Meadow Portage, where the Indians directed a trader who was with them, to build his house, and remain during the winter. This they did in order that they might know where to bring their skins or other products of hunting for barter or for sale. We left here all our canoes, and went up into the country to hunt for beaver, among the small streams. The Indians gave to my brother and myself a little creek, with plenty of beaver, and on which they said that no one else would be allowed to hunt. My mother gave me three traps, and instructed me how to set them, by the aid of a string tied round the spring, as I was not yet able to set them with my hands as the Indians did. I set my traps overnight, as I had been instructed, and in the morning I found beavers in two of them. Being unable to take them out of the traps myself, I carried home the beavers and traps, one at a time, upon my back, that the old woman might assist me. She was highly gratified and delighted at my success. In truth she had always been kind and considerate, often taking my part when the Indians would attempt to ridicule or annoy me.

We remained in this place about three months, in which time we were as well provided for as any of the band; for if our own game was not sufficient, we were sure to be supplied by some of our friends, as long as anything could be killed. The people that remained to spend the winter with us were two lodges, our own making a third; but we were afterwards joined by four lodges of Cree Indians. These people are related to the Ojibbeways and Ottawwaws, but their language is somewhat different, so much so as not to be readily understood. Their country borders on that of the Assineboins, or stone-roasters, so called from their custom of cooking their food by help of heated stones. One tribe of the Ojibbeways is, in the same style, called spit-roasters, from their being chiefly in the habit of roasting their meat on wooden spits. The Crees are not relations to the Assineboins, to whose country they are nearest; but although not natural allies, they are for the most part friendly and at peace with them, and are more or less intermixed by marriage and business relations.

After we had been about three months in this place, game began to be scarce, and we all suffered at times from hunger. The chief man of our band, who was called As-si-ne-boinainse, or the little Assineboin, proposed that we should move, as the country seemed exhausted of game. Our necessities by this time had become extreme. The evening before our intended removal, my mother was in low spirits, and had been talking much of her losses and misfortunes, and of the distress we were now suffering. In the night I was awakened by the loud speaking and singing of the old woman, and on listening I heard that she now and then addressed the Great Spirit with much earnestness. In the morning very early she told us all to get up, and put on our moccasins, so as to be ready to start. She then called my brother, Wa-me-gon-a-biew, to her, and in a rather low voice said to him: "My son, I dreamed a dream last night, after I had been praying to the Great Spirit. A man appeared to me, and said: 'Net-no-kwa, to-morrow you shall cat bear flesh.' I dreamed it was in a place like an open meadow, not far from the path we are to travel to-day. If you go, and search for that place, you will certainly find a bear."

Now, my brother was not very dutiful, nor did he regard what our mother said, although she was a great believer in dreams. Going out of the lodge, he laughed at her, and said to some other Indians: "The old woman says we are to cat bear to-day; but I do not know who is to kill it." The old woman heard him, called him back, and reproved him; but she could not prevail on him to go alone to seek the bear. The Indians now had all moved on towards the place where they were to encamp that night. The men went first by themselves, each carrying some portion of the baggage, and when they reached the place, they threw down their loads, and went to look for game. Some of the younger ones, and I among them, remained with this baggage until the women should come up. While waiting here, I had my gun with me, and I began to reflect on what my mother had said about her dream. I had heard what she said to my brother. At length I resolved to go in search of the place she had described, and without mentioning my purpose to any one, I loaded my gun and went back on our track. I soon met one of the women, wife of one of my mother's brothers. She had lately been very unfriendly, thinking we were a burden upon her husband, who had to help to support us. She asked me what I was doing on the path, and whether I expected to kill Indians, as I carried a gun. I made no answer, and going on I watched everywhere for any opening in the track that might lead to the meadow. I saw at a break in the bushes a round, flat, hollowed place, that looked as if it might have been formerly a pond, though now partly covered with underwood. I went towards it, when suddenly I fell up to my middle in the snow. I extricated myself with some difficulty, and walked on. Remembering then that I had heard Indians speak of sometimes killing bears in their holes, it occurred to me that possibly it was a bear's hole into which I had fallen. So returning, and looking down, I saw the head of a bear lying close to the bottom of the hole. He was perfectly still, in his winter sleep; so I placed the muzzle of my gun nearly between his eyes, and fired. As soon as the smoke cleared away I took a piece of stick and thrust it into the wound, and being quite satisfied that the bear was dead, I laid hold of him to try to pull him out of the hole. But being unable to do this, I returned home, following the track I had made in coming out.

As I came near the camp I met the same woman whom I had seen in going out, and she immediately began to ridicule me. "Have you killed a bear, that you come back so soon, and walk so fast?" I thought to myself: "How does she know that I have been after a bear?" Then I thought that perhaps my mother, on missing me on her arriving at the camp, might have said something about her dream. But I passed on without replying, and went into my mother's lodge. She said at once: "My son, look into that kettle, and you will find a mouthful of beaver meat, which a man gave me since you left in the morning. You must leave half of it for Wa-me-gon-a-biew, who has not returned from hunting, and has eaten nothing to-day." I accordingly ate part of the beaver meat, for I was very hungry, and when I had finished, observing an opportunity when she stood by herself, I whispered in her ear: "My mother, I have killed a bear." "What do you say, my son?" "I have killed a bear." "Are you sure you have killed him?" "Yes." She watched my countenance for a moment, and then caught me in her arms, and for some time kissed and hugged me with great earnestness. I then told her what my aunt had said to me, both going and returning, and this being told to her husband when he came in, he not only reproved her, but gave her a severe beating. Some men were sent back with me to fetch the bear. Being the first I had killed, there was much congratulation, and it was cooked all at once, and the hunters of the whole band invited to feast with us, according to the custom of the Indians.

I do not pretend to explain my mother's dream; but from her belief in it, in connection with her prayers, and from many things I have observed among the Indians, which some may ridicule as superstitions, I am sure that most of them have ideas of the supernatural, and possess certain religious feelings or instincts in their nature, without which to work upon it would be little use for the white missionaries and teachers to attempt to give them better religious instruction.

On the following day one of the Crees killed another bear and a moose, and a large portion was sent to my mother's lodge. For some time we had plenty of food. Soon after the Crees left us to go to their own country. They were friendly and hospitable people, and we were sorry to part with them. We went a few days later to the place where we had left the trader, and arrived there on the last day of December, as I remember that the following was New Year's Day.

We remained for some time by ourselves at a little distance from the trading-house; at length, one day the trader sent a messenger to come to his lodge. We found there Peshaw-ba, a celebrated war-chief of the Ottawwaws, who had come some years before from Lake Huron. He had heard, it appeared, in his own country of an old Ottawwaw woman, who, with a family of two women, two boys, and three little children, having lost their men by death, were on the Ass-ineboin, and suffering from poverty. He had come, with three companions, whose names I remember were Waus-so, the lightning; Sag-git-to, he that terrifies all; and Sa-ning-wul, he that stretches his wings. All the Indians are known by distinctive names of this sort. The oldest of these three, Waus-so, himself a famous warrior, had fallen sick, and had been left at some distance behind. Pe-shaw-ba had traced us from place to place, by the reports of the Indians, and at last found us at Prairie Portage. He was a large, handsome man, although now aged. When we entered he immediately recognised Net-no-kwa as a relative, whom he had known long ago. Looking then at us, he said: "Who are these?" She answered: "These are my sons." He looked closely and intently at me, and motioned me to come nearer. My mother anticipated any questions by telling who I was. He inquired particularly as to the time and circumstances of my capture, which had happened after he left Lake Huron. The only remark he made to me was that if Ke-wa-tiu had lived he would now be about my age.

In two or three days we started together for the country of Pe-shaw-ba, which was far off.

The snow was deep, and our route being, for the most part, across open prairies, we were not able to travel when the wind was very high, as it sometimes was. When we commenced our journey, we had very small stock of provision, but soon found plenty of buffalo, which was fat and in good condition. Although the snow was deep, the buffalo could still feed, pushing aside the snow with their heads, and reaching the pasture beneath. We had thrown away our mats made of flags, or ruk-kwi, as we called the reed of which they were woven, the long journey requiring us to carry as few things as possible. The buffalo hides now came to be very serviceable, for we spread them over our lodges, and becoming hard and frozen they formed strong shelter from the snow and wind. In calm weather we commonly encamped with no other covering than our blankets, one of which every Indian always carries. Throughout the journey, Pe-shaw-ba and Sa-ning-wul each carried one of our sister's little children on their backs. Thus we travelled on diligently, as the weather would permit, for about two months and more. In the middle of our journey we passed the trading-house and fort at Mouse River. Our general direction was a little north of west, and we came at length to a log hut near the bank of Clear Water Lake, where Pe-shaw-ba and his three companions had lived for some time after leaving Lake Huron. They had lived there alone, the chief having left his wife at his own home, as had the other men, if they were married. On our reaching the log-hut the chief opened his bundle, and took out numbers of beaver and other skins, dried food, and various articles, all of which he delivered to our women, saying: "We have long been our own squaws, but we must be so no longer. It is your business to dress the skins, dry our meat, make our moccasins, and leave us to hunt." The old woman took charge of Pe-shaw-ba's property, calling him her son, and treating him as such. The daughter and daughter-in-law took charge of the other men. In hunting I was the companion of Pe-shaw-ba, who was kind to me, and took pleasure in trying to teach me to be a great hunter. It must have been late in winter when we got to Clear Water Lake; but the weather was still so cold that water carried out of the lodge froze immediately. When going out to hunt we started before sunrise, and did not return till after it was dark. At noon the sun scarcely rose to the height of the tops of the trees, though these were not high in that place. The country was chiefly prairie, with occasional clumps of low cedar and pine-trees.

Our camp at Clear Water Lake was not very far from the country of the Mandans, on the Missouri. From Mouse River a man may walk to the Mandan villages in four days. Just before the leaves began to appear in spring we started with all our peltries or stock of skins, and large quantities of dried meat and dried beaver tails, to come down to the trading-house on Mouse River. In that country there is no birch or cedar fit for making canoes, so that we were compelled to make one for our journey of green or new moose skins, which being sewed with great care and stretched over a proper frame, then allowed to dry, make a strong and good canoe; but in warm weather it will not last long. In a canoe of this kind, which would carry perhaps about five tons, half as much as a common Mackinac boat, we all embarked, taking whatever belonged to us; the intention of Net-no-kwa and Pe-shaw-ba being to return to Lake Huron.

We descended the Little Saskatchewan for several days. On this river we found a village of Assineboins, with whom we stopped a short time. None of us could understand them except Waus-so, who had somewhere learned to speak their language. When we came from the Little Saskatchewan into the Assineboin River, we came to the rapids, where was a village of about a hundred and fifty lodges of Assineboins, with some Crees. We had begun to feel the want of provisions, and therefore stopped here to kill sturgeons, which were abundant at this place. In two days from these rapids we came to Monk River, where both the North West and the Hudson's Bay Company have trading-houses.

Here Pe-shaw-ba and his friends began to drink, and in a short time expended all the peltries they had made in their long and successful hunting. In one day a hundred beaver skins were bartered for liquor. It is a shameful thing that such barter was allowed. The price was then six beaver skins for one quart of rum, but the traders mixed much water with it, and more liquor was called for. After the time of drunkenness was over we began to make birch canoes, still intending to continue on our journey. But at this time the Assineboins and Crees and other Indians of that part of the country, with whom the Mandans had made peace, were invited by the Mandans to come to their country and join in a war against a people called by the whites Minnetarees, and by the Ojibbeways called A-gutch-a-ninne, or the settled people. They lived in settlements about two days distant from the Mandans. Waus-so, hearing of this, resolved to join the war party then assembling at Mouse River. Pe-shaw-ba and Net-no-kwa endeavoured to dissuade him, but the old warrior was the more determined to go. Pe-shaw-ba began to feel the excitement, and at length all the men went, even down to my brother, leaving me only with the three women and three children. They left the canoes unfinished, and all set out in a warlike spirit But the expedition, for which the Mandans had summoned aid from such remote regions, came to nothing. The tribes, some of whom had hereditary enmities far stronger than their feeling against these new foes, quarrelled among themselves on the way. The project was thus discovered, and the A-gutch-a-ninne were left at peace in their own village.

After they had gone I started with Net-no-kwa and the remainder of the family for Lake Winnipeg, as we expected the war party to be absent a long time. We were compelled still to use the old moose-skin canoe, as none of the birch ones were finished, and we were tired of remaining at Mouse River. We had loft the trading-house but a short time when we espied a sturgeon, which, by some accident, had got into such shoal water, on a sand-bar, that part of his back was to be seen above water. I jumped out of the canoe and killed him with little difficulty. As this was the first sturgeon I had killed, the old woman thought it necessary to stop and celebrate a feast of first-fruits, though, being alone, we could invite no guests to partake of it. The mouth of the Assineboin was a place at that time much frequented by the Sioux war-parties, who lay concealed there, and fired upon such as were passing. We did not approach the place until dark, intending to pass through late at night. It was, accordingly, after midnight when, carefully avoiding either shore, we floated silently out into Red River. The night was very dark, and we could discern nothing distinctly on shore; but we had scarcely entered Red River when the silence was broken by what seemed the hooting of an owl on the left bank of the Assineboin. This was quickly answered by another hoot on the right bank, and presently a third was heard on the side of Red River opposite the mouth. "We are discovered," said Net-no-kwa in a scarcely audible whisper, and she made me put the canoe about with utmost silence. In obedience to her direction we ascended with the greatest caution, endeavouring to keep near the middle of Red River. I was in the bow of the canoe, keeping my head as low as I could, and was carefully watching the surface of the water before me, hoping to be able to see and avoid any canoe or other object that might approach, when I saw a little ripple on the surface of the water, following a low, black, moving object, which I at once concluded to be the head of a man swimming across stealthily in front. As he was not coming towards the canoe I pointed to the moving object, and we speedily agreed that we should pursue, and, if possible, kill the man in the water before he got to the shore. A strong sturgeon spear was handed to me, and we commenced the pursuit, the women plying the paddles well. But the goose (for it was really a wild goose chase) soon became alarmed, and rose in flight, followed by its brood of young ones. When we perceived our mistake we retraced our course up the river with somewhat less of fear, but still we could not venture to continue our way. I tried to make light of the timidity of the women, but I do not know to this day whether the hooting of three owls or signals of a war-party of Sioux frightened us back. We returned several miles, and expecting that a party of traders would pass before long, we determined to wait for them. Fortunately there were many young geese and ducks, so that we had plenty of fresh provisions while waiting.

When the traders came, according to our expectation, we went down to the house at Winnipeg, where we remained two months. When they were about to return to the Assineboin, we purchased a bark canoe and accompanied them. We had a good many beaver skins, and Net-no-kwa bought a keg of rum with some of them for Pe-shaw-ba, who had said to her that "he would come back from fighting very thirsty." We expected we would be back to the Mouse River before their return from the war expedition.

In the Assineboin River, about two days' distance above the Prairie Portage, is a place where the Indians frequently stop. Here we saw some little stakes in the ground with pieces of birch bark attached to them, and upon these the figures of animals and some other marks. Net-no-kwa immediately recognised the totems or marks of Pe-shaw-ba, Waus-so, and their companions. They had left them to inform us that they had been at the place, and as directions to enable us to find them. We therefore left the traders, and taking the course indicated by the marks which Pe-shaw-ba had caused to be made, we found him and his party at the distance of two days from the river. They had returned from the abortive war expedition to the trading-house on the Mouse River, and stayed there till they had finished the canoes which they had left incomplete. They descended to the place where the marks were left, knowing that there were good hunting-grounds near. We found that they had plenty of game in the camp, and they had also taken a great number of beavers. We continued here, therefore, until the ice became too thick for beaver trapping, and then went to the prairie in pursuit of buffaloes. When the snow began to have a crust upon it, the men said they must leave me along with the women, as they were going to Clear Water Lake to make canoes, but they would kill some food for our supply during their absence. Waus-so, who was a great hunter, went out by himself and killed one buffalo; but in the night the weather became very cold and stormy, and the buffaloes came in to take shelter in the woods where we had our camp. Early in the morning Net-no-kwa called us up, saying there was a large herd not far off from the lodge. Pe-shaw-ba and Waus-so, with three others, took up stations indifferent directions, so that the herd could not all escape if alarmed. They would not allow me to go out, and laughed when they saw me putting my gun in readiness; but Net-no-kwa, who was ever ready to befriend me, after they were gone, led me to a stand not far from the lodge, near which, her sagacity taught her, the herd would probably run. The Indians fired, and all failed to kill. The herd came past my stand, and I had the good fortune to kill a large cow. It was my first success in buffalo hunting, and gave great gratification to my mother. Shortly afterwards, having killed a considerable number, and made a good store of food, the Indians left us: myself, the old woman, one of the young women, and three children, six in all, with no one to provide for them but myself. The dried meat lasted for some time, but I soon found that I was able to kill buffaloes, and we had no want of fresh food. On one occasion an old cow which I had wounded ran fiercely at me, although she had no calf, and I was barely able to escape from her by climbing into a tree. She was enraged not so much by the wound as by the dogs; and it is, I believe, very rare that a cow attacks a man unless she has been worried by dogs.

As spring came on we went up the Mouse River for about ten miles, to woods where we made maple sugar. The weather rapidly became mild, and once I was in great danger from the breaking of the ice. The beavers had begun to come up through the holes on to the ice, and sometimes went on shore. I was watching near one of these holes, and shot one as it came up. Running hastily along the ice to secure him I broke through; my snow shoes became entangled with some brush on the bottom and had nearly dragged me under, but by great exertion I at length escaped.

When the leaves began to appear on the trees, Pe-shaw-ba and the men returned in new birch canoes, bringing with them many beaver skins and other valuable peltries. Old Net-no-kwa was now anxious to return to Lake Huron, but Waus-so and Sa-ning-wul would not go, and Pe-shaw-ba was unwilling to part with them. Sag-git-to, one of the men had fallen into a very bad state of health. Pe-shaw-ba said to the old woman, "It is not good that Sag-git-to should die here, at a distance from all his friends. Since we see he cannot live much longer, I think it best for you to take him and the little

children, and return to Lake Huron. You may be able to reach
the rapids, at Sault St. Marie, before he dies." Conformably to
this advice, our family divided. Pe-shaw-ba, Waus-so, and Sa-
ning-wul remained; Net-no-kwa and the two other women,
Sa-git-to, my brother Wa-me-gon-a-biew, and myself, with a
little girl the old woman had bought, and three children,
started to return to Lake Huron. The little girl was brought
from the country of the Fall Indians, by a war party of Ojibbeways, from whom Net-no-kwa bought her to be a helper for
herself and the children. The Fall Indians live near the Rocky
Mountains, and wander much with the Black Feet; their language being unlike that of both the Sioux and the Ojibbeways.

These last, and the Crees, are more friendly with the
Black Feet than they are with the Fall Indians. The girl was
now about ten years of age; but having been for some time
among the Ojibbeways had learned their language.

When we came to Rainy Lake we had ten packs of beaver,
of forty skins each. Net-no-kwa sold some other peltries for
rum, and, I am sorry to say, was drunk for a day or two. We
here met some of the traders' canoes, on their way to Red
River. Wa-me-gon-a-biew, who was now eighteen years old,
being unwilling to go to Lake Huron, determined to go back
to the north with the traders. The old woman said much to dissuade him; but he jumped into one of the canoes as they were
about to start, and although, at the request of the old woman,
they endeavoured to drive him out, he would not leave the
canoe. Net-no-kwa was greatly distressed, although he did
not at any time show much affection for his mother. She could
not make up her mind to lose her only surviving son, and
determined on returning with him. The packs of beaver skins
she would not leave with the traders, not having sufficient
confidence in their honesty. We therefore took them to a
remote place in the woods, where we made a sunjegwun, or
deposit, in the usual manner. We then returned to the Lake of
the Woods. From this lake the Indians have a route to go to

Red River, which the white men never follow, by the way of the Muskeek or swamp carrying place. We went up the Swamp River for several days, and then dragged our canoes across a swamp for one day. This swamp is only of moss with small bushes, and it quakes as people pass over it. Then we put our canoes into a small stream, which they call Begwion-usk, from the plant cow-parsley, which abounds there. Thence we descended into a small lake, bearing the same name. It has only two or three feet of water, and over most of the surface it is scarcely a foot in depth; but all this time the whole lake was covered with ducks, geese, swans, and other birds. Here we remained some time, and made four packs of beaver skins.

We were now quite alone, no Indians or white men being within four or five days' journey from us. Here we had packs to put in cache or deposit, as we were about to leave the country; and the ground being too swampy to admit of burying them in the usual manner, we made a sunjegwun of logs, so tight together that a mouse could not enter it, and in this we left our packs and other property which we could not carry. If any Indians had found it, they would not have broken it up, and we had no fear of any white traders passing that way. Indians, when they have not had much dealing with the white traders, have not learned to value these peltries so highly as to be tempted to steal from one another. At the time of which I am speaking, and in that part of the country, I have often known a hunter leave his traps for many days in the woods, without visiting them, or feeling any anxiety about their safety. It would often happen that one man having finished his hunt, and left his traps behind him, another would say:

"Where are your traps?" and have leave to use them, as would others in succession, and yet in the end they are sure to return to their first owner.

Chapter IV.

COMPELLED BY HUNGER TO MOVE FREQUENTLY TO NEW HUNTING-GROUND—WITH FRIENDLY CREE INDIANS AT RED RIVER—THE GRAND PORTAGE—WA-ME-GON-A-BIEW, ELDEST SON OF NET-NO-KWA, IN TROUBLE—HIS MARRIAGE—MOOSE HUNTING—STORIES ABOUT THE MOOSE—ELK HUNTING—MARTEN TRAPPING—PORCUPINE STORIES—THE CHIEF WAGE-TOTE AND HIS DAUGHTER—AN INDIAN CAROUSAL AT THE TRADING STATION—A SOLITARY CANOE VOYAGE—THE HAUNTED CAMPING GROUND—LEGEND OF THE TWO DEAD BROTHERS AND THEIR GHOSTS—MY FEARFUL NIGHT BIVOUAC ON THE HAUNTED GROUND.

When the snow had fallen, and the weather began to be very cold, so that we could no longer kill beaver, we began again to suffer from hunger. My brother exerted himself, and was sometimes successful; but the supply was very uncertain. Our suffering compelled us to move, and we went toward Red River, hoping either to meet some Indians, or to find game on the way. One lodge of Ojibbeways we met with, but they were extremely inhospitable, a rare thing with Indians when others are really in want. They would only supply us with any food in exchange for our silver ornaments, which we were forced to part with. Net-no-kwa was very indignant, and forbade us to give anything more, and we moved away from them. After some days we came upon tracks of hunters, and found the head of a buffalo which they had left, and with which we were glad to stay the pangs of hunger. Following this track we came to an encampment of some of our friends on Red River. This was a band of Crees, whose chief, the Little Assineboin, I have formerly mentioned. He and his people received us in a very cordial manner, and supplied our wants. We stayed with them nearly two months, when the buffalo and other game becoming scarce, the whole camp began to suffer. It was necessary to move, and it was thought advisable to separate, and go in different directions. Net-no-kwa determined to go with her family to the trading-house of a Mr. Henry, who was afterwards drowned in the Columbia River by the upsetting of a boat in an exploring expedition. This trading-place was near where a settlement was afterwards made, called Pembinah. We hunted all the remainder of the winter with the people of the fur-traders. In the spring we returned to the lake where we had left our canoes. We found all our property safe, and having gathered all that we took from our sunjegwuns or caches, and all we brought from Red River, we found we now had eleven packs of beaver, of forty skins each, and ten packs of other skins. It was now our intention to return to Lake Huron, and to dispose of our peltries at Mackinac. We had, besides, the large sunjegwun at Rainy Lake, near the trader's station, though the site had been concealed from him. On reaching this place we found the sunjegwun had been broken up, and not a pack nor a skin left. We saw a pack in the trader's lodge, which we believed was one of our own; but did not dare to say so, as we could not prove it, they being all so much alike. The old woman did not hesitate to affirm to us that the trader had stolen the packs. It was a great disappointment, for this, along with our other packs, would have been disposed of for what would have made us rich for a long time.

When we reached the small house at the other side of the Grand Portage to Lake Superior, the people belonging to the traders urged us to put our packs in the wagons or carriages, and so have them taken across. But the old woman, knowing that if they were once in the hands of the traders, it would be difficult, if not impossible to get them again, refused to comply with their request. It took us several days to carry all our packs across, as the old woman would not suffer them to be carried in the traders' road. Notwithstanding all this caution, when we came to this side the Portage, two traders, I remember their names, Mr. Macgillivray and Mr. Shabboyea, by treating her with much attention, and giving her some wine, induced her to place all her packs in a room which they gave her to occupy. At first, they endeavoured by friendly solicitation to induce her to sell her furs; but finding her determined not to part with them at that time, a young man, Mr. Shabboyea's son, attempted to seize them by force; but the old man interfered, and reproved his son for his conduct Thus Net-no-kwa was enabled to keep possession of her property; and might have done so till her arrival at Mackinac, but for a sad event which occurred. An Indian, called Bit-te-gish-sho, or crooked lightning, arrived with a band of his people from Middle Lake. With these people my brother became very intimate, and formed an attachment with the daughter of the chief, although we knew nothing of it at the time. When we were about to start for Sault St. Marie, and the baggage was in the canoe, Wa-me-gon-a-biew was not to be found. We sought everywhere for him, and it was not till after some days that we heard, from a French trader, that he was on the other side of the Porttage, with the family of the Crooked Lightning. I was sent for him, but he would not return to Net-no-kwa. Knowing his obstinate disposition, the old woman began to cry. "If I had two of my own sons," she said, "I would let this one go; but as he is the only one left, and his father too is dead, I must go with him." She gave to the widow, her sister's daughter, who had lived with her from a child, five packs of beaver, one of which was for her own use; the other four, together with sixty other skins, she told her to take to Mackinac, and deliver them according to her direction. This she did, coming down in the trader's canoe, and delivering the skins to Mr. Lapomboise, agent of the North-West Company, and took his due bill, as she was told it was, for the amount. But this bill was subsequently lost, by the burning of our lodge, and neither Net-no-kwa nor any of her family ever received anything for these skins.

The remainder of our property met with a still more disastrous fate. The old woman, much vexed by the conduct of her son, brooding again over her past losses, and disappointed of her hopes of returning to Lake Huron, forgot her usual dignity and self-possession, and abandoned herself to drink. In the course of a single day she sold one hundred and twenty beaver skins, with a large quantity of buffalo robes, and other valuable articles, for rum. When she thus broke out, she used to make all the Indians about her also drink. Of all the great stock of peltries, the produce of so long toil, and saved through so many long and perilous journeys, there remained one blanket, three kegs of rum, and the poor and almost worn-out clothes on our bodies. I did not, on this as on other occasions, witness the wicked and wanton waste of our peltries and other property with that indifference which the Indians seem always to feel; but I was then helpless to prevent the disaster.

Our return being determined upon, we started with Bit-te-gish-sho and some other Indians for the Lake of the Woods. Here we were overtaken by cold weather while making a canoe. Net-no-kwa resolved to remain there, though most of the others went on. Here it was found that the attachment of Wa-me-gon-a-biew to the daughter of the Crooked Lightning was not too strong to be broken; and, indeed, it is somewhat doubtful whether the anxiety of the traders at the Grand Portage to possess themselves of our packs had not as much to do with occasioning our return as anything on the part of this young man.

After these people had left us, we found our condition too desolate and hopeless to remain there by ourselves, being so ill-provided against the approaching winter; so we repaired to Rainy Lake trading-house, and obtained credit to the amount of one hundred and twenty beaver skins, and thus furnished ourselves with clothing, blankets, and other things necessary for the winter.

It would weary my readers to give in detail the various movements and occupations, summer and winter, in the next few years. They were much after the fashion of those already described. Most of the movements and changes of encampment among the Indians are regulated by the sheer necessity of supporting life. Hunger drives them forth when food is failing, and they are drawn hither or thither by the prospect or hope of finding plenty in other quarters. Sometimes there may be a desire to see friends or relatives, or to visit particular places from other motives; but for the most part it is in order to get food that removals are made and wanderings renewed. Hunting is their main business, first for the meat, and also for the skins of those animals that are of value. These they take to the trading posts which are scattered over the regions frequented by hunters. Here they obtain by barter the blankets, clothes, kettles, and other things required in their lodges. By far the largest part of the product of their winter and spring hunts is expended on whisky or rum. These debauches are frequently attended by mischievous or fatal quarrels, and always followed by poverty and hunger, which compel them to begin again their life of toil. I seldom was tempted to such excesses, but had to share the poverty all the same. I had then no other prospect before me, and I had become attached to hunting both as a business and an amusement. There were no Indian settlements in those days, as there are now.

Some incidents of my early hunting days I well remember, and may be interesting to relate. When our lodge was near the trading-house at Rainy Lake, we found early one morning a moose track. My brother and I started in pursuit, taking with us several dogs, and accompanied by an Indian whose lodge was near. After following the track more than an hour, the Indian was tired, and the dogs returned with him. It was not far from noon when we came up with the moose just as it was making for a lake which was frozen over. The ice being in some parts quite smooth, the moose could not run so fast as on land, and my brother, who was very swift-footed, along with one dog, overtook him, and he was easily killed. I think that I have not till now mentioned moose hunting. The Indians consider the moose more shy and more difficult to take than any other animal. He is far more vigilant and cautious than the buffalo or caribou, and fleeter than the elk, though clumsier in his appearance and gait. In the most violent storm, when the wind and the creaking or falling timber are making the loudest and most incessant roar in the forest, if a man, either with his foot or with his hand, breaks the smallest dry limb of a tree, the moose distinguishes the sound. If he is standing browsing, and the hunter has stealthily been able to creep near the place without being seen, if the slightest noise is made, the moose hears it, and though he does not always run, he ceases eating, and rouses his utmost attention. If, in the course of an hour or so, the man lies dead still, and avoids making the least noise, the animal may begin to feed again, but seems not to forget what he had heard, and is for hours more vigilant than before.

There is an opinion prevalent among the Indians that the moose, among the methods of self-preservation with which it seems better acquainted than most other animals, has the power of remaining a long time under water. I do not believe this; but I may tell the following anecdote as illustrating the general belief in this power as ascribed to the moose. Two men, whom I knew very well, after a long day's absence on a hunt, came into camp at night, and stated that they had been on a moose track, and had chased him into a small pond, and that they had seen him wade to the middle of it, and disappear from their sight. Choosing positions from which they could command a view of the whole circumference of the pond, they sat there, and watched and smoked till the evening. During all this time they never saw the slightest motion of the water, or other sign of the position of the moose. At length, discouraged and wearied with watching, they gave up hope of taking him, and returned home. Not long afterwards an Indian related that on that evening he had seen and followed a moose track, and had traced it to the same pond; but having also observed the tracks of two men, made apparently at the same time as those of the moose, he concluded that they must have killed it. Nevertheless, approaching cautiously to the margin of the pond, he sat down to rest. Presently, while thus quietly seated, he saw the moose rise slowly in the middle of the pond, which was not very deep, and wade towards the shore where he was. When sufficiently near, he shot him in the water, and he was loaded with the meat when he came to our lodge and told this story. I do not pretend to explain it; but it is much more likely that there was some weak place in the account of the hunters than that the moose could live for hours under water. He may have been submerged partly, while keeping his head so as to be able to breathe, till their watching was less vigilant. The story is only worth telling as proof of the cunning with which the moose is credited.

Moose hunting

In the open chase it is almost impossible to overtake him, his pace is so swift and his strides so long. The best chance is in snow, when the surface is not hard. The animal's legs sink in the snow, while the hunter moves quickly over the surface with his snow shoes.

In the prairie country of the north-west, towards the Assineboin and Saskatchewan lands, the elks chiefly abound. Between these two rivers is another called Elk River, from their abundance in that region. There are brine springs and salt lakes in that quarter, which may partly account for the animals resorting thither in large numbers. I once, when with an Indian hunter a good distance up the Assineboin, saw a herd of probably two hundred elk in a little prairie which was almost surrounded by the river. We stationed ourselves in the gorge, which was not more than two hundred yards across. The herd having been alarmed, and unwilling to venture on the smooth ice in the river, began to run round and round upon the little prairie. It sometimes happened that one was thrust within reach of our shot, and in this way we killed two. In our eagerness to get nearer, we left our place of conceal-ment, and advanced so far toward the middle of the prairie that the herd divided, a part being driven on to the ice, and a part escaping to the high ground beyond the gorge which we had left. The hunter followed the latter herd, and I ran on to the ice. The elks on the river, slipping on the smooth ice, and being much frightened, crowded so close together that the ice broke with the weight; and as they waded towards the oppo-site shore and endeavoured to rise upon the ice, it continued to break before them. I ran hastily and thoughtlessly along the brink of the open place, and as the water was not so deep as that the elks could swim, I supposed I could get those I killed, and continued firing. When my balls were all expended, I drew my knife and killed one or two with it; but those that I had shot in the water were in a few minutes swept under the ice, and I got not one of them. Only one, which I struck after he rose upon the surface close to the bank, I saved. This, in addition to the others we had killed on shore made four, a poor result out of not less than two hundred that were there.

On another occasion we were on the river in our canoe, when the dogs, which we had not taken on board, but were running on the shore, started a solitary elk, which took to the water. We drove him on shore again with the canoe, and my brother keeping charge of it, I gave chase, and succeeded in killing what proved to be a fine fat buck.

I may observe that elk and caribou are never found together. The country between Lake Winnipeg and Hudson's Bay is low and swampy, and that is the home of the caribou. More to the west, towards the Assi-neboin and the Saskatchewan, is the prairie land where are found elk and buffaloes.

Marten hunting has not much adventure in it, as with larger game; but, being done by trapping, success is obtained only by considerable skill and experience. Its favourite haunt is in pine forests. It feeds on whatever it can catch by craft or stealth, young birds, eggs, marmots, rabbits. The trap used by Indians was chiefly the fall trap. A half-circle of stones being built up, a heavy tree or beam is laid across the entrance, one end being raised and supported by a movable prop. A bit of rabbit or other bait is hung on a projecting stick made fast into the back of the semi-circle of stones. The marten can only get at the bait by creeping under the tree, and on seizing it, and finding himself unable to pull it down, he backs out, tugging the string by which it is attached along the stick. In this effort he loosens the support of the tree, which falls on him, and kills him, but without doing any harm to the fur. The further north the darker and better are the skins.

In trapping the beaver, the otter, and different sorts of game, various contrivances are used, but there is not much interest in the mere description of them. In hunting expeditions other animals are met with, besides those which are sought for trading purposes. For instance, here are some of my recollections of the porcupine.

Early one morning, I was lying wrapped in my blanket by a deep buffalo path, which came down through a prairie to the little creek where we were then encamped. It was late in the fall, and the thick and heavy grasses of these prairies having been long before killed by the early frosts, had become perfectly dry. To avoid setting fire to this dry grass, we had kindled our fire in the bottom of the deep path, where it passed through the corner of the bank. Some of the Indians had got up, and were sitting part on one side and part on the other side of the path, preparing something for breakfast, when our attention was called to some unusual sound, and we saw a porcupine coming slowly and slouchingly down the path. I had heard much of the stupidity of the animal, but never had an opportunity of witnessing it till now. On he came, without giving any attention to surrounding objects, until his nose was actually in the fire; then bracing stiffly back with his fore feet, he stood so near the flame, that being driven towards him by the wind, it actually singed the hairs on his face. Still he stood there for some minutes, stolidly opening and shutting his eyes. At length one of the Indians, tired with looking at him, hit him a blow with a piece of moose meat he had on a little stick to roast. Another man killed him with his tomahawk, and we roasted and ate some of the meat, which was very good. The Indians then, in conversation respecting the habits of this animal, related, what I have since seen, that as a porcupine is feeding in the night, along the bank of a river, a man may sometimes take up some of his food upon the blade of a paddle, and holding it close to his nose, he will eat it, without even perceiving or appearing to perceive the presence of man. When taken, they can neither bite nor scratch, having no defence nor protection, except what is afforded by their barbed and dangerous spines, which they erect with great force and swiftness. Dogs fear them, and can rarely, if ever, be induced to attack them; if they do, severe injury and suffering, if not death, it is said, will be the certain consequence of wounds by the spines.

On another occasion, when out in camp on a war expedition, we were on the alert on account of the proximity of some Sioux Indians, from whom we feared a night attack. More than half the night had passed, and not one of us had slept, when we heard a sudden rushing outside, and our dogs came running in, not making any noise, but in terrible fright. I said that the time was come for us all to die together. I placed myself in the front, and raising the door a little, put out the muzzle of my gun, and sat in momentary expectation of the approach of the enemy. In the silent night footsteps were distinctly audible, not regular but at intervals, as if some one were stealthily advancing; but the darkness was so great that as yet I could see nothing. At length a small black object, not larger apparently than a man's head, was seen moving slowly and directly toward my lodge. Here I experienced how much imagination or alarm influences the correctness of sight; for this object, at first appearing small, as it came on, seemed at one time to enlarge itself to the height of a man; and again, upon steadily looking at it, to lessen to the size which it really was. Being now convinced it was only some small animal, I stepped out, and finding it to be a porcupine, I despatched it with a blow, that it might not again raise alarm, as in our case it had done by sending the dogs flying into our lodge.

I am now about to narrate an important event of my early years, my marriage to an Indian wife. I have already told of the marriage of my brother Wa-me-gon-a-biew with the daughter of Crooked Lightning, and of the troubles that befell us on that occasion, when we lost all the property that we then had. The whole affair had so many painful associations, that I was the less inclined to follow his example. I was now, it is true, about twenty-one years of age, and few of the Indian young men remain single so long. But I was contented with my way of life, and happy, except when we had to experience the pains of want and of hunger. I was now a good hunter and loved a hunter's life, and it was a pleasure as well as my duty to provide for my old mother Net-no-kwa, and the women and children that formed her family. No thought or wish for a change disturbed me.

About this time, when on our way to a trading-house, we met with an old Ottawwaw chief, called Wa-ge-to-tah-gun (he that has a bell), more commonly called Wa-ge-tote. He was a relative of Net-no-kwa, and had then three lodges and two wives. One of his sons also was there with his wife. He was pleased to meet with Net-no-kwa, and he made us remain near him for two months. Every morning he came to our lodge, as he went out to hunt, and asked me to accompany him. He always gave me the largest portion of what we killed. He took much pains to teach me how to take moose and other animals which are difficult to kill. Wa-me-gon-a-biew, with his wife, who were still with us, left us here and went to Red River.

The spring having come, the Indians in the neighbour-hood were all preparing to take their skins and other property to the trading-house. Knowing what had happened on previous occasions, and feeling strongly the foolishness of wasting our peltries in purchasing what was not only useless but hurtful to us, I urged Net-no-kwa not to go there, but to accompany me to another hunting station. I am happy to say that I had influence enough to dissuade her, and we prepared to go in a different direction. She went to see Wa-ge-tote, to take leave of him, and to thank him for his kind hospitality. When she returned, I readily perceived that something unusual had happened. She was quiet and rather mysterious; and presently she took me to one side, and began to speak to me. "My son," she said, "you see that I am now getting old; I am scarcely able to make you moccasins, to dress and preserve your skins, and do all that is needful about your lodge. You are now able to take your own place as a man and a hunter, and it is right that you should have some one who is young and strong, to look after your property, and to take care of your lodge. Wa-ge-tote, who is a good man, and respected by all the Indians, will give you his daughter.

You will thus gain a powerful friend and protector, who will be able to assist us in time of difficulty; and I shall be relieved from much trouble and anxiety about our family." Much more she said, in the same strain; but I told her at once, and without hesitation, that I could not comply with her request. I had hitherto never entertained the thought of marrying among the Indians, still thinking that somehow and some time, before I became old, I would marry among the whites. At all events, I assured her I could not now marry the woman she proposed for me. She still insisted that I must take her, stating that the whole affair had been settled between Wa-ge-tote and herself, and that the young woman herself had been spoken to, and had said she was not disinclined to the match. She pretended that after what had been arranged with Wa-ge-tote she could not do otherwise than bring her to our lodge. I said, if she did so, I would not treat her or consider her as my wife.

The affair was in this situation the morning but one before we were to separate from Wa-ge-tote and his people. Without coming to any better understanding with the old woman, I rose early, and went out with my gun. I stayed out all day, but was too much annoyed and troubled to attend much to hunting. Returning in the evening to the lodge, I carefully reconnoitred the inside before entering, intending, if the young woman was there, to go to some other lodge to sleep; but I saw nothing of her. Next morning Wa-ge-tote came to my lodge to see me, he expressed all the interest in me which he had really been in the habit of showing, and gave me much friendly advice and many good wishes. When he left, Net-no-kwa came to me, again urging me to marry the daughter, but I gave no consent. I believe now that it was she, and not Wa-ge-tote or the daughter, who had been anxious for the match, if indeed she had even been spoken to on the subject. The old woman no doubt saw it would be a convenient as well as proper alliance, so far as she and her household were concerned; but I had no feeling upon the subject, and I did not understand the making-up of matches by parents and guardians for convenience, and without respect to the mutual affection or even acquaintance of young persons. That my thoughts were correct I am the more sure, as I heard not long after that Wa-ge-tote's daughter was married soon to another man.

This affair, though it came to nothing, had the effect of bringing the question of marriage more seriously under my consideration, and may have prepared the way for what did take place at no distant period. But some important events occurred before that time which I must narrate; all the more as they brought me to a condition of health, and of mind, which may have made me the more ready to seek the companionship and comfort belonging to married life.

Leaving Wa-ge-tote, his daughter and his band, we went to the hunting-ground which I had chosen. Wage-tote himself I parted from with true regret, for he had taken a great liking to me, and had taught me many useful things, being a skilful and experienced hunter. Late in the fall we moved to a trading station, where many Indians met the trader, not at his house, but at some distance near a lake. Here he encamped for some days, and having brought with him a large quantity of rum, he rightly thought it better to get the Indians to buy and drink what they could before he went to his house, as they would give him less trouble at his camp. I had the prudence to purchase the most needful things for the winter, such as blankets and ammunition, as soon as we met him. After we had completed our trade, it had been the annual custom for Net-no-kwa to make a present to the trader of ten fine beaver skins, in return for which she was in the habit of receiving a chiefs dress and ornaments, and a ten-gallon keg of spirits. On this occasion when the trader sent for her to deliver his present, the old woman had already been drinking so hard that she was unable to go. In this emergency I felt it necessary to go and receive the articles. I put on the chief's coat and ornaments, and taking the keg on my shoulder, carried it home to our lodge, placed it on one end, and knocked out the head with an axe. I was thoughtless at the moment, and excited with the whole affair, the spirit of revelry prevailing all through the camp. On knocking in the head of the keg I addressed all who were capable of listening: "I am not one of those chiefs who draw liquor out of a small hole in a cask; let all who are thirsty come and drink" I am sorry to say that I set the example, and this second time that I had joined the Indians in drinking I was guilty of far greater excess than the first time. Our keg was soon empty, and then I and those who were able to stagger forth went to other lodges where liquor could be had. It was now late at night, but the noise of drunkenness was heard in every part of the camp. Next day, when Net-no-kwa recovered sufficiently to speak, she asked me whether I had received the chief's dress and the keg of rum. When I told her that the keg had been emptied, she actually grew angry because I had not reserved some for her, and then reproached me severely, censuring me not only for ingratitude to herself, but for disgracing myself by getting drunk. The Indians told her she had no right to complain of me for doing as she herself had taught me, and then in order to pacify her they soon contributed rum enough to make her again completely drunk.

Such scenes took place regularly at every trading station. I am told that by order of the government and of the trading companies these abuses have been put an end to in the stations under their authority; but there will always be excessive drinking where the sale of spirits is permitted, and I am describing what I myself witnessed, and sometimes took part in, when I was among the people as one of them.

When all the peltries were disposed of, so that the Indians had to discontinue drinking, they began to disperse to their hunting-grounds. Our family was about this time increased by the addition of a poor old Ojibbeway woman and two children, who being destitute of any male protector had been taken up by Net-no-kwa. I hunted with considerable success that season, when Net-no-kwa determined to return to the trading-house at Menaukonoskeg, while I should go to the trading-house at Red River to purchase sonic necessary articles. I made a pack of beavers, having been very successful in trapping them, and started alone in a small buffalo-skin canoe, only large enough to carry me and my pack, and descended the Little Saskatchewan.

During this solitary journey a strange incident occurred. There is on the bank of that river a place which looks like one where the Indians would always choose to encamp at. In a bend of the river is a beautiful landing place; behind it a little plain, a thick wood, and a small hill rising abruptly in the rear. But this tempting-looking site is utterly shunned by the Indians, and regarded with a superstitious terror. No Indian will land his canoe, much less encamp at "the place of the two dead men." The legend is, that many years ago, when there was an encampment here, a quarrel arose between two brothers, who had she-she-gwi or rattlesnakes for their marks or totems. One drew his knife and slew the other; but the bystanders instantly killed the murderer, for fratricide is deemed a crime as horrible as it is rare among them. The two brothers were buried in one grave.

I had heard the story of the two brothers, and as they bore the same totem as myself, it having been given to me by Manito-o-gheezik when I came with his family, I suppose they were probably related to us. I had heard it said that if any man camped near their graves, as some had done soon after they were buried, the dead men would be seen to come out of the ground, and either react the quarrel and the murder, or in some other way so annoy and disturb the visitors that they could not sleep. Yet the place when I saw it had a strange fascination for me. With a mixed feeling of curiosity and of bravery I pulled my little canoe to the shore. I thought to myself I should break the spell, and be able to tell the Indians that I not only stopped, but slept quietly, at a place which they shunned with weak and superstitious dread.

The sun was going down as I landed. Pulling up my canoe, I soon kindled a fire, and after eating my supper lay down to sleep. How long I lay I cannot tell, but I saw the two dead men come out of the ground and sit down at the fire opposite to me. Their eyes were fixed intently upon me; but they neither spoke, nor smiled, nor frowned; only gazing on me. I rose up from the ground where I lay, and was going to sit opposite to them by the fire, when I saw them not. The night was dark and gusty, but while looking and listening, I saw nothing and heard nothing except the wind in the trees. It is likely that I fell asleep again, for presently I saw the same two men standing below the bank of the river, their heads just rising to the level of the ground where I had made my fire. They were looking at me as before. While I was watching them they seemed to rise up, and came and sat opposite me again by the fire. This time they were laughing and speaking to one another, and they looked as if they were about to rush upon me. I tried to speak to them, but my voice failed me; I tried to rise and flee, but my limbs refused to move; at length one of them said, "Look over the top of the hill behind you." I turned and looked, and saw a horse fettered, and standing looking at me. "There," said the ghostly voice, "is a horse which I give you to ride on your journey to-morrow; and as you pass here on your return home, you can call and leave the horse, and spend another night with us." By this time I was wide awake, and no more I saw or heard anything, save the still red embers of the fire, and the moaning of the wind in the trees under the hill. I could not lie down to sleep again, but watched for the morning, and was pleased then to find that, with the darkness of the night, these terrifying visions vanished.

In the morning, instead of going down to the river I went towards the hill, when I observed tracks and other signs. Following a little distance I saw a horse tethered by its foot, and knew it as belonging to the trader I was going to see; I knew also that several miles might be saved by crossing from this point on the Little Saskatchewan to the Assineboin, instead of following the bends of the river. So I left my canoe, and having put my load on the horse, I led him towards the trading-house, where I arrived next day.

In reflecting calmly about this strange night adventure, the explanation seems simple enough. My mind had been full of the story I had heard of the dead men and of their apparitions. It was natural enough that in my sleep I saw the ghosts, and in dreams we imagine that we hear as well as see what is unreal. There was neither sight nor sound after I was awake, and this twice over. The only thing that puzzles me is my having been told by one of the spirits about the horse. I fancy now that in my relief next morning, after the horrible excitement of the night, the welcome meeting with the horse got confusedly mixed with the vivid remembrances of the dream. I said nothing at the trader's house, but on my return home, and afterwards, the account I gave of what I had seen and suffered that night was eagerly listened to, and confirmed the superstitious terrors of the Indians. I know that in all subsequent journeys through that country, I carefully shunned "the place of the two dead men."

Chapter V.

***MY MARRIAGE WITH "THE RED SKY OF THE
MORNING"—CURIOUS COURTSHIP—INDIAN
MARRIAGE CUSTOMS—ALONG WITH MY
BROTHER I ACCOMPANY A WAR EXPEDITION—
WAR CEREMONIES—RULES IN CAMP AND ON
MARCH—DIVINATION AND OMENS—WANT OF
WATER IN THE JOURNEY—DISCOVERY OF
SPRINGS—GREAT HERD OF BUFFALOES ON THE
PRAIRIE—BULLS FIGHTING—A COUNCIL OF
WAR—DISPUTES AMONG THE CHIEFS—WITH-
DRAWAL OF MANY FROM THE EXPEDITION—
RETURN HOME WITHOUT ATTACKING THE
SIOUX.***

At the end of the next fall, on going to Mouse River trading-house, I heard that some white people from the United
States Government had been there, to purchase some articles
for the use of their party, then living at the Maudan village. I
regretted that I had missed the opportunity of seeing them;
but as I had received the impression that they were to remain
permanently there, I thought I would be able at any time to
make an occasion to visit them. I have since been informed
that these white men belonged to the party of Governor Clark
and Captain Lewis, then on their way to the Rocky Mountains
and the Pacific Ocean. As the date of that expedition must be
given in American history, I mention the matter, as it gives
clue to the period to which my recollections of Indian life
belong.

In a preceding chapter I said I was going to tell you about my marriage, and it is time that I finish that statement. It was in the following spring, when about to leave our winter quarters, an old man, a chief of the Metai, came to our lodge, bringing a young woman, his granddaughter, together with the girl's parents. She was a handsome girl, young and healthy; but Net-no-kwa did not think favourably of her. She said to me: "My son, these people will not cease to trouble you if you remain here; and as the girl is by no means fit to become your wife, or my daughter-in-law, I advise you to take your gun and go away. Make a hunting camp at some distance, and do not return till they have time to see that you are decidedly disinclined to the match." I took her advice, and the old man apparently relinquished his hope of marrying me to his granddaughter.

After some time I returned, and was standing by our lodge one evening, when I saw a good-looking young woman walking about, and smoking. She observed me, and presently came up, and asked me to smoke with her. I answered that I did not smoke. This was the case, for I had been told when first among the Indians that the healthiest men and the best hunters never smoked. Yet I was not surprised to sec her smoking, for it is common among Indian women, whether young or old. She said she saw that I was averse to touching her pipe, and would not smoke with her. I did not wish to be discourteous, so I took her pipe, and smoked a very little just to please her. She remained for some time talking, and I thought her agreeable. After this, we talked frequently, and I became gradually attached to her.

I mention this because it was to this woman I was married, and because the beginning of our acquaintance was not after the usual manner of the Indians. Among them it commonly happens that when a young man marries a woman, even of his own tribe, he has had no previous personal acquaintance with her. They have seen each other in the village; he has looked at her in passing; but it is probable they have never spoken together. The match is planned and made up by the old people, and when the proposed marriage is made known to the young pair they usually find in themselves no objection to the arrangement, as they know, should it prove disagreeable mutually or to either party, the proposal can at any time be broken off.

My conversations with Mis-kwa-bun-o-kwa (the red sky of the morning), for such was the name of the young woman who had offered me her pipe, was soon noised about the village.

The old chief hearing of it, and inferring that I, like other young men of my age, was thinking of taking a wife, came one day to our lodge, leading by the hand another of his granddaughters. "This," he said to Net-no-kwa, "is the handsomest and best of all my descendants; I come to offer her to your son." So saying, he left her in the lodge, and went away. This young woman was one whom Net-no-kwa had always treated with marked kindness, and she was considered one of the handsomest in the band. The old woman was therefore now in some embarrassment, for she could say nothing to the old chief against his granddaughter. But at length she found an opportunity to say to me: "My son, this girl which O-shusk-koo-koon offers you is handsome and good, but you must not marry her, for she has that about her which will in a very short time bring her to the grave. It is necessary that you should have a wife who is strong and free from any disease. Let us, therefore, make the young woman a handsome present, for she deserves well of us, and send her back to her father." She accordingly gave her presents to a considerable value, and she returned home. Less than a year afterwards she died of decline, as Net-no-kwa had anticipated. In the meantime Mis-kwa-bun-o-kwa and myself were becoming more and mere attached to one another. The recent experiences of Wa-ge-tote's daughter and the other chief's two granddaughters convinced me that I was expected no longer to remain single, and I now had my own inclination on the side of the general feeling in the matter. I said nothing to Net-no-kwa, but like a prudent sagacious old woman as she was, she was well aware of what was going on, and I found that she did not disapprove, but rather favoured my intention. This I discovered by the following incident. I had been visiting at the lodge of my young mistress, and having stayed very late, I stole quietly into our lodge, and went to sleep. In the morning I was awakened very early, at the first appearance of dawn, by a smart rapping on my feet. Looking up I saw the old woman standing by my couch, with a stick in her hand, and she said to me: "Up, get up, young man, who art about to take to yourself a wife. Get up and start after game. It will make the young woman think far more highly of you to see you bring home a load of meat early in the morning, than to see you idling about the village, dressed ever so gaily, dangling after her, when the hunters are all gone out." I could make no answer to this, so putting on my moccasins, I took my gun and went out. Returning before noon with as heavy a load of fat moose meat as I could carry, I threw it down before Net-no-kwa, saying: "Here, old woman, is what you called for in the morning." She was much pleased, and commended me for my exertion. I was now satisfied that she was not displeased on account of my attachment to "the Red Sky of the Morning," and I was much gratified on finding that I had her approval. Many of the Indians have little respect or care for aged people, but though Net-no-kwa had her faults and was now decrepid and infirm, I felt the truest regard for her, and continued to do so while she lived.

I now redoubled my diligence in hunting, and commonly came home with meat early in the day, and always before night. I then dressed myself as gaily as I could, and walked about the village, often blowing the pe-be-gwan or flute. For some time Mis-kwa-bun-o-kwa, as if sure of having gained my affection, and perhaps vain of her conquest, began to pretend she hesitated about marrying me This went on till there really arose some abatement of ardour on my side, and I treated her as coolly as she treated me. I began then also to bethink myself of the responsibilities of married life, and my desire to bring a wife home to my lodge gradually abated. I sought to avoid her, and to break off communication with her, but a lingering inclination was too strong to make me come to any regular rupture. When she saw my growing indifference she sometimes reproached me, sometimes sought to move me by tears and entreaties, and all her coy coquettish-ness had disappeared. Still I said nothing to the old woman about bringing her home, and I felt unwilling to take the decided and irrevocable step of making her my wife.

At this time I had occasion to go to the trading-house on Red River, and did not return till the third day. On arriving at our lodge I saw Mis-kwa-bun-o-kwa sitting in my place. As I stopped at the door of the lodge, taken aback and hesitating to enter, she hung down her head and was silent; but Net-no-kwa greeted me in a tone harsher than was her wont in seeing me after absence. "Will you turn back from the door of the lodge," she said, "and put to shame this woman, who is better than you are? This affair is your seeking, not mine or hers. You have followed her about the village, and caused her to be spoken of along with you; and now you would treat her as one who sought to thrust herself upon you!" I was in part conscious of the justness of Net-no-kwa's reproaches; and the sight of the now submissive young woman touched my heart, so I went and sat by the side of Mis-kwa-bun-o-kwa, and the old woman smiled and spoke a blessing on our affection. I found afterwards that in my absence the good old woman had taken up the matter in earnest, without consulting me; and had made her bargain and her arrangements with the parents of the young woman, and brought her home, rightly judging that my indecision would be thus brought to an end, and that it would not be difficult to reconcile me to the measure. A wise and kind interference is often of great importance under similar circumstances. In this case, when the slight difficulties were brushed aside, the disturbed affections resumed their sway, and we loved one another as before.

Soon after my return from Red River we moved to the woods, and encamped there. Besides myself and wife, and the family of Net-no-kwa, was my brother Wa-me-gon-a-biew, who had returned with a second wife, one of the granddaughters of the old chief Wa-ge-tote. There was also an Indian hunter Wau-be-nais-sa, with his wife and several children, a friend of my brother, and who had been engaged by Net-no-kwa to hunt for her family when we were absent. We directed our course towards the Craneberry River (Pembinah), wishing to select near that place a favourable spot for the women and children to remain encamped. My brother and I had resolved to join a war party, which we heard was then in preparation to go against the Sioux. I had till now never left the peaceable business of a hunter, but the exciting narratives of war expeditions led me to wish to witness such scenes. When we had chosen a suitable place for the camp, we applied ourselves diligently to hunting, that we might leave enough of dried meat to supply the wants of our families when we went away.

We had killed a considerable quantity of meat, and the women were occupied in drying it, when, feeling curious to know the state of forwardness of the war party at Pembinah, and how soon they would start, my brother and I took our horses and rode down, leaving Wau-be-nais-sa with the women and children. When we got to Pembinah we found forty men of the Muskegoes ready to start on the following morning, and though we had come without our moccasins and unprepared for fighting, I determined to go forward along with them. There were a good many Ojibbeways and Crees also assembled, and prepared for advancing, but they seemed in general to be unwilling to go in company with the Muskegoes, a race not held in very high repute by most of the other Indians. My brother tried to dissuade me from going, urging that we had better put it off, and accompany the Ojibbeways later on in the season. But I assured him I would by no means lose the present opportunity, inasmuch as we could both go now and also in the fall with the Ojibbeways. As it turned out, my curiosity was somewhat disappointed, so far as the sight of war was concerned, as I shall presently relate, but the journey enabled me to gain new experience and to witness some things that I would not otherwise have seen.

I saw, for instance, and began to attend to some of the ceremonies of what may be called the initiation of warriors, this being the first time I had been on a war party. Such ceremonies, I am told, exist in most nations, and vary in their character; and they may perhaps vary among different Indian tribes. I refer only to some of the things that I observed at this time. The young warrior puts black war paint on his face, and wears a peculiar cap or head-dress. He must always in marching follow the older warriors, stepping in their tracks, and never preceding them. However long or fatiguing the march, he must neither eat, nor drink, nor sit down to rest by day. If he halts for a moment, he turns his face towards his own country that the Great Spirit may see it is his wish to return home again.

At night they observe a certain order in their encampments. If there are bushes where they halt, the camp is enclosed by these stuck into the ground so as to include a square or oblong space, with a passage at one end, which is always that towards the enemy's country or camp. If there are no bushes, they mark the ground in the same manner with small sticks or with the stalks of the weeds which grow in the prairie. Near the entrance to this gate or opening is the head chief and the old warriors, succeeded in order by younger men, according to age or prowess, or reputation in war; and last of all, in the extreme end of the enclosed camp, the men with blackened faces who are making their first war expedition. All sleep with their faces towards their own country, and on no consideration, however uneasy their position or however great their fatigue, must any change of posture be made. No two must lie upon or be covered by the same blanket. During marches the older warriors, if they ever sit down, must not sit on the bare ground, but at least have some grass or bushes under them. They are very careful not to wet their feet, and if obliged to cross a stream or a swamp they keep their clothes dry, and whip their legs with bushes or grass when they come out of the water. They must never walk in a beaten path, but if obliged to do so they put on their legs some sort of medicine, which is carried for the purpose. Any article belonging to any of the party, such as his gun, his blanket, his hatchet or toma-hawk, his knife or war-club, must never be stepped over by any other person, nor must any one step over the body or limbs of any other who is sitting or lying on the ground. Should this rule or usage be inadvertently violated, it is the duty of the one who has been stepped over, or to whom the article stepped over belongs, to seize the offender and throw him to the ground, not in anger but to maintain the rule; and the person seized must suffer himself to be thrown down, even when much stronger or older than the other. The vessels which they carry, to eat or drink out of, are commonly small bowls of wood or of birch bark. They are marked across the middle, and they have some way of distinguishing the two sides; in going out they invariably drink out of one side of the bowl, and from the other in returning. On the way home, when within one day of their village, they suspend all these bowls on trees, or they throw them away on the prairie.

Various other observances and usages I noticed, some of them painful, and others troublesome, such as, of the latter, never to scratch the head or any part of the skin with the fingers but with a small twig or stick; and never must the bowl one eats or drinks out of, nor the knife he cuts with, be used by another. There may be diversity of observances and cere-monies, as I have stated, but it may be well thus to note some which I saw or heard of.

I ought to have mentioned, that in encamping at night, the chief who conducts the party sends some of his young men a little in advance to prepare a piece of ground where religious ceremonies and divination is to be performed for various purposes, chiefly to ascertain thereby the position of the enemy. I do not believe that there is any truth in these divinations, which have probably been invented and are maintained by the chiefs and the prophets and diviners, to make mystery, and to keep up thereby authority over the people. But there are many such observances, both in time of peace and of war. In preparing to encamp, when the young men go forward, they clear a piece of ground, removing the turf from a rectangular oblong space, and with their hands break up the soil, making it fine and soft, and then enclosing this place with poles or pieces of stick. The chief, on being informed that it is ready, goes and sits down at the end opposite to that of the enemy's country. Two small roundish stones are placed before him, and he is supposed then to engage in prayer to the Great Spirit to show the direction where the enemy is to be found. A crier then goes to some of the principal warriors and bids them come to the chief, and to smoke in the enclosure. It is dark by this time, and after awhile a light is made, and they examine the position of the two round stones, which have been moved by the people in the little space. From the direction in which they have been shifted, they infer the course they are to pursue in the morning. This is evidently a very clumsy and rough sort of divination, and liable to trickery as well as to error. However, it is not my purpose to criticise but only to narrate. After this process, offerings of cloth, beads, tobacco, or whatever the chiefs and men may choose to leave for sacrifice, are exposed during the night on a pole; also the je-bi-ug or memorials of dead friends or relatives, which are taken back in the morning and retained in order to be thrown into the midst of the fight, or thrust into the bodies of their enemies, ripped up by their knives. Warriors will carry with them to battle locks of hair of a lost child, or toys, or other home relics; and throwing these on the field are inspired to greater energy, and excited to greater passion of fierceness or revenge.

I am more convinced that the divination processes which I witnessed arose from craft, in that A-gus-ko-gaut, the Muskego chief whom we accompanied on this occasion, professed himself to be a prophet of the Great Spirit, like one who in after-years appeared among the Shawnees, and obtained great influence and notoriety. A-gus-ko-gaut had some time before lost his son, and in this expedition he carried the je-bi, with the determination to leave it in a bloody field of battle. But his design and the whole expedition came to an ignominious conclusion by the interference of an Ojibbeway chief, Ta-bush-sha, which means, he that dodges down, or the dodger, who the next morning overtook us from Pembinah, along with twenty warriors. This ambitious and restless chief, on arriving at the place of rendezvous, and hearing that a band of Muskegoes had started, was indignant that the lead should be taken by a people so despised by him, and was unwilling that one of them should head an expedition against the Sioux. He was a cunning man, and on arriving at the camp he dissembled, and professed nothing but good-will and friendliness; saying he had hastened to the aid of his brethren the Muskegoes. A-gus-ko-gaut could not have been ignorant of the character of the dodger, and may have suspected his designs; nevertheless, he received him with apparent cordiality, and bid him welcome.

We all journeyed onward for several days, when in crossing some wide prairies the want of water was sorely felt, and the necessities of thirst caused some of the rules which I have described to be broken or disregarded. The principal men were acquainted with the general features of the country we had to pass, and knew that water could be reached not very far ahead; but most of the older warriors, being on foot, were exhausted with fatigue and thirst. In this emergency, it became necessary that such of the party as had horses, among whom were Wa-me-gon-a-biew and myself, should go forward and search for water, and when it was found, make such signal as would inform the main body what course to take.

There was no thought then about new warriors never preceding the old. I was in the very front, and among the first to discover a place where water could be had; but before all the men could come up it, the sufferings of some of them had been excessive. Those who had arrived at the spring continued to discharge their guns during the night, the sound of which guided the direction of the advance, and no doubt cheered their fainting hopes. Not till morning did some stragglers totter to the place, utterly exhausted, and some of them in a condition of temporary madness.

While we rested at this spring, an old man, Ah-tek-oons, or the little caribou, made a divination, and afterwards announced that in a particular direction which he pointed out was a large band of Sioux warriors, coming straight towards us; that if we could turn to the right or the left, and avoid meeting them, we might proceed unopposed to their country and destroy their villages; but that if we stayed where we were, or went straight on, they would meet us, and from their numbers we must all be cut off. Ta-bush-sha affected to place the most implicit reliance on this prediction; but the Muskego chief, and the Muskegoes generally, would not listen to it, and we remained where we were two or three days longer.

There began now an incipient murmur of discontent, fostered certainly by the inactivity of the people, and perhaps helped by fears caused by the prediction of the dodger. Some even talked of leaving A-gus-ko-gaut, and going back to their own country. The only thing that caused some excitement was the discovery, by our scouts, of a solitary Indian, who fled immediately on being seen, and was supposed from this circumstance to be one of a Sioux war party. The sight of that one man caused endless conversation and conjecture in the camp. Nothing more was ever seen or heard of him, but his apparition caused increased vigilance, especially at night. It was necessary, however, to move to considerable distances from the camp. Food was beginning to get scarce, and the hunters had to go out in search of game. At first we kept ourselves as quiet as possible, but in the necessity for getting food some of the Muskegoes, with whom I was glad to join, rode out in open day in search of buffaloes, and we were successful in killing some. We had to go to long distances, and one night we found ourselves too far off to return, and slept where we were, with only such shelter as our clothes and the grass afforded.

After we had lain down and our ears were near the ground, there was heard a noise, which has been familiar to me since, but which then I heard for the first time. It was the tramp of a vast herd of buffaloes. When we sat up, or stood up, we could hear nothing, but on putting our ears close to the ground the same strange dull sound was heard. I would not have known what it was, but one of the Muskegoes told me, and then I could picture to myself the tramp of the great herd which could thus cause the earth to quake, and to utter a sound far off. In the morning when the light dawned we could see nothing of them, although we could command a rich view of the prairie. But as we knew they could not be very far off, eight of our number, of whom I was one, were selected to go in the direction whence the sound seemed to come; and if we killed any, we were to bring the meat to a point agreed upon, where we expected to have to stay the next night.

In the morning, we could still hear, by applying our ears to the ground, the same dull thud and noise as on the previous night, and it seemed about the same distance, and in the same direction as before.

We started early, and rode some hours before we saw anything passing over the trackless, boundless, sea-like prairie. At length we descried, apparently eight or ten miles off, a long dark line, drawn across the edge of the sky, like a low shore seen across a lake. The distance of the herd when we heard them first must have been at least twenty miles. We had been advancing towards them, but they also were on the move, so it was some hours before we reached the margin of the herd. As we approached, the noise became terrible. To the sound of the deep tramp of thousands of feet, and the noise caused by the knocking together of the two divisions of the hoof, as they raised their feet from the ground, was added the loud and furious roaring and bellowing of the bulls, engaged everywhere throughout the moving mass in fierce and furious conflicts. We knew that our approach would not cause the alarm and stampede at such a time—for it was the rutting season—that it would have done at any other time, so we rode directly towards them. The first we came up with and killed was a sorely wounded bull, which scarcely made any effort to escape from us. He had been terribly gored, and had wounds in his flanks into which I could have put my hands. As we knew that the flesh of the bulls at this season is not good to eat, we did not seek to kill them, though as we came near we might have shot several, so intent were they on their own fierce battles. Some of us now dismounted, leaving our horses in the care of the others, who were willing to stay back for that purpose, while we crept into the herd to try to kill some of the cows. I got separated from my companions, and before I had an opportunity of shooting a cow several bulls were fighting very near me. In their fury they were totally unconscious of my presence, and came rushing towards the place where I was, that in alarm I took refuge in one of those holes in the prairie ground, which are not uncommon in parts frequented by buffalo herds, and which they dig themselves to wallow in. Seeing them coming near to me, and fearing to be overwhelmed, I fired, in hope of dispersing or turning them aside, and only succeeded in doing so after killing two of them. The firing alarmed the cows, and they went off swiftly out of range, so that I perceived I should not be able to kill any in this direction. I therefore came out of my pit, and going back for my horse, I rode to a distant part of the herd, where my companions had succeeded in killing a fat cow. From this cow, as is usual, the rest of the herd had quickly moved off, except one bull, who stayed to guard her, and who, when I rode up, still kept the Indians at bay.

"Ah, you warriors," in my excitement I said; "you are going far from your country to an enemy's land, to despoil his homes, and you cannot take his wife from that old bull, who has nothing in his hands!" So saying I rushed past them, and rode directly for the bull, then not more than two hundred yards distant. He no sooner saw me approaching, than lowering his head he came plunging full charge at me, with such impetuosity that, knowing the danger to my horse and myself, I turned aside with a jerk, and fled at full speed. The Indians I could hear laughing loudly at my repulse; but they did not give over their less incautious attempts to get at the cow. By dividing the attention of the bull, and creeping up to him on different sides, he got confused and discouraged, and they at length gave him a fatal shot.

While we were cutting up this cow, the herd were at no great distance, and an old cow, which the Indians supposed to be the mother of the one we had killed, taking the scent of the blood, came running with great violence directly towards us. The Indians were alarmed by the sudden rush, and fled, some of them not having their guns in their hands, but only their knives. I had just re-loaded mine, and had it ready for use. Throwing myself down close to the body of the dead cow, and behind it, I waited till the other came within a few yards, when I fired. She turned, gave one or two jumps, and fell dead. We now had the meat of two fat well-conditioned cows, about as much as we wanted or could carry; accordingly we repaired without further delay to the appointed place, where we rejoined our party. They had already appeased their hunger by the meat of a deer which they had killed while waiting for us.

On our return to the camp we found that others had been successful in the chase, and there was that day something like a general feast. After they had eaten, Ta-bush-sha sent some of his men to call all the people together, as if for a council, and when they were assembled he arose and harangued them with a loud voice:

"You Muskegoes," he said, "are not true warriors, although you have come from your own country far off, to find the Sioux, as you say; but though hundreds of these enemies are at no great distance, you never can find them, and will remain till they fall upon you and kill you." More to this effect he spoke, his design evidently being to create hesitation and disunion, and thus to frustrate the plans of A-gus-ko-gaut, the Muskego chief. In closing his address he declared his determination to abandon an expedition so badly conducted, and to return to Pembinah with his twenty warriors.

When he had ended, up rose and out spoke Pe-shew-o-ste-gwon (the wild cat's head), orator and councillor of A-gus-ko-gaut, the Muskego: "Now," he said, "we see plainly why our brothers, the Ojibbeways and Crees, were not willing to come with us from Red River. You are near your own country, and it is of no importance to you whether you meet the Sioux now, or in the fall; but we have come a very great distance; we bear along with us, as we have long borne, those that were our friends and children, but we cannot lay them down, except we come into the camp of our enemies. You know very well that in a party like this, although it is large now, if only one turns back, another and another will follow, until few or none are left. And it is for this reason that you have joined us; that you may draw off our young men, and thus compel us to return without having done anything."

After he had thus spoken, Ta-bush-sha, whatever he may have felt, made no sign, nor spoke any word, but rose, and turning his face towards his own country, departed with his twenty men.

The chief of the Muskegoes and the principal men sat silently together, and then they saw one and another of their own young men get up and follow the Ojibbeways.

In the first moments, the departure of Ta-bush-sha roused some indignation in the breasts of some of the Muskegoes, and two or three of them actually raised their guns and fired after the retiring Ojibbeways. Some of these were preparing to resent this, but their leader, being always a cool and prudent man, repressed their ardour, for if blood had been shed they might all have been slain by the more numerous Muskegoes. So they departed in silence, and those who had fired upon them returned to the camp. As for the old chief, A-gusko-gaut, with a few of his faithful councillors he continued to sit upon the ground, upon the same spot where he had listened to the speech of Ta-bush-sha; and when he saw his band gradually fall away, till only five remained out of sixty, the old man bowed his head and wept.

I had retired to a little distance from the chief, and remained there during the whole time. When I saw the result of the Ojibbeway dodger's intrigue, and that the old man was deserted by his own people, I felt pity and indignation. I went up to the chief, and told him, that if he was willing to go on himself, I would accompany him, if no other would. My brother Wa-me-gon-a-biew had already gone with the deserters. The other men who remained sitting with him were his personal friends, and would have gone if he had wished it; but he said he feared we could do very little if so few in number, and the Sioux would certainly cut us off when they learned the weakness of our party.

Chapter VI.

RETURN BY THE MOUSE RIVER TRADING STATION—MEET A BAND OF CREE INDIANS HAVING A BLOOD FEUD WITH OUR FAMILY—THEY RECOGNISE MY BROTHER WA-ME-GON-A-BIEW, AND TRY TO TAKE HIS LIFE—MY LIFE IN PERIL WHILE SAVING HIS—BEAR HUNTING ADVENTURES—CHASED BY A SHE BEAR WHOSE CUB I HAD SHOT—NARROW ESCAPE IN A BEAR'S PIT—VARIOUS HUNTING EXPEDITIONS.

So the expedition was abandoned, and every man sought to return home by the most speedy and convenient way, no longer paying the least regard to anything except to his own safety and comfort. I soon overtook my brother, and with three other men we formed a party to return in company. We chose a route different from that taken by most of the others, and finding game abundant we did not suffer from hunger. In four days we reached Large Wood River, which runs from a mountainous region, taking a long course through prairie, and some miles passing underground, finally joining the Red River. Near this river we killed one of the common red deer, said to be abundant near the Ohio, but which are rarely seen so far north. When we reached home I had only seven balls left, and as there was no trader near I could get no more; but I was extremely careful, and on several occasions, after shooting a moose or elk, I recovered the ball, which does not always pass through, and may be used again. With my seven balls I killed double the number of game. When the supply began to diminish, towards the fall, I went to the trading-house at Mouse River to get ammunition and various goods that we required in our lodge. My brother went with me, and when there, he told me he had determined to go and live by himself with his family. He had spoken to Net-no-kwa, who preferred remaining with me.

Wa-me-gon-a-biew, while outwardly friendly, had long shown a want of affection to me, and I have had occasion to mention his want of respect and consideration for the old woman. Still we had lived as brothers all these years; and now an event occurred which enabled me to save his life, and to give him at least good ground for knowing my friendship and regard for him as the son of Net-no-kwa.

At the Mouse River trading-house we met with some members of a family that had quarrelled, in times long past, with the predecessors of our house. These family feuds are kept up from father to son, and for generations the fire of revenge may be smouldering, ready to burst forth if opportunity comes, even if no new provocation is given. These men did not know me, but they in some way recognised in my brother the son of a hostile house. They belonged to a band at the trading station, strangers to us, and too powerful for us to resist openly.

Some one warned us that these men had been heard to threaten to kill my brother. As we could not avoid being thrown more or less into their power, I thought it best to try to conciliate their goodwill, or, at least, purchase the forbearance of some of them by a present, and by using the influence of hospitality. So we procured two kegs of whisky, and took them to this band, disguising our having heard of any ill-will or ill-design on their part. One of the kegs I gave specially to the head of the family who nursed the old feud, and had made the threat of which we heard. The other keg was broached at once by the band, and as some of them probably knew nothing of the feud, we began apparently to be all very jovial together.

While the drinking was going on I noticed one man, who, with great show of cordiality, invited and urged my brother to drink with him, and pretended to drink along with him. In order the more effectually to disarm suspicion and throw my brother off his guard, the fellow began to act like a drunken man, though I could see that he was quite sober, and knew that he had taken very little liquor indeed. It was not difficult to see through his design, and I determined to be on the watch, and to protect my brother, if possible, from the mischief plotted against him.

We had, in hope of securing the friendship of the Cree family, made our fire very near theirs, and as I saw that Wa-me-gon-a-biew was becoming too drunk to have much discretion, I withdrew him to our camp. The man who had pretended to be drunk could not decently throw off his disguise in a moment, which he must have done had he hindered my withdrawal of my brother. He let us go; but we had scarce reached our lodge, and I had just laid him down, when I found myself surrounded by a number of men, with guns and knives, and they spoke openly of killing Wa-me-gon-a-biew. Fortunately, as it now turned out, our present of spirits had nearly overcome the senses of all this menacing band, with the exception of the man already mentioned, who had evidently been charged with the duty of the assassination, and who alone being sober, I regarded as the most formidable of the band. Two of them approaching as if to stab Wa-me-gon-a-biew, I stepped between and prevented them; upon which they seized me by the arms, which I allowed them to do without any resistance on my part. I knew that if they were going to stab me, they must let go at least one hand each, and I could then better make an effort to escape from them. I grasped firmly in my right hand, concealed under my blanket, a large and strong knife, on which I placed great reliance. Very soon after they had seized me, the Indian on my left, still holding my left hand by his, raised his knife in his right hand to strike me in the ribs. His companion, who was more drunk, having felt his belt for his own knife, found that he had dropped it, and calling to his companion to wait till he could find his knife that he might kill me, let go my right hand and went towards the fire to look for his knife. This was my opportunity, and with a sudden spring I disengaged myself from the one who still held my left hand, at the same time showing him a glimpse of my knife. I was now free, and could have escaped, but I could not leave Wa-me-gon-a-biew in a situation where to be left alone was certain death. The Indians seemed for a moment astonished at my resistance and escape, and not less so when they saw me catch up the helpless body of my companion, and at two or three leaps pass out of their reach and place him in a canoe. I lost no time in getting to the trading-house, which was not far from their camp. Why they did not fire upon me before I was out of the light of their camp fire, I cannot tell; the whole thing was over in a short time: perhaps they were intimidated at seeing me so well armed, so active, and so entirely sober, which last circumstance gave me an evident advantage over most of them.

Wa-me-gon-a-biew for some time showed himself fully sensible of the risk I had run in saving his life, and had more brotherly feeling towards me. He soon afterwards left me, according to his previous determination, and I went to live by myself, at a place on the Assineboin River. A few days after I had been there, A-ke-wah-zains, a brother of Net-no-kwa, came to visit at our lodge. He had not been with us long, when we one day espied a very old man coming up the river in a small wooden canoe. A-ke-wah-zains, immediately recognised him as the father of the young men from whom I had so lately rescued my brother. The old man came promptly to the shore when called, but it soon appeared that he was quite unaware of what had passed between his sons and us. When I told A-ke-wah-zains all about it he was excessively enraged, and, but for my interference and entreaty, he might have killed the old man on the spot. I was content to allow him to take a good deal of the rum which the old man had brought out of his canoe, to which I helped him to return immediately, and urged his departure, as I knew it would not be safe to remain among us after his liquor had begun to have its effect.

The same evening A-ke-wah-zains asked me for my gun, which was a long, heavy, excellent one, in exchange for his, which was short and light I was unwilling to exchange, although I did not as yet know how great was the disparity between the two pieces; and although Net-no-kwa was unwilling I should exchange, I did not see how to refuse, because such refusal of a request made by an older to a younger man is rare among the Indians. So I had to part with my own gun, and go out with the old man's piece. My first adventure with it proved its worthlessness. I chased a bear into a low poplar tree, after firing several times without appearing to do him any harm. I was at last compelled to climb into the tree, and put the muzzle of my gun close to his head before I could kill him.

A few days afterwards, as I was hunting, I started at the same moment an elk and three young bear cubs; the latter running into a tree. I shot at the bears, and two of them fell. As I thought one or both of them must be only wounded, I sprang forward immediately towards the trunk of the tree, but had scarcely reached it when I saw the old she-bear come jumping in an opposite direction. She caught up the cub which had fallen nearest her, while she stood on her hind feet, holding it as a woman holds her child. She looked at it for a moment, sniffed the ball hole which was in its belly, and perceiving it was dead, dashed it down, and came directly towards me, gnashing her teeth and now walking so erect that her head stood as high as mine. All this was so sudden that I had scarcely re-loaded my gun, when she was close to the muzzle, having had only time to raise it. I now saw the necessity of a lesson I had been early taught by the Indian hunters, and which I rarely neglected, namely, after discharging my gun, to think of nothing else before loading it again. Firing at so close quarters left the bear no chance, and she instantly was rolled over.

At this period I had a good deal of practice in bear-hunting. They seemed to be plentiful in the woods. I killed above twenty, notwithstanding the poorness of my gun. One old she-bear was quite white, and had four cubs, one white with red eyes and red nails, like herself, one brown, and two black. In size and other respects she was the same as the common black bear, being what is called an albino. The fur of the black is not so highly valued as the red by the trader. I had a narrow escape on one occasion. I came upon a bear in his hole, not very far from our lodge. I shot him, and waiting for the smoke to clear away, as he was lying perfectly still at the bottom, I supposed he was dead, and jumped down to prepare to draw him out. My body filling the hole so as to exclude the light, I did not perceive he was still alive till I laid my hand upon him. On this, he turned and sprang upon me; I retreated as fast as I could, but he was equally nimble, and as I ran I could feel his breath at one time warm on my neck while snapping his teeth, so near did he get. He might have seized me then, and I cannot understand why he did not, I had caught up my gun as I leaped from the mouth of the den. He still pursued, though I had made a spurt when the sensation of his breath so near had startled me, and had now gained a little distance. My first fire wounded him and caused him to stop, and I soon killed him. I was ever afterwards very cautious about going into bears' holes without first being certain that the animals were dead.

As the sugar season came on we went to Buffalo-Hump Lake, two days' journey from the head of the Pembinah River, to hunt beavers. We took our wives to the hunting grounds, but left Net-no-kwa, with the children to make sugar. It was our object to kill beaver enough to enable us to purchase each a good horse, intending to accompany the war-party against the Sioux in the ensuing summer.

In ten days I killed forty-two fine and large beavers, and Wa-me-gon-a-biew nearly as many. With these we went to the

Mouse River trading-house to buy horses. Mr. McKie had promised me, the last time I was there, to sell me a very strong and beautiful horse of his which I had seen, and I was much dissatisfied when I found that the horse had been sold to the North-West Company. I told him that since the horse had gone there, the beavers might go there also. On crossing to the other side I bought a large grey mare for thirty beaver skins. This was in some respects as good a horse as the other, but it did not please me so well. Wa-me-gon-a-biew also bought a horse from the Indians, and then we returned to Great Wood River, to look for old Net-no-kwa, but she had gone to Red River, whither we followed her. My horse caused me much trouble, as will appear by-and-by, but I must not anticipate.

We remained some time at the mouth of the Assineboin River, and many Indians gathered round us; among them some of my wife's relations, whom I had not before seen. Among them was an uncle, who was a cripple, and had for years scarcely been able to walk. He had heard of me only that I was a white man, and supposed that I could not hunt. When he saw my wife, he said to her, "Well, I hear you are married; does your husband ever kill any game?" This he said in a sneering incredulous tone, and my wife answered him in the same spirit: "Yes," said she, "if a moose or elk has lost his road, or wants to die, and comes and stands at our door or in his path, he will sometimes kill him!" "Oh, he has gone to hunt to-day, has he not? If he kills anything, I beg you will give me the skin to make some moccasins." This he said in derision; but on my return, on being told, I gave him the skin of the elk I had killed that day, to make his moccasins, at which he was much surprised and pleased. Continuing to be successful the next few days, I gave game to all my wife's relations, and soon heard no more of their ridicule, but was regarded by them with respect.

After some time the game was exhausted, and we found it necessary to disperse in various directions. I went about ten miles up the Assineboin, when we found two lodges. These people were also relatives of my wife. When we first arrived, the wife of the chief man happened to be cooking a moose's tongue for her husband, whom she expected soon to return from hunting. This she gave us immediately, and would perhaps have farther relieved our want, had not the men arrived. After this they gave us nothing; although the children were crying, and there seemed plenty of meat about their lodges. It was now late, and I was too much fatigued to go out hunting that evening; nevertheless, I would not suffer our women to purchase meat from them, as they wished to do. I saw these people considered us poor and helpless; and by an inhospitality unusual among Indians even towards complete strangers, they meant to treat us in a way that we must move away from quickly. So, at the earliest appearance of dawn in the morning, I took my gun, and, standing at the door of the lodge, I said purposely in a loud voice, "Can none but Po-ko-taw-ga-maw (which was the chief's name) kill game?" My wife came out of the lodge and handed me a piece of dried meat which she had made her sister take for me. By this time several of the people had come out of the lodges, and I threw the piece of meat from me among the dogs, saying, "Shall such food as this be offered to my wife and children, when there are plenty of elks in the woods?" Before noon I had killed two fat elks, and brought back to the camp a heavy load of meat.

There was a wonderful change from that time in their treatment of us, and we were pressed to stay, which we did for the short time it was convenient for us. We wanted to select some good skins of elk and moose for making moccasins. Those taken in the woods make better leather than the skins of animals in the open prairies, which are less strong and suited for this purpose.

Chapter VII.

SOME ACCOUNT OF INDIAN RELIGIOUS CERE-
MONIES—JUGGLING IMPOSTORS—FEASTS AND
FESTIVALS—WAR FEASTS—MEDICINE
HUNTS—PROPHETS, SEERS, AND MEDICINE
MEN—THE METAI—SONGS, CHANTS, AND LEG-
ENDS—THE STORY OF THE RAG AND SNOW-
MAN—WOMEN'S WORK AND PLACE IN THE
INDIAN LODGE.

As we were travelling one day through the prairie we saw at a distance, coming in our direction, a man loaded with baggage, and having two of the large drums called Ta-wa-e-gurt-num, used in the observances of the religious ceremony called Waw-be-no. We looked to our young women for an explanation, as we soon recognised the approaching traveller to be no other than Pich-e-to, one of the band of inhospitable relatives we had lately left. The face of Squaw-shish, the Bow-we-tig girl, betrayed the consciousness of some knowledge respecting the motives of Pich-e-to. He soon came up, with his two drums, and stopped with us. Old Net-no-kwa was not backward in inquiring what had brought him, and when she found that his designs extended no farther than to the Bow-we-tig girl, she gave her consent to the match, and they were married, continuing with us for some time. He behaved quietly, and did not, when with us, make any parade of the religion of which he was a professor. I remember only that one night when there was a great thunderstorm, Pich-e-to became terribly alarmed, and got up and offered some tobacco to the thun-

s if it were the voice of a living being, and entreating it
op. This was from his own personal fear and superstition,
d had nothing to do with the Waw-be-no, a false and mischievous religion then in some vogue among the young
Ojibbeways and other tribes, although discountenanced by
the older and more respectable Indians.

The ceremonies of the Waw-be-no are attended with
much noise and irregularity. The feasts differ from all other
Indian feasts in being held in the night, and in the exhibition
of many tricks with fire, by the chiefs of the sect. The initi-
ated take red-hot embers in their hands, and sometimes put
hot stones in their mouths. Sometimes they put powder on the
insides of their hands, first moistening them to make it stick;
then by rubbing them on coals, or a red-hot stone, they make
the powder burn. Occasionally one of the principal performers has a kettle brought and set down before him, which is
taken boiling from the fire, and before it has time to cool he
plunges his hands to the bottom, and brings up a piece of flesh
that had purposely been put there. He then, while it is yet
smoking or steaming hot, tears the flesh with his teeth, dancing and capering about all the time.

These performances prove that the founders of this sect
are a set of juggling impostors, who have persuaded the ignorant that they possess supernatural power. It is on the same
principle that medicine men and prophets obtain honour and
influence, the knowledge possessed by them being made
power. In the case of the Waw-be-no fire-eaters and fire-han-
dlers, the knowledge is that of a preparation of certain herbs,
which make the parts to which it is applied less sensible to
heat. One of these plants is a species of yarrow or millefoil;
another grows on the prairies. These plants they mix and
bruise, or chew together, and rub over their hands and arms.
The yarrow poultice is a common remedy for burns; but when
mixed with some other herb, not so well known, the mixture
certainly gives to the skin, even of the lips and the tongue,
wonderful power of resisting the effects of fire.

The Waw-be-no is not, however, confined to these juggling exhibitions. The performers are a crafty and unprinci-
pled set, and the night festivals are the source of much evil,
excited by the singing and dancing, and drink when they can
get it. The drum is made of a portion of the trunk of a tree,
hollowed by fire, and with skin tied tightly over it. There is no
music, but much noise and disturbance. No wonder that the
sedater Indians set their faces against the Waw-be-no, which
gradually fell into disrepute.

Indian games. Boat race.

I may here introduce some account of the other chief
feasts and festivals common among the Indians. Before the
whites introduced regular trade for the proceeds of their hunting, and brought among them the general use of intoxicating
drinks, the assembling for feasts was the principal and most
favourite source of excitement in times of peace. When game
was plentiful feasts were frequent, and the man who gave
many feasts was accounted a great man. They used to assemble for feasting on many special occasions. I have already
mentioned the custom of feasting when a young hunter kills
his first animal, and the greater the game, such as a moose or

a buffalo, the greater the entertainment. There are feasts also at marriages, at the naming of children, and in celebrating other family events. There is also the feast with the dead, eaten at the graves of deceased relatives or friends. At these each person, before he eats, cuts off a small portion of flesh, and casts it into the fire, round which they sit. The smoke and smell of these offerings, they say, attracts the Je-bi or spirits to come, unseen, and to eat with them.

The war feast is, as its name implies, one of a special and occasional kind. It is made before starting, or on the way to the enemy's country. There may be four, or eight, or twelve, or any even number of warriors to partake of it, but never an odd number, which would bring evil luck. The whole animal, whether deer or bear, or whatever it is, being cooked, they are expected to consume the entire carcase. Any man who fails to eat his share is liable to the ridicule of his gormandizing companions, and compelled to do his best (or worst), just as in other countries it is said that people compel their comrades to drink to excess. If a man can eat no more, and none of the others volunteer to help to consume the portion, he is compelled to give tobacco or something as a forfeit, and if there are others at hand they are called to finish the food. They are very careful throughout this feast that no bone of the animal eaten shall be broken, the reason assigned being that they may signify to the great Spirit their desire and hope of returning home to their own country with their bones uninjured. The bones are carefully tied up and hung on a tree, after the flesh is stripped off as clean as possible.

Under the name of the Metai are included the feasts and ceremonies belonging to the most important of the Indian ideas of religion. There is no order or caste of priests among them. The medicine men who subsist and gain influence, partly by some knowledge of the use of remedies, but chiefly by practising on their credulity, have the nearest resemblance to a priestly caste. They sell charms or medicines for ensuring success in war, or in hunting, or in gaining the affection of the females, and for other purposes. Sometimes a man has ascendency through pretending to interpret dreams, or to receive revelations from the great Spirit, and is reverenced as a prophet or seer. If there are no medicine men or prophets of great repute at hand, some of the aged men, esteemed to possess wisdom and experience, are chosen as chiefs for the Metai. The guests are invited by a Me-zhin-no-way, or business man of a chief, who delivers to each a small stick, as a form of invitation. In the south, small pieces of cane are thus used; in the north, quills are sometimes substituted, which are dyed and kept for the purpose. No verbal message is delivered with this symbol. Dogs are always included in the food at the feast, from a belief that, as they are most useful animals to man, they will be more acceptable to the divinities than any other animal. They believe that the food they eat on these occasions, in some way ascends, in invisible offering, to the Great Spirit. Songs are sung during the feast and addresses made by the old men, mostly traditional narratives, intermixed with strange accounts of various persons of their mythology, and occasional moral or prudential precepts and exhortations. Whenever the name of the Great Spirit is referred to, all the audience, if still in sober condition, respond by a cry of Kwa-ho-ho-ho-ho! the first syllable uttered in quick loud tone, the after syllables fainter and quicker till ended in a low breath or whisper. The songs are chiefly rhapsodies of personal boasting, as to knowledge or adventure, by which the aged astonish or encourage the younger guests. As many of the ceremonies are fast becoming obsolete, and as they vary in different parts, it would be waste of space to go into greater details. I have been led to say thus much, in consequence of the reference to the Waw-be-no, when Pich-e-to came to us, and took as his wife the Bow-we-tig girl, who had lived with us since she was adopted by old Net-no-kwa.

Sometimes, when sitting round the camp or the lodge fire, stories or legends are told, interspersed with songs. Adventures of war or the chase, and affairs of love, are principally the subjects of these stories. There is often a great amount of humour shown, and at times the tale, as fables ought to do, is made to convey a practical lesson. Here is one which teaches young girls the danger of coquetry, and gives warning against undue admiration of unknown strangers, and of finery of dress.

There lived, once upon a time, in a village of the Ojibbeways, a noted beauty, who was the admiration of all the young hunters and warriors of the tribe. She was particularly admired by a young man, who from his good figure, and the care he took in adorning his person, was named Ma-mon-dá-gin-ine, which we may interpret Beau-man.

This young man had a companion and friend, whom he made a confidant of his affairs. "Come," said he, one day, in a sportive mood, "let us go a-courting to her who is so handsome; perhaps she may fancy one of us." But she would listen to neither of them, and treated them with cool indifference. When the handsome young man rallied from the rebuff, and endeavoured again to press his suit, she put together her thumb and three fingers, and gracefully raising her hand towards him, opened them contemptuously in his face. This gesticulation with the thumb and fingers denotes supreme scorn, and decided rejection, so that the young hunter had to withdraw, confused and abashed. His pride was deeply wounded, and he was the more piqued because this had been done in the presence of others, and the affair was soon noised abroad, and became the talk of every lodge circle. Being of a very sensitive disposition, the rejection of his suit so preyed upon him that he became melancholy. He was moody and silent, sometimes for days together scarcely speaking a word, and taking little or no food. At last this told upon his health, and he became ill, and kept to his bed. No efforts could rouse him from this state. Feeling abashed and dishonoured, he no longer wished to go abroad, and could scarcely endure to be seen by his relatives in their own lodge.

Presently the time came for moving and breaking up the camp, for the winter hunting season was over, and the spring warned them to go towards the place of their summer encampment. No persuasion could induce the young man to arise, and prepare for departure. As they saw him so determined, they put some dried food within reach, and left him there, lying upon his deerskin couch. The last to leave him was his boon companion and friend, a relative of his own, who has already been mentioned as also an admirer of the Indian belle. But even *his* voice was unheeded, and as soon as the sound of his retiring footsteps ceased, the stillness and solitude of the wilderness reigned around.

But now, when all had departed, and the young man felt that no help was near, and that death must soon come to him if he remained where he lay, his thoughts became troubled within him. He began to pray to his moneto or guardian spirit, who heard his appeal, and put into his mind a plan by which he might punish and humble the haughty girl who had brought him so low. The idea worked in his mind, and soon roused him to action. The evil spirit had prompted him to carry out a stratagem, in order to obtain revenge.

Rising from his couch, he walked over the ground of the deserted camp, and gathered all the bits of cloth, feathers, and other scraps of finery which he could see. The motley heap of gaudy but soiled stuff he cleaned as best he could, and with much labour put them into shape, and clothed them with coat and leggings, trimmed with beads, and decorated after the fashion of his tribe. He had a spare pair of moccasins, which he also garnished with beads, and got ready a bow and arrows, and a frontlet and feathers for the head. The mass was still very loose and rough looking, so he searched for bones, and scraps of meat, and offal, and dirt of all kind to fill up spaces, cementing the whole with snow, which he could knead in its half-thawed state, and which would soon harden into a solid mass. So, having filled the clothes with these things, and pressed the mass firmly together, it appeared in the form of a tall, well-framed man, attired in gala dress, as if for the chase. And the evil spirit, his guardian and counsellor, gave a certain amount of life to this Moowis, or Rag and Dirt man, who had thus been fashioned.

"Now, follow me," said the Beau-man, "and I will direct you, and tell you what to do."

So they followed the trail of the tribe, and came up to their camp in the evening, when the failing light was all the better for the deception about to take place. As they entered the camp, all were pleased to see the young man, and said that he already looked more like himself again. But he obtained little notice, for all eyes were struck by his companion; tall, silent, and dignified; with clothes so many-coloured, and covered with such profusion and variety of ornament, for the Indians do not estimate intrinsic value, but judge by the gaudy show that is made. The chief invited the stranger to his lodge, and prepared for him a feast of moose hump, and the finest venison.

No one of those who saw the attractive stranger admired him more than Ma-mon-dá-go-kwa, the Indian belle. She fell in love with him at first sight, and got her mother to invite him to their lodge, on the evening after his arrival. The Beau went with him, for it was under his patronage that he had been introduced; and in truth he had his own motive for going, for he had not wholly lost his feelings of admiration for the fair one, against whom he was nevertheless conspiring, by help of necromantic art. He was prepared to reserve himself for any favourable turn that affairs might possibly take. But no such opportunity occurred. Moowis attracted all attention, and every eye and heart were alert to entertain him. He was placed in the most prominent seat in front of the fire, and was the observed of all observers. The heat began to make him feel uncomfortable; as well it might, for there was risk of his being resolved into his original elements of rags and dirt and snow, and so his true character be revealed. He pulled a boy to him, and put him as a screen from the fire. He shifted his position frequently, and by turning this way and that way, by dexterous manoeuvres and timely remarks, evaded the pressing invitation of his host to sit still and enjoy himself. At last, in fear of speedy dissolution, he placed himself near the door of the lodge, and by so doing increased the admiration of the forest maiden, who could not but praise the brave spirit of endurance which could resist the paralysing cold in that part of the lodge.

Presently the mother pressed him to cross to the inmost part of the lodge, and to take the coveted *Abinos*, or bridegroom's seat. The Beau, on seeing this, perceived that his own chance was over, and that Moowis had triumphed. He therefore withdrew, as did the other guests one by one, and Moowis remained as one of the family. Marriage is a very simple ceremony among the Indians, and there are no banns to be asked or forbidden. The dart with which the belle had often delighted to wound others, she received into her own heart. She had married not a true man, but an image.

As the morning dawned the stranger arose, and took his weapons, saying he must depart. "I must go," said he, "for I have important business to do before I can settle myself in a lodge, and there are many hills to mount and streams to cross before I come to the end of my journey." "I will go with you," she said. "It is too far," he replied, "and you are not able to undergo the toils and encounter the perils of the way." "It is not so far but that I can go," she said; "and there are no toils nor dangers that I am not ready and willing to share with you."

Moowis said he must go and bid his friend farewell. He went and told him that the girl wished to accompany him on the journey. For a moment, pity filled the heart of the rejected Beau. He regretted that she should thus have cast herself away upon an image and shadow, when she might have been mistress of a good lodge and of a true man. "But it is her own folly," he said; "she has turned a deaf ear to the counsels of prudence, and she must submit to her fate."

That same morning the image set forth, and his wife followed behind at a distance, as is always the custom among Indians. The way was rough and difficult, and she could not keep up with his rapid pace; but she struggled hard and perseveringly to follow him. He had been for some time out of sight, when the sun now shone with piercing heat, and commenced upon his snow-knit body the work of dissolution. He began to melt away, and to fall in pieces. As she followed him, piece after piece of the raiment which she recognised as his, and the ornaments by which she had been dazzled, were found in the path. Then she saw his moccasins, and his leggings, and his coat, and the feathers of his head-dress. As the heat unbound them they fell assunder, and they all returned to their original dirty and base condition. The way led over rocks, across marshes, and through forests. A high wind arose and seemed to whirl from all points of the compass, so that she got confused and lost her way. Here and there she still found rags, and bones, and beads, and feathers; but Moowis she never caught sight of. The whole day she spent in wandering in her vain search, for she had long lost every track, and night overtook her wearied and in despair. With bitter cries she bewailed her fate, but none heard her, and she perished in the woods of cold and hunger." Moowis, Moowis, you have led me astray, you are leading me astray, and here I must perish!"

Then the Indian girls take up the refrain, at the end of the tragic story, and sing:—

"Moowis! Moowis!
Dost than deceive me?
Hear my moan;
Do not, do not leave me
All alone, all alone!"

The mention of the Abinos, or the bridegroom's seat, in this story, leads me to add a few remarks about the arrangements of the Indian lodge. It was by the mother that he was installed in that seat, and made a member of the family. The lodge is the precinct of the wife's rule and government. She assigns to each member his or her ordinary place to sleep and put their effects. These places are permanent, and only changed at her will, as when there is a guest, either by day or night. In a space so small this system keeps order, and the husband, who is lord in the field and the forest, does not interfere with the affairs of the lodge, where he is more like guest than master. His chief duty is to find food, which the women prepare for the feast or the meal. Hunting is his chief business, with the defence of the village, the preparation of implements of hunting or war, of canoes for travelling, and other outdoor work. The women dress the skins, weave the mats from rushes, gather firewood, and perform other domestic work less suitable for men. They also take a principal part in corn-planting and gathering, and in sugar-making at the season, when they go to the woods where maple-trees abound.

The usual notion of the women being almost like slaves of the men is not in accordance with fact. In he lodges where I have lived the mothers and wives have rather ruled the men, and some of them, such as Net-no-qua, have been looked up to with respect and obeisance by all the tribe. The labours which the women are seen to undertake are assumed at their own will, and in accordance with ancient usage. White people, who have seen an Indian squaw toiling along behind her husband, burdened apparently with a heavy load, while he stalks along smoking his pipe, have perhaps judged hastily as to their relation. In this one matter of the wife trudging in the rear, the origin of the custom is entirely due to superstition. It is an un-propitious omen if a woman ever walks in the path before a man. If she cross his track when he is about to set out on a hunting or a war expedition, his luck is gone. In journeying, it is natural that the man should be in advance; but the position of the squaw is not meant to denote inferiority, but is the result of the superstitious feeling alluded to. Besides, she is much fitter for bearing burdens than the erect, quick-stepping hunter or warrior. She has been accustomed to carry the children slung on her back, and the habit of bearing the papooses enables her to carry easily the baggage which would impede and weary the man.

Let me close these remarks with telling of a burden once carried by an Indian woman, of which little was thought by her own people, but which has caused her to be spoken of with wonder and praise by white men, on hearing of it. It is certainly a remarkable instance of filial duty and affection.

Gitchi-naigow, a Chippeway chief, had long been celebrated as a leader and ruler in his tribe. He had been a friend of the French in the time of their supremacy in Canada, and took part in the struggle that followed the capture of Quebec in 1759. The French called him Le Grand Sable, or The Great Sand Chief. He was one of the assailants in the memorable capture of the old Fort Mickilimackinac, in 1763. After the wars were ended, he lived many years in the region of the Upper Lakes. He shifted his lodge, as the seasons changed, from the open shores of Lake Huron and Lake Michigan to the thick woods where the Indians seek shelter from the wintry winds. More than eighty years had now whitened the locks of the aged chief, and he felt that the time of his journeyings must soon be over. He accompanied his people for the last time, during the early spring, from the borders of the water to the maple forests, where they stay till the budding leaves show that the sweet sap is no longer available for making into syrup for sugar.

When they began to pack up their effects to return to the lakes, it was evident that the old man had no more strength to bear the journey. His daughter, Nodowáqua, the wife of Saganash, determined to carry him on her back, that he might yet once more see the refreshing waters. She took her long and stout deerskin apecun, or head-strap, which she fastened round his body, and, bending under the load, with the strap across her forehead, she rose and set out on the path with the others. Resting occasionally by the way, she bore him safely to the shores of Lake Michigan, a distance of more than ten miles. It was the old man's last journey. He died and was buried on the shores of the lake.[1]

The above story must have been put in by the Editor. The original "narratives" was published in 1830.

---

1.   The daughter lived to a good old age, and in 1833 she told the story of her father's last journey to Mr. Schoolcraft at Mackinac.

Chapter VIII.

NEW WAR EXPEDITION AGAINST THE SIOUX—
UNITED BANDS OF OJIBBEWAYS, OTTAWWAWS,
AND ASSINEBOINS—FOLLOWING THE TRAIL OF
THE SIOUX—THE INDIAN WAR-WHOOP—
RETREAT OF THE SIOUX—HORSE-STEALING—
IN SEARCH OF MY HORSE, STOLEN BY ASS-
INEBOINS—CURIOUS RENCONTRE ON A PRAI-
RIE—INDIAN LODGES—HOSPITABLE USAGES—
FAMILY AND VILLAGE LIFE.

At this time there were fresh rumours of a war party preparing to go against the Sioux, and we again resolved to
accompany it. We therefore went toward the prairie land, in
order to kill buffaloes, that we might make dry meat sufficient
for our families during our absence. After we had killed and
dried large quantities of meat, we erected a sunjegwun, or a
scaffold, where we deposited as much as we thought would
supply the wants of our families till our return. Before we had
entirely finished the preparations for our journey, we were
suddenly fallen upon by a war party of about two hundred
Sioux, who killed some of our people. A small party of Assineboins and Crees had already gone out towards the Sioux
country, and, falling by accident on the trace of this war party,
had dogged them for some time, coming repeatedly near
enough to see the crane's head, used by their chief instead of
stones, in the nightly divination, which I have already
described as customary among the Indians to discover the
position of an enemy. This little band of Assineboins and

Crees had not courage enough to fall upon the Sioux, but they sent messengers to the Ojibbeways, by a circuitous route. These came to the lodge of the principal chief of the Ojibbeways, who was hunting in advance of his people. He scorned to display fear. By retreating at once to the trader's fort, he might have escaped the danger that was imminent. He made some preparation to move, but his old wife, being then jealous of a younger one now in higher favour than herself, reproached him, and complained that he cared more for the young woman than for herself. He said to her: "You have for a long time annoyed me by your jealousy, and by your complaints; I must hear no more of it. The Sioux are near, and I will wait for them." He accordingly remained, and continued hunting. Early one morning he went up into an oak-tree that stood near his lodge, to look over the prairie for buffalo, and in descending he was shot by two young men of the Sioux, who had been in concealment near the place great part of the night. It is probable they would have fallen upon him sooner but for fear. Now the trampling of horses was heard, and the men who were with the chief had scarce time to run out of the lodge, when the two hundred Sioux were upon them. There was fighting for some time, but in the end all the Ojibbeways there, about twenty in number, were killed, except Aisainse (the little clam), a brother of the chief, and two women with one child.

The Ojibbeways at the fort soon heard of it, and the trader at Pembinah gave them ammunition to pursue the party that had killed the chief, who was his father-in-law. A large body assembled, four hundred in all, of whom one hundred were Assineboins, the remaining three hundred being Ojibbeways and Crees, with some Muskegoes. My brother and I accompanied them. In the course of the first day after we left the fort, nearly one hundred Ojibbeways deserted and went back. In the following night the Assineboins left in considerable numbers, having stolen many horses, and among them four belonging to me and Wa-me-gon-a-biew. I had only five pairs of moccasins, intending to make the whole journey on horse-back, and I felt it a great misfortune to have lost my horses. I went to Pe-shaw-ba, who was chief of the band of Ottaw-waws to which we belonged, and told him I intended to make reprisals from the small number of Assineboins still with us. He would not consent, saying, very justly, that this would raise a quarrel which would entirely interrupt and frustrate the designs of the whole expedition. His advice, though I knew it to be good so far as the interest of the whole was concerned, did nothing to remove my private grievances, and I went from one to another of the Ottawwaws, and those I considered friendly among the Ojibbeways, endeavouring to persuade them to join me in taking horses from the Assineboins. None would consent except a young man named Gish-kau-ko, a rel-ative of him by whom I had been taken prisoner. He agreed to watch with me the thirteen Assineboins who still remained in the camp, and if opportunity offered, without directly using force, to assist me in taking horses from them to replace those which their people had stolen from me. Soon after, I saw eight of these thirteen lingering in the camp one morning, and I believed it was their intention to leave us and turn back. I called Gish-kau-ko to watch them with me; and, sure enough, as soon as most of the Ojibbeways had moved forward, these men got on their horses, and turned their faces to go home. We resolved to follow and still to watch. As we knew we could not take the horses by force, as they were well armed, we left our arms, and followed them with nothing in our hands. Perceiving that they were followed, one of them dis-mounted, and waited to hold a parley with us; but they were too wary and cautious to give us any opportunity of taking their horses. The others had now also halted. We tried entreat-ies, to give us two of the horses for the four that had been sto-len by their brothers. As this had no effect, I told them that their five companions whom they had left behind would not be safe among us; but this threat, instead of having any good effect, only induced them to send a messenger on their swiftest horse to warn these men to beware of me. We returned to the main party on foot, and took the first opportunity of visiting the camp of the five Assineboins; but they had taken alarm on the arrival of the messenger, and had fled with their horses.

At a lake near Red River we came on the path of the retiring Sioux, by whom the Ojibbeway chief had been killed. We found the dead body of a young Sioux, which the Ojibbeways beat and kicked, and took the scalp. Pe-shaw-ba forbid me and the young men of his party to join in such unmanly and unworthy outrages. The trail being quite recent, we thought we could not be more than two or three days behind the Sioux.

At Lake Traverse, our numbers had diminished to one hundred and twenty; of these three were half-breed Assineboins, about twenty Crees, and as many Ottawwaws, the rest Ojibbeways. Many of the original party had been discouraged by unfavourable divinations; among others, one by Pe-shaw-ba, the Ottawwaw chief, made on the first night after we left Pembinah. He told us that in his dream he saw the eyes of the Sioux, like the sun; they saw everywhere, and always discovered the Ojibbeways before the latter came near enough to strike them. Probably he said this to incite to greater watchfulness, but it had the effect of discouragement, as if he had not confidence in his own side, and may have caused some of the numerous desertions so early in the journey. He also told, as part of his dream, that he had seen all our party returning, unharmed, and without bearing any scalps of enemies; but he said that on the left-hand side of Lake Traverse, opposite our road, he saw two lodges of Sioux by themselves, which he intended to visit on his return.

Due west from Lake Traverse, at the distance of two days' travel, is a mountain called O-ge-mah-wud-ju (chief mountain), near which is the village to which the war party we were pursuing belonged. As we approached this mountain, we moved in a more cautious and guarded manner, most commonly lying hid in the woods during the day, and travelling at night. When at last we were within a few miles, we halted in the middle of the night, and waited for the approach of the earliest dawn, the time the Indians usually choose for an attack.

Late in the night, a warrior of high reputation the Black Duck, took the reins of his horse in his hand, and walked on towards the village. Having seen him thus advancing I joined him, and he allowed me to accompany him. We arrived at early dawn at the little hill which sheltered our approach from being seen in the village. Raising his head cautiously to reconnoitre, the Black Duck saw two men walking at some distance in front of him. As they evidently had not observed him, he descended the hill a little, to meet our advancing people, and then tossing his blanket in a peculiar manner thereby made a signal to the Ojibbeways to rush on. Instantly there was a tearing off of leggings, stripping off and throwing down of blankets, and the whole band leaped to the feet of Black Duck, with whom they moved silently and swiftly over the crest of the hill, and soon stood on the site of the village. After passing the crest of the hill they saw the two men, who instead of flying came calmly towards them; and turned out to be two of the young men of their own band. They had left the main party when they halted in the night, and without giving any notice of their intention, had gone forward at once to reconnoitre what they supposed to be the position of the enemy. But they had found the Sioux village deserted many hours before, and they had walked about, scaring away the wolves from among the rubbish; then they slowly returned to meet their own people advancing. It was well for them that the light by this time allowed them to be at once recognised, for the band, after their silent advance, as soon as they topped the hill, had raised the Sas-sah-kwi, or war-whoop, as they came down the slope with a rush.

The loud and piercing sound of the Indian war-whoop, especially if raised suddenly and heard unexpectedly, has a most thrilling effect. It intimidates and depresses the weak, or those who are surprised without arms in their hands, while it rouses the spirit of those who are defiant and ready for battle. I have observed, on many occasions, a surprising effect upon animals. I have seen a buffalo so terrified by it as to fall down in his steps, being able neither to run, nor to make any resistance. I have seen a bear so terror-stricken as to quit his hold in climbing a tree, and fall to the ground in utter helplessness.

Although the village was found deserted, the chiefs were not willing to relinquish the object of the journey, and we followed along the trail of the Sioux. We found at each of their encampments the place of divination, from the appearance of which we were able to infer that they knew accurately our position from day to day. Though retiring, they still kept on the alert. There was now, among the young men of the expedition, an increased disposition to desert. The chiefs laboured to prevent this by appointing certain persons whom they could rely upon, to act as sentinels, both in the encampments and during the marches; but this measure, so far from being effectual to stop desertion, seemed rather to increase it, perhaps because the young men dislike and despise the idea of restraint of any kind. They became more dissatisfied and troublesome after we had crossed the head of the river St. Peter, getting into regions not known to them. The traders have a fort somewhere on the upper part of the river, to which the Sioux had retired. When we got within a day's journey of this fort, fear and hesitancy became manifest throughout our band. The chiefs desired to send some of the young men forward to examine the position of the enemy, but none of them offered themselves for this service.

We remained for two days in the same place, and took advantage of the time for supplying the wants of those who were deficient in moccasins or other necessary articles. It is the custom during a war expedition, if any one's supply of ammunition, or moccasins, or other necessary part of dress should have failed, to obtain from others what he needs. If he wants moccasins, he takes a single one in his hand and walks about the encampment, pausing a moment before each of his companions, as he hopes he may supply his need. He has no occasion to say anything, as those who happen to have an overstock are usually glad to furnish him. Should this method fail, the chief of the party is appealed to, who then dresses himself in his war dress, and accompanied by two or three young warriors, goes through the camp, and from those who have the greatest quantity takes what may be necessary of the articles required.

On the morning of the third day we broke up the camp and turned back. We returned towards the village at the Chief Mountain, in case any of the people might have gone back there. If they had been, we could not have surprised them, for our young men had lost all discipline, and those who had horses rode noisily and recklessly forward. After leaving the Chief Mountain, and advancing some distance on the plains towards home, we found that we were watched and followed by a party of nearly a hundred Sioux.

At a river named Gaunenoway, rising from the Chief Mountain, and running into Red River, several days' journey from Lake Traverse, there was a quarrel between Pe-shaw-ba and an Ojibbeway chief, Ma-men-o-guaw-sink, on account of a horse which I thought I had a right to take from some Crees, whom I knew to be friends of the Assineboins who had robbed me of mine. This chief having killed a Cree was anxious to do something to gain friends among that people. It happened that Pe-shaw-ba and myself were travelling together at a little distance from the main body, and I was leading the horse which I had taken, when Ma-men-o-guaw-sink came up to us, accompanied by some of his friends, and fiercely demanded the horse. Pe-shaw-ba, who probably did not know all the circumstances, but was ready to stand by his own followers immediately cocked his gun, placing the muzzle close to the Ojibbeway chief's heart, and so intimidated him by threats and reproaches, that he desisted. The Ottaw-

waws, seeing their chief thus engaged, now stopped, and Pe-
shaw-ba remaining at their head, fell in the rear of the body,
in order to avoid further trouble on account of this horse, all
of them apparently unwilling that I should give it up.

There were four men of this war party who walked in six
days from the Chief Mountain to Pembinah, but others of our
band, although with horses, took ten days for the journey.
When I arrived at Pembinah, I found my family had gone to
the mouth of the Assineboin. After the separation of our
party, my special friends having left my route at Pembinah,
my horse was stolen from me at night. I knew who had taken
him, and as the man was encamped at no great distance, I
took arms in my hands and went in the morning to retake him.
On my way I met Pe-shaw-ba, who peremptorily forbade me
to proceed. He was a prudent and good man, and remembering how he had taken my part about the horse before, I knew
he had reasons for interfering now. I might have gone on to
take the horse, contrary to his order, but I did not choose to do
so, and returned along with him on my way.

I had no moccasins left, and felt the more angry at the loss
of my horse, for my feet became swollen and wounded, and I
had yet two days' long walk. I found my family in great want,
as my absence had extended to nearly three months. The time
had been wasted in long and toilsome marches, all resulting in
nothing, as war expeditions often do, even when enemies
meet, which we never did. It was necessary for me to go out
to hunt immediately, although the condition of my feet made
the effort painful. Fortunately I succeeded in killing a moose
the first time I went out. The next day snow fell to a considerable depth, which made the capture of game more easy, and
we soon had plenty of food.

I had been at home but a short time when I heard that the
Assineboins had boasted of taking my horse. As I was preparing to go in pursuit of them, an Ojibbeway, who had often
tried to dissuade me from any attempt to recover him, gave

me a horse on condition that I would not attempt to retake my own; accordingly, for some time I said no more about it.

Having spent the winter at the mouth of the Assineboin, I went to make sugar at Great Wood River; but here it was told me that the Assineboins were still boasting of having taken my horse from me. With some persuasion I prevailed upon Wa-me-gon-a-biew to accompany me in an attempt to recover him.

At the end of four days' journey we came to the first Assineboin village, ten miles from the Mouse River trading-house. This village consisted of about thirty lodges. We were observed before we came to the village, as the Assineboins, being a revolted band of the Sioux nation, and now allied with the Ojibbeways, are in constant apprehension of an attack from the Sioux, and therefore, always station some men to watch for the approach of strangers. The quarrel which resulted in the separation of the band of the Bwoinnug, or Roasters, as the Ojibbeways call the Sioux, originated in a dispute about a woman, and happened some years before, as we were told. So many Ojibbeways and Crees now live among them that they are most commonly able to understand something of the Ojibbeway language, though their own dialect is very unlike it, resembling closely that of the Sioux.

One of the men who came out to meet us was Ma-men-o-guaw-sink, with whom Pe-shaw-ba had quarrelled some time before on my account. When he came up to us, he asked where we were going. I told him, "I am come for the horses which the Assineboins stole from us." "You had better," said he, "return as you came, for if you go to the village, they will take your life." To these threats I paid no attention, but inquired for Ba-gis-kun-nung, the men of whose family had taken our horses. They replied that they could not tell where he was; that he and his sons had, soon after the return of the war party, gone to the Mandans, and had not yet come back; that when they came among the Mandans, the former owner of my mare, recognising the animal, had taken her from the son of Ba-gis-kun-nung; but that the latter had remunerated himself by stealing a fine black horse, with which he escaped and had not been heard of since.

Wa-me-gon-a-biew being discouraged, and perhaps intimidated by the reception we met in this village, endeavoured to dissuade me from going further; and when he found he could not prevail, he left me to pursue my horse by myself, and returned home. I would not be discouraged, but determined to visit every village and camp of the Assineboins, rather than return without my horse.

I went to the Mouse River trading-house, where I was well-known, and having explained the object of my journey, they gave me two pounds of powder and thirty balls, with some knives and small articles, and directed me how to reach the next village. As I was pursuing my journey by myself, I had occasion to cross a very wide prairie, on which I saw at a distance something lying on the ground resembling a log of wood. As I knew there could be no wood in such a place, unless it were dropped by some person, I then thought it was probably some article of dress, or a blanket, or possibly the body of a man who might have perished when on a journey or when out hunting. I made my approach cautiously, and presently discovered that it was a man lying on his belly, with his gun in his hand, and waiting for wild geese to fly over. His attention was fixed in the direction opposite to that on which I approached, and I came very near him without his being aware of my presence, when he rose and discharged his gun at a flock of geese. I now sprang forward; the noise of hawk bells and the silver ornaments of my dress notified him of my approach, but I caught him in my arms before he had time to make any resistance. His gun being unloaded, he felt he was helpless; and seeing himself captured he cried out "Assineboin," to which I answered "Ojibbeway." We were both glad we could treat each other as friends, and although we could not converse on account of the dissimilarity of our dialects, I motioned him to sit down on the ground beside me, with which request he immediately complied. I gave him a goose I had killed shortly before, and after resting a few minutes, signified to him that I would accompany him to his lodge. A walk of about two hours brought us in sight of his village, and when we entered it I followed him to his lodge.

Here I witnessed a curious custom, not common to other Indians. As I entered the lodge after my companion I saw an old man and old woman, who at once covered their heads with their blankets, and my companion disappeared into a small division of the lodge merely large enough to admit one, and to conceal him from the remainder of the family. Here he remained, his food handed to him by his wife; but though secluded from sight he maintained by conversation some intercourse with those without. When he wished to pass out of the lodge, his wife gave notice to her parents, and they concealed their heads, and again in the same manner when he came in. This formality is strictly observed by the married men among the Assineboins, and I believe among all the Bwoin-nug, or Dah-ko-tah, as they call themselves. It is known to exist among the Omowhows of the Missouri. If a man enters a dwelling in which his son-in-law is seated, the latter conceals his face until he departs. While the young remain with the parents of their wives, they have always this separate lodge within, or there is a partition made by suspending mats or skins. Into this little compartment the wife reclines at night; by day she is the organ of communication with those without; the man retaining as little intercourse as possible with the family. A man rarely, if ever, mentions the name of his father-in-law, and it is considered highly indecorous to do so.

This custom does not exist in any shape among the Ojibbeways, and they look upon it as a very foolish and troublesome one. I was describing it long afterwards to a white man, who laughed, and said, "It was right for a young couple to begin early to be independent of the family from which the wife is taken, and it was best for a mother-in-law to have her mouth covered." I only mention what I myself observed.

The people of this lodge treated me with much kindness. Notwithstanding the great scarcity of corn in the country they had a little reserved, which they cooked and gave. The young man told them how much he had been frightened by me in the prairie, at which they all laughed heartily. This village consisted of twenty-five lodges, but although I inquired of many of them, none of them knew where Ba-gis-kun-nung was to be found.

There was another village, they told me, at the distance of about a day's journey; he might be there. I remained a little longer at the lodge of the young man I had found in the prairie, and then went out to start for the next village. Geese were flying over, and I raised my gun and shot one. It fell in the midst of a number of Assineboins. Seeing there a very old and miserable looking man, I motioned to him to go and get it. But he must first come up to me to express his gratitude by a method I had not before seen used. He came up, and placing both his hands on the top of my head, passed them several times down the long hair that hung over my shoulders, at the same time muttering something in his own language that I could not understand. He then went and took up the goose, and returning, he communicated to me by signs which I had no difficulty to understand, that I must go to his lodge and eat with him before I could leave the village. While he was roasting the goose, I went about from lodge to lodge to look at their horses, thinking I might see mine amongst them, but I did not. Some of the young men of the village accompanied me, but without any arms, and all seemed friendly; but when I was ready to start for the next village I noticed that one of them, mounted on a fleet horse, started to precede me.

When I arrived at this village no one took the slightest notice of me, or even seemed to see me. They were a band with which I had previously had no acquaintance, and I could perceive that they had been prejudiced against me. Their chief was a distinguished hunter, who I heard was soon afterwards killed. He had been absent from home unusually long, and by following his track they found he had been attacked by a grizzly bear on the prairie and was killed.

Chapter IX.

FAILING TO FIND MY OWN HORSE, I TAKE ONE BELONGING TO THE ASSINEBOIN CHIEF—A QUESTION OF CONSCIENCE—PURSUED BY THE INDIANS—HAVE TO ABANDON THE HORSE AND HIDE IN THE BUSH—AFTERWARDS I TAKE THE HORSE OF A NOTED HORSE-STEALER—JOIN A WAR PARTY—ASSAULT ON A MANDAN FORTI-FIED VILLAGE BY SIOUX WARRIORS—SCALPS AS TROPHIES—THE SHAWNEE PROPHET— VISIT FROM ONE OF HIS EMISSARIES—SUCCESSFUL BEAVER TRAPPING.

Finding the people of this band decidedly unfriendly, I went into none of their lodges, but stood about, watching their horses to see if I could discover mine among them. I had heard at the last village of a young horse belonging to the chief, noted for its beauty and fleetness, and I soon recognised this animal, known to me only by description. Thinking that I was only taking what was fairly due from a chief one of whose people had taken my horse, I resolved to try to possess myself of this one. I had a halter under my blanket, and watching a favourable opportunity, I slipped it on the head of the horse, mounted him, and fled at full speed. I was excited to this action principally by a feeling of irritation at the unfriendly conduct of the people of the village, and of their chief, for it had not been my intention to take any horse but the one which belonged to me. But in the state of mind I then had, the feeling of right was subverted, as is often the case, by the reasoning that it was not wrong to take from those who were connected with the robber of my horse.

When the horse and myself were out of breath, I stopped to look back, and the Assineboin lodges were scarce visible, looking only like little specks on the distant prairie. I now reflected that I was doing wrong, conscience resuming its sway, for I was stealing away the favourite horse of a man who had never personally injured me, though he had refused the customary dues of hospitality. I got down and left the horse; but had scarce done so, when I saw thirty or forty men on horseback, who had before been concealed in a depression of the prairie; they were in pursuit, and very near me. I had just time to fly to a little thicket of low hazel bushes, when they were upon me. They rode about for some time, searching, and this delay enabled me to get into closer concealment on the ground among the bushes. At length most of them dismounted, the others holding their horses, and dispersed themselves in various directions, seeking for me. Some came very near me, and then turned off in other directions. My position was such that I could watch them without exposing myself. One young man began singing his war-song, and laying aside his gun, came straight towards the place where I lay, with only his war club in hand. I thought I must have been discovered, for he advanced till not above thirty or forty paces from me. My gun was cocked and aimed at his heart. It was a terrible moment, for even if I had killed him the others would have immediately made an end of me. But when within about twenty paces he stopped, then turned and went back. It is not probable that he saw me; but perhaps the thought of his being watched by an unseen enemy, with a gun, and whose position he could not ascertain till almost over him, had overcome his valorous spirit. They continued their search for a time that seemed painfully prolonged, but at length after talking awhile, they gathered together for returning, taking back the chief's horse to the village.

I travelled towards home, rejoicing in my escape, and without halting for the night, either on that or the succeeding one. I arrived in the evening of the third day at the Mouse River trading-house. The traders, when I told them my adventure, said I was a fool for not having brought the chief's horse. They had heard much of his qualities, and would, as they said, have paid me a high price for him.

In the Assineboin village, ten miles from this trading-house, I had a friend called Be-na (pheasant), and when I had passed through I requested him, while I should be absent, to endeavour to discover my horse, or at least to ascertain, and be able to tell me, where I could find Ba-gis-kun-nung. When I returned there, after visiting Mouse River trading-house, Be-na took me immediately to a lodge where a couple of old women lived, and looking through a crevice, he pointed out to me the lodge of Ba-gis-kun-nung, and those of his four sons. Their horses were feeding about, and among them we distinguished the fine black one they had brought from the Mandans in place of mine.

Wa-me-gon-a-biew had been to the trading-house, but returned to the village before I arrived, and was now waiting for me at the lodge of some of the sons of Taw-ga-we-ninne, who were his cousins, and were very friendly to him. He had sent a messenger to Ba-gis-kun-nung, offering him a gun, a chief's coat, and all the property he had about him, for a horse to ride home. When I heard of this I reproved him, and told him if Ba-gis-kun-nung had accepted his presents, it would only have occasioned additional trouble to me, as I should have been compelled to take not only a horse but these presents also.

I went, soon after my arrival at the village, to Ba-gis-kun-nung, and said to him, "I want a horse." "I shall not give you one," he answered. "I will take one, then." "If you do, I will shoot you." With this I returned to the lodge of Be-na, and made my preparations for starting early in the morning. Be-na gave me a new buffalo robe to ride home upon, and I got from an old woman a piece of leather thong for a halter, having left mine on the chief's horse. I did not sleep in Be-na's lodge, but with our cousins, and very early in the morning, as I was ready to start, I went to Be-na's lodge, but he was not awake. I had a very good new blanket, which I spread over him without making any noise; then, along with Wa-me-gon-a-biew, I started. When we came in sight of the lodge of Ba-gis-kun-nung, we saw the eldest of his sons sitting on the outside, and watching the horses. My brother endeavoured to dissuade me from the design of attempting to take one, since we could not do it without being seen, and had every reason to believe they were prepared to take violent measures to prevent us from succeeding in the attempt. I told him I would not listen to his advice, but consented to go with him some distance on the road, and lay down our baggage; then we were to return together and take the horse. When we had proceeded as far as I thought necessary, I laid down my load; but Wa-me-gon-a-biew, seeing me resolved to go back, began to run. At the same time that he ran from the village, I ran towards it, and when the son of Ba-gis-kun-nung saw me coming, he began to call out as loud as he could in his own language. I could only distinguish the words, "Ojibbeway" and "horse." I answered, "Not altogether an Ojibbeway." The village was instantly in motion. In the faces of most of those who gathered round, I could see no settled determination to act in any way; but there was encouragement in the countenances of Be-na and a number of Crees who were about him. There was a manifest hostility only in the Ba-gis-kun-nungs. I was so excited that I could not feel my feet touch the ground, but I think I had no fear. When I had got my halter on the head of the black horse, I stood for a moment hesitating to get on him; as in the act of doing so I must, for the moment, deprive myself of the power of using my arms, and could not avoid exposing myself to an attack behind. But recollecting that anything like indecision would at this time have an unfavourable effect, I gave a jump to mount the horse, but jumped so much higher and further than was necessary, that I fell sprawling on the ground on the other side of the horse, my gun in one hand and my bow and arrows in the other. I regained my feet as quickly as I could, and looked round to watch the motions of my enemies; but presently an universal shout of laughter, in which all joined but the Ba-gis-kun-nungs, gave me some confidence, and I proceeded deliberately to mount. I knew that if they could have ventured to make an open attack upon me they would have taken the opportunity when I was lying on the ground and in a position not ready to make any dangerous resistance. The hearty and general laughter of the Indians convinced me also that what I was doing was not generally offensive to them.

When I turned to ride off, I saw Wa-me-gon-a-biew still running like a frightened turkey; he was almost out of sight. When I overtook him, I said: "My brother, you must be tired and out of breath, I will lend you my horse." Just then we saw two men coining on horseback from the village to pursue us. Wa-me-gon-a-biew was alarmed, and would have rode off, leaving me to settle the difficulty with the two men as I could; but perceiving his intention, I called to him to leave the horse, which he did, and resumed his flight on foot. When the two men had approached within about half a mile of me, I got down from the horse, and taking the halter in my hand, stood with my face to them. They stopped at some distance from me, and looking round in the other direction I saw Wa-me-gon-a-biew had hid himself in the bushes. The two men stood in the road for some time, and I remained facing them, holding the horse. Many people from the village I could see standing on a little elevation near the lodges, watching what would be done. The two Ba-gis-kun-nungs, getting tired of standing, then separated, and one came round upon one side, the other on the other side of me. It was then, I thought, they would approach, and get an opportunity of shooting me down; but they went on upon either side and joined each other again on the path, between me and Wa-me-gon-a-biew. Perhaps they thought he was in ambush ready to fire on them. Evidently they lacked courage, so getting on the horse I rode toward them; but they turned out of my way, and went back toward the village. In this affair I found Wa-me-gon-a-biew more cowardly than it was usual even for him to be; but it happened that the leading men in the village were not sorry that I came to take a horse from Ba-gis-kun-nung and his sons. They were considered troublesome and bad men; hence I was able to carry through this affair alone, and without any help from Wa-me-gon-a-biew.

After the two men had turned back, my brother joined me from among the bushes where he had lain concealed. We found that night the lodge of our old friend Waus-so, who used formerly to live with Pe-shaw-ba. The horse I had taken I left tethered in the woods, not wishing to tell Waus-so of what I had done. But during the night, after I had gone to sleep, Wa-me-gon-a-biew began to relate to him all that happened the preceding day, and when he came to hear of my jumping over the horse, of which I had told my brother, the old man waked me with his loud and hearty laughter.

Next morning we continued our journey towards our home. I had for some time two horses, and to a friend who visited us I offered one, but as he was not going straight home he deferred taking it till he should be returning. In the meantime the horse I intended for him died, so that I had only the black horse, to which I had become much attached. But when the man returned, having journeyed a long way, I could not do otherwise than give him this one, much to my regret, and to the annoyance of my wife, who was vexed at my thus parting with what I had got with so much trouble. However, I could not see my friend, who was much esteemed by me, go away disappointed.

Three months after this the Crees sent tobacco to the Ojibbeways, with invitations to accompany them to the Mandans, and join in an attack on some of the Bwoin-nug or Sioux, in the country of the Missouri. As these preparations were making, I received a message from Ba-gis-kun-nung that he did not wish to have me join the war-party. This amounted to a threat to take my life if I went, but I paid no attention to it.

In six days I could go from my place to Turtle Mountain, where the Crees were assembling in considerable numbers. I had been waiting nearly a month when Wa-ge-tote arrived with sixty men, on his way to the rendezvous. Here eight of us joined him, and gave what assistance we could, in provision, to his party, who had been starving for some time. Soon we were all equally suffering; we had travelled on two days when twenty young men were selected to go to hunt buffalo. Wa-ge-tote insisted that I must go with them, but I declined. He urged it upon me repeatedly, and at last taking my load upon his shoulders, he said, "My nephew, you must go, and I will carry your load for you till you join us again." I went forward a short distance, and had the good fortune to kill an elk. The Indians fell on it like hungry dogs, and soon not a particle of flesh was left, though I believe not more than half of those that were in a starving condition tasted of it. The twenty men who had been sent out returned without having killed anything. They now became so weak from hunger, that numbers were left behind, being unable to walk. For many days we had no other food than the roots of the grass berry, a root called pomme blanche by the French. I was myself about to fail, when late one night, as all were asleep, an old man, a relative of my wife, waked me and put carefully into my hand a small quantity of pemmican, which he had concealed about him. This enabled me to reach the Turtle Mountain, to which place, probably, about half of Wa-ge-tote's band had arrived at the same time. Of those that had parted from us, some returned to their own country, and others were no more heard of.

The Assineboins and Crees, whom we had expected to meet at Turtle Mountain, had left it some time before, and we had followed on their trail but a few days when we met them returning. They related to us that they had arrived at the Mandan village just as a party of Sioux had reached the same place, with a design to attack the town. The Mandan chief said to them, as soon as they came, "My friends, those Sioux have come hither to put out my fire. They know not that you are here. As they have not come against you, why should your blood flow in our quarrel? Remain, therefore, in my village, and ye shall see that we are men, and need no help when they come to fight us at our own doors."

The Mandan village was surrounded with palisades, and close to these Sioux fought most of the day. At length an intermission occurred, and the Mandan chief, calling to the Sioux from the inside, said to them, "Depart from about our village, or we will let out upon you our friends, the Ojibbeways, who have been sitting here all day, and are now fresh and unwearied."

The Sioux answered, "This is a vain boast, made with a design to conceal your weakness. You have no Ojibbeways in your house, and if you had hundreds we neither fear nor regard them. The Ojibbeways are women, and if your village were full of them we would the sooner come among you."

The Crees and Assineboins, hearing these taunts, became irritated, and ran out to attack the Sioux with such vehemence that they gave way and fled in all directions. The Ojibbeways, although they had little share in the fight, were allowed to have some of the scalps taken during the day, and one of these fell into the hands of our chief, Wa-ge-tote, who had never been near the conflict, and with this trophy he returned towards his own country.

When we reached Turtle Mountain on our return we were again all suffering the extremity of hunger, and many were unable to proceed farther. We were, therefore, compelled to stop, and of the whole party there were found only four who had strength and resolution enough remaining to undertake to hunt. The four were an old man called Gitch-e-weech (big beaver-lodge), two young men, and myself. The old man was in high spirits, and expressed his confidence that he would be successful. He said he had spent most of the night before in praying, and was sure that the Great Spirit would hear his prayer and supply our need. We all started at the same time in the morning, but went to hunt in different directions. I hunted all day without finding anything, and so weak was I that I could traverse but a very small extent of ground. It was late when I came in; the two young men were in before me; all were in despair; but old Gitch-e-weech was still absent At a very late hour he arrived, bending under a heavy load of meat, having killed a moose. We went to the place next day where the moose had been killed, and the rest of the meat was soon disposed of.

Near this place Wa-me-gon-a-biew discovered a large quantity of property which had been left by a band of Assineboins, as a medicine sacrifice. Property left in this way may be taken by any friendly band finding it. But the offerings made to ensure success in war may not be taken from the place where they are left. Wa-me-gon-a-biew having climbed a high tree when he made this discovery, and having pointed out the place to the Indians at once, was so tardy in coming down, that every blanket, every piece of cloth, and indeed, everything of value was seized and appropriated before he got a chance. He said little of his disappointment, though it was evident enough. He went aside, and sat by himself on a log. Disturbing with his foot a pile of dry leaves, he found buried under it a brass kettle, inverted, and covering a quantity of valuable offerings made to the earth. These he of course seized upon for himself, and his portion was more valuable than that of any other. The blankets, robes, and other things were suspended in trees, and the quantity was larger than is usually seen in places where such offerings are made. The Assineboins had held a metai or religious ceremony here on their way to the country of the Sioux.

From this place I travelled to my home, and finding all there as usual, I remained some time hunting, and was successful in obtaining a plentiful supply of food.

It was while I was living here at Great Wood River that news came of a prophet among the Shawnees who had been favoured by a revelation of the will of the Great Spirit. I was hunting in the prairie, at a great distance from my lodge, when I saw a stranger approaching. At first I was apprehensive of an enemy, but as he drew nearer his dress showed him to be an Ojibbeway; yet when he came up there was something very strange and peculiar in his manner. He signified to me that I must go home, but gave no explanation of the cause. He refused to enter into any conversation, and would not even look at me further. I thought he must be crazy, but nevertheless I turned towards my lodge in his company. On arriving we smoked together, still in silence, but at last he began to tell me that he had come with a message from the prophet of the Shawnees. "Henceforth," said he, "the fire must never be suffered to go out in your lodge. Summer and winter, day and night, in calm or storm, you must remember that the life in your body and the fire in your lodge are the same in nature and in origin. If you suffer your fire to go out, at the same time your life will be at an end. You must not suffer a dog to live, kill them all. You must never strike man, woman, or child. The prophet himself is coming to shake hands with you; but I have come before, that you may know what is the will of the Great Spirit, communicated to us by him, and that the preservation of your life depends on your entire obedience. From this time we are neither to get drunk, nor to steal, nor to lie, nor to go against our enemies. While we yield obedience to these commands of the Great Spirit, our enemies, even if they come to our country, will not be able to see us; we shall be protected and made happy."

I listened to all he had to say, for he seemed in earnest; but I told him, in answer, that I could not believe we should all die, in case our fire went out; that in many instances it would be difficult to avoid punishing our children; and that dogs were so useful in helping us to hunt and to take animals, that I could not believe the Great Spirit wished to deprive us of them. He continued talking till near midnight, and then went to sleep in my lodge.

I happened to wake the first in the morning, and perceiving that the fire had gone out, I called to him to get up, and to see how many of us were still living, and how many dead. He was prepared for the ridicule I was attempting to throw upon his doctrine, and told me I had not yet shaken hands with the prophet. His visit was merely to prepare me for that event, and to make me aware of the obligations I would make and the risks I would run by entering into the engagement implied in taking in my hand the message of the prophet.

I seemed incredulous, but confess I did not feel altogether easy in my unbelief. I had heard that very many of the Indians received the doctrine of this man with reverence and with fear. Distress and anxiety appeared in the countenances of the people near our lodge. Many killed their dogs, and resolved to practise obedience to the commands of the prophet.

Without saying anything, I took an opportunity of going to the trading-house, hoping to see white men, believing that if the Great Spirit had any communications for men, they would be given, in the first instance, to white men. The traders said that a revelation had been given, and was written in a sacred book; but they did not say more about it at that time. They ridiculed, however, and despised the idea of a new revelation of the Divine Will having been given to a poor Shawnee. Thus I was confirmed in my unbelief. Nevertheless, I did not openly avow my opposition, only I refused to kill my dogs. The Ojibbeway envoy stayed some time in our neighbourhood, and gained the attention of the principal men so effectually that a time was appointed for a public adherence by many of them to the cause of the prophet. When the lodge had been prepared for the ceremony, I went along with the others to observe the proceedings. I saw something carefully concealed under a blanket, in shape and size bearing resemblance to the form of a man. But while we remained no use was made of this figure, and no one went near it, or raised the blanket which was spread over. After a long address, in which the chief points of the new revelation were stated and urged, the man showed four strings of beans, which he said were made of the flesh itself of the prophet. These were presented, with much solemnity, to each man in the lodge, and he was directed to take hold of each string at the top, and draw the bean-like substances gently through his hand. This was called shaking hands with the prophet, and was considered as an engagement to obey his injunctions, and to accept his mission. All the Indians who touched the beans had previously killed their dogs, and they gave up also their medicine bags and other charms, and expressed their readiness to comply with whatever should be required of them.

The excitement and discussions caused by this strange visitor had a bad influence on our people. They were gloomy and depressed, as if with superstitious awe. Some of the most brave and active became indolent, and as there were considerable numbers gathered at and near the place, want of food soon was manifest, and a famine threatened. I set out with my dogs to hunt, and soon got a supply for my lodge. I took care to argue again with the Indians as to the folly of having killed the dogs, which the Great Spirit must have given to help in hunting for supporting our lives. The prophet had disappeared when the famine began. He had told the Indians never to use flint and steel, and never to give fire to one another, if that in our own lodges was extinguished. I told them that it could not be pleasing to the Great Spirit to see any lying hungry and cold for want of exerting themselves. The use of flint and steel appeared to excite them so much, as if a sharp defiance of the prophet's warnings, that I avoided using this way of striking a light, and I kindled my fire by rubbing two pieces of dry cedar wood, in which I became very expert. I think there was some improvement so far as anger and violence were concerned, and the desire for war was not expressed as formerly; there seemed less craving for drink also, which might be caused by their thoughts being otherwise directed, and by the want of anything to take to the trading-houses where drink was obtained. Hunger compelled them to resume more activity, and gradually fires were lighted again; dogs were procured and increased; the women and children were kept in order as before, with the help of beating when necessary; and the Shawnee prophet was remembered as a troublesome impostor. I heard afterwards of similar panic and mischief being caused among distant and scattered Ojibbeway villages, but I never heard it conjectured that there was any purpose to unite these Indians in the accomplishment of any purpose. The whole affair showed how easily superstitious fears may be excited, and strange actions performed under their influence, such as the killing of their faithful and useful dogs by these Indians. As to the good precepts mixed with the folly, such as forbidding to lie and steal and make war, it is possible that the prophet had heard something of the religion of the white men in a confused way, and repeated those precepts in which the voice within us agrees with the alleged revelation of the Great Spirit. This I thought, not at the time, but long afterwards, when I came to know more of the religion of the whites, as I shall presently relate.

After the excitement of this affair had somewhat subsided, I went with a large party of Indians to some of the upper branches of the Red River to hunt beaver. I know not whether our people were emboldened by the promise of the prophet that we should be invisible to the Sioux, but we went much nearer them than we had formerly ventured into their country. It was here, in a border region, where both they and ourselves had been afraid to hunt, that we now found beaver in the greatest abundance. Here I, without the aid of my gun, took one hundred large beavers in a single month, by trapping merely. My family had now increased, but I was able alone to supply all their wants.

Chapter X.

I LIVE IN A SOLITARY LODGE—OCCASIONAL ALARMS—I JOIN A BAND OF OJIBBEWAYS, OF RED RIVER, UNDER A CHIEF BE-GWA-IS—A HUNTING EXCURSION TOWARDS THE SIOUX COUNTRY—ENMITY OF WA-GE-TOTE, BROTHER OF THE CHIEF—FRIENDSHIP OF WAB-KE-ZHE, AN OTTAWWAW WHO HAD LIVED MUCH AMONG THE WHITES—JOIN HIS BAND—HUNTING ADVENTURES—LETTER FOUND CONSISTING OF MARKS ON A PIECE OF BIRCH-BARK—WA-ME-GON-A-BIEW AGAIN IN TROUBLE—DEATH OF MY OLD FRIEND PE-SHAW-BA—A PROPHET'S REVELATION—LITTLE CLAM AND HIS BAND KITTED BY THE SIOUX.

At length, however, the beaver got scarce, and I had to use my gun again. The first time I went out with it I shot an elk. When the report was heard at the lodge, my people were startled, and fled to the woods, believing the Sioux had fired upon me. A few days after, I myself got a fright from a similar false alarm. I had killed a moose, and was cutting it up, when I heard a gun not more than two hundred yards from me. I knew that I had advanced nearer to the frontier of the Sioux than any Ojibbeway, and I did not believe there was any of the latter tribe living near me. I therefore believed this must be the gun of a Sioux, and immediately called out to him, as I supposed he must have heard my firing; but no answer was returned. I watched about me more anxiously than before, and as evening was coming on I went home as silently and cautiously as I could. On the following day, I ventured to examine in the direction of the place where I had heard the gun, and found the tracks, which proved to be those of an Ojibbeway, who had fired upon a bear he was pursuing, probably with too much eagerness to have heard my call. Soon after this I found many tracks, and ascertained that I was not far from a place where the Ojibbeways had built and fortified a camp.

Three times I received messages from the chiefs of the band living at this camp, urging me to go there, as the situation of my lodge was exposed and dangerous. Disliking to live in a crowd, I did not attend to this offer until I discovered the tracks of some Sioux, who had evidently been reconnoitering my camp. Then I took advantage of this offer.

The Sioux from time to time came near and looked at the place, but did not venture to attack it. When the spring came all the Ojibbeways left in a body; but I was compelled to remain, having charge of some packs for a trader, which I could not remove. The chiefs warned me, and said the Sioux would certainly know when the main body had gone, and would fall upon me when thus left behind. Having seen nothing of them for some time I did not feel alarmed, though I could not wholly disregard the friendly warning. At night I closed the entrance to my camp as effectually as I could, and cautioning my family to remain very quiet, I stationed myself by the stockade or wall to watch. The night was not far advanced, when by the light of the moon, which then shone brightly, I saw two men, who came directly towards the usual entrance, but finding it barricaded they began to walk round and examine the fence. Fear strongly prompted me to fire and shoot them without hailing; but remembering that possibly they might not be Sioux, I took an opportunity, when I could get my gun pointed at them without my being much exposed, to hail them. They proved to be the trader on whose account I had stayed back, accompanied by a French trader. I gladly opened my fort to let them in, and thus reinforced we spent the remainder of the night quietly. Next morning we moved out, taking the trader's packs, following the path of the Ojibbeways.

I did not wish to rejoin this band, and after leaving the traders I went to camp by myself in the woods for a time. Then I joined some other Ojibbeways, of Red River, under a chief called Be-gwa-is. The hunters of this band had been for some days trying to kill an old buck moose, who had become notorious among them for his shyness and cunning. The first day I went out I saw this moose, but could not kill him; I killed another, however, and returned the next day after the buck. It so happened that the weather and wind were favourable, and I killed him. I think it was only a fortunate shot, but the Indians, after their own want of success, gave me credit for superior skill, and I was thenceforth reckoned the best hunter in that band.

We now started, twelve of us, under Be-gwa-is, to go towards the Sioux country, to hunt beaver, leaving our families behind. On this hunt all the Indians became snow-blind, and I being the only one for a time able to hunt, had to provide for the whole band. As the snow went off in the spring, they began to recover. We separated into three parties, one of which was attacked by the Sioux, who killed a man and carried off another as prisoner. The band with whom I was, heard of this from the two who escaped when the Sioux fell upon them, and becoming panic-struck fled with all the speed they could make. I happened to have hurt my foot with my axe, and was unable to travel fast, but they paid no regard to my situation. I followed as I was able, and at night came up with them, finding them miserable and starving in their comfortless camp; for these were disciples of the prophet, and did not venture to strike a fire. Rain and sleet had fallen, although the spring was now advancing, and the weather was very cold. As soon as I could I got away from this cheerless band, and found my way back to where I had left our women, who were employed for some time in making sugar, as the sap rose in the maple-trees in early spring.

After our spring hunting there was again talk about going against the Sioux, and a party assembled, among those who lived immediately about me. Wa-me-gon-a-biew and I joined them, but instead of going against our enemies, we spent the greater part of the summer among the buffalo. In the fall I returned to Pembinah, my intention being to go thence to the wintering ground of a trader who had some time before proposed to assist me in getting to the States. I now heard of the war between the States and Great Britain, and of the capture of Mackinac, and this intelligence deterred me from any attempt to pass through the frontiers of the United States territory, which were then the scenes of warlike operations.

In the ensuing spring there was a very general movement among the Ojibbeways of the Red River towards the Sioux country, but the professed design was only to hunt. I travelled with a large band under the direction of Aisainse (the little clam). His brother, Wa-ge-tote, was a man of considerable importance. We had ascended Red River about a hundred miles when we met Mr. Hanie, a trader, who gave us some rum. I lived at this time in a long lodge, having two or three fires, and I occupied it in common with several other men and their families, mostly the relatives of my wife. It was midnight, or after, and I was asleep, when I was suddenly waked by a man seizing me roughly by the hand, and raising me up. There was still a little fire burning, and by the light it gave I recognised, in the angry and threatening countenance that hung over me, the face of Wa-ge-tote, the brother of the Little Clam, our principal chief. "I have solemnly promised," he said, "that if you come with us to this country, you shall not live; up, therefore, and be ready to answer me." He then went on to Wah-zhe-gwun, the man who was sleeping next to me, and used to him similar threatening and insolent language; but by this time, an old man, a relation of mine, called Mabnuge, who slept beyond, had comprehended the purpose of his visit, and raised himself up, with his knife in his hand. When Wa-ge-tote came to him, and was beginning the same threatening language, he got a sharp answer with the point of the old man's knife. He then returned to me, drew his knife, and threatened me with instant death. "You are a stranger," he said, "and have come among us, with your family, to feed yourself with what does not belong to you. You have visited our best hunting grounds, and have destroyed many animals intended for our sustenance. Go back, therefore, from this place, and be no longer a burden to us, or I will certainly take your life." I answered him that I was not going to the country they were now about to visit, but that if I were, it was my right to go where I pleased, and I would maintain my right." By this time I was standing up to defend myself, and at that moment old Mab-nuge came also beside him, with his knife in his hand, and drove the quarrelsome half-drunken Wa-ge-tote out of the lodge. The rum given by the trader had caused this disturbance. We saw the man no more for some time; he probably felt ashamed of himself when sober in the morning. His brother, the Little Clam, told us to think nothing of what he had said.

Here a messenger overtook us, to bring to the Ottawwaws the information that the chief known as the Black Bird, from L'Arbre Croche, had arrived from Lake Huron, to call us all home to that country. So we turned back, and one after another left tilt only the Ojibbeways remained, and they met with others of their people on their way towards the Sioux country. Aisainse, the Ojibbeway chief, was returning one evening from a successful hunt, having killed two elks, and on the following morning, his wife with her young son, started out to dry the meat. They had proceeded a great distance from the lodge when the lad discovered a Sioux band at no great distance, and called out to his mother, "The Sioux are coming." The old woman drew her knife, and cutting the belt which bound the boy's blanket to his body, told him to run for home with all his strength. She then awaited the approach of the war party. The lad heard the firing of guns, and the old woman was no more heard of. The boy reached the fort near Wild Rice River in a state of great exhaustion. Another party of Ojibbeways fell in with some Sioux, but succeeded in driving them off, chiefly through the valour of Little Clam, Aisainse, whose wife had been killed in the way just narrated. Another Ojibbeway chief man, Ta-bush-shish, had been hunting in a different direction, accompanied by only one, and had heard distant firing, either where the old woman had been killed, or where Aisainse was fighting, and had returned home. The Indians said of him, as they often say of a man after his death, that he had some presentiments or forewarnings of his fate. On reaching his lodge the previous evening in the fortified camp, he had been met by the abusive tongue of an old wife, who had been jealous of the attention bestowed on a younger rival. On this occasion he said to her: "Scold away, old woman, for I hear you now for the last time." Later in the evening some one arrived who had skulked and fled from the fight in which the Little Clam was engaged. Ta-bush-shish said to one of his friends, Be-na, the Pheasant, "Is it not a shame to leave Aisainse outside, with only a few men, while so many of his friends are staying here safely in the camp?" The two went out together, and following a track it brought them to a place where a party of Sioux had lighted a fire, round which they were sitting. They crept as near as they could, but not finding a favourable opportunity to fire, they went forward on the path which they were sure the Sioux must take, and lay down in ambush in the snow. It was night, but not very dark. When the Sioux began to move, and a number of them came near the place where they had concealed themselves, both rose up and fired, Be-na instantly fleeing in a different direction from Ta-bush-shish, as they had arranged to do. When at a considerable distance, and finding that he was not pursued, he stopped to listen, and occasionally heard a gun fired, and sometimes distinguished the shrill and solitary sah-sah-kwi or signal cry of Ta-bush-shish, shifting from place to place, probably in hope that they might rejoin one another. But presently he heard several guns discharged at the same moment, and immediately after, the shouts and whoops of the Sioux at the fall of their enemy. They had just discovered his place of concealment. All was silent soon, and he then returned to the camp.

It was on the same day, as we afterwards learned, that the warriors from Leech Lake, to whom Wa-ge-tote had joined himself, fell on some Sioux lodges at the Long Prairie. They fought for most part of two days, and many were killed on both sides.

Wah-ka-zhe, brother of Black Bird, the chief from L'Arbre Croche, met those Ottawwaws who returned from Red River at Lake Winnipeg. He had been ten years in the Rocky Mountains and the country near there, but now wished to return to his own people. He had been in the course of his life much in company with whites, and was well acquainted with the different methods of gaining a living among them. I had much conversation with him. He told me that I would be much better situated among the whites, but that I could not become a trader, as I was unable to write. Nor could I be a farmer, because my habits had made me unfit to submit to the steady constant labour necessary for success. There was but one situation exactly adapted to my habits and qualifications, that of an interpreter. The idea, therefore from this time occupied my thoughts and excited my hopes.

Among other subjects of conversation he gave me an account of a missionary who had come among the Ottawwaws about the lakes, and urged them to abandon their own religion and adopt that of the white men. I had met white men on different occasions, but never had heard them speak on the subject of religion, except that time when I went to seek information about the Shawnee prophet. They seemed wholly occupied with their trading. I longed to meet this or some other missionary from whom I could learn something of the religion held by them. But this opportunity did not come till some time after.

Wah-ka-zhe being the most considerable man among us at this time, it devolved upon him to direct our movements; but either from indolence, or from his good opinion of me, he determined that not only himself but all his band should, for the winter, be guided by me. As we had no object beyond subsistence and I was reckoned a very good hunter, and knew this part of the country better than any other man of the band, his advice was indeed not impolitic, and I undertook the leadership. I advised that we should go to spend the winter at the Be-gwi-o-nush-ko River. This is a tributary which enters Red River about ten miles below Pembinah. At the time I speak of, the country on either side of it was well stocked with game. We lived here in great comfort and plenty, and Wah-ka-zhe often expressed his satisfaction at having chosen me to direct the movements of his band. When part of the winter had passed we were brought into trouble by the violent conduct of Wa-me-gon-a-biew. He had on former occasions, at different places, got into quarrels, and in one rencontre had part of his nose bitten or cut off. His temper had, perhaps on this account, been getting worse than ever. He was now talking of sacrificing Wah-ka-zhe, on account of being in some degree connected with the man who, many years before, had killed his father, Taw-ga-we-ninne. I remonstrated with him strongly against his present purpose. Nevertheless he went one day, with his knife in his hand, to the lodge of Wah-ka-zhe, with the intention of killing him. Muk-kud-da-be-na-sa, a son of Wah-ka-zhe perceived his intention and prevented him, and offered to engage Wa-me-gon-a-biew in single combat. He declined this, and was accordingly taunted by many with cowardice, a charge which I think he richly deserved, when he retained the vindictive feeling against the old man. I not only reproved him, but proposed that he be driven from the band, and no longer considered as my brother. But Wah-ka-zhe was a friendly and considerate man, and, unwilling that further trouble or disturbance should be made, forgave his offence.

Another son of Wah-ka-zhe was reckoned one of the best hunters among the Indians of this band, and there was between us a friendly rivalry in hunting. He killed nineteen moose, one beaver, and one bear, while I killed seventeen moose, seven bears, and very many beavers; but he was considered the better hunter, moose being the most difficult of all animals to kill. There are many Indians who hunt through the winter in that country, and kill not more than two or three moose, and some are never able to kill one.

We had plenty of game at the Be-gwi-o-nush-ko River, until another band of Ojibbeways came upon us, in large numbers, and in a starving condition. While we were in this situation, and many of those who had recently joined us were on the point of perishing with hunger, a man called Gish-kaw-ko, the nephew of him by whom I was first taken prisoner, went a-hunting, and in one day killed two moose. Knowing my reputation as a hunter he asked me to go out with him, and get some meat for ourselves and our own people; signifying at the same time his intention to keep his success concealed from the remainder of the band, and especially from the new comers: but I refused to have any part with him in such a transaction. I immediately started with the chief's son, and one or two others, and we killed four bears, which we distributed among the hungry.

It was soon found necessary, as our company was now so large, to disperse in various directions. With Wah-ka-zhe, his son, the Black Bird, and one other man, I went and encamped at about the distance of two days' journey from where we had been living. We had very bad luck in hunting, and were so reduced to straits, that my companions thought it necessary to have recourse to a medicine hunt. To myself and to the son of the old man, as the best hunters, a little bag of medicine was given, consisting of certain dried roots, pounded fine, and mixed with red paint. This was to be applied to the little figures of animals we wished to kill. These figures, or idols we might almost call them, are often carried by the Indians, and if they have them not, a rude sketch is made on birch bark or other surface, representing the animal, and this is marked with the medicine paint. This is supposed to secure good success.

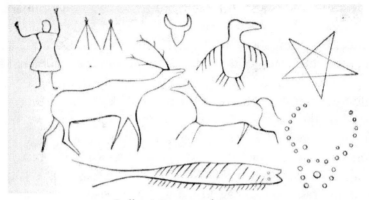

Indian totems, or charms.

A somewhat similar kind of medicine charm is used when an Indian wishes some injury or disease to come upon another. He draws a figure of his enemy, and the part representing the heart is pierced with a sharp instrument if death is desired, and the figure is smeared with the medicine. These drawings on birch bark or wood are called muzzi-ne-neen (plural muzzi-ne-neen-ug). After our medicine incantation we started with much confidence of success, but Wah-ka-zhe followed, and overtaking us at some distance, cautioned us against using the medicine which Wah-gitch-e-gum-me had given us, as he said it would be the means of mischief and misery to us, not at present, but when we came to die. We therefore did not make use of it; but nevertheless, happening to kill some game, Wah-gitch-e-gum-me thought himself, on account of the supposed efficacy of his medicine, entitled to a handsome share of it. Such is the power of imagination in those who are credulous. We might not have the same luck another time, whether with or without the medicine charm, and seeing that hunger was likely to press heavily upon us, I separated from the rest, and went to live by myself, feeling confident that by so doing I could always ensure a plentiful supply of food for my own family.

About the usual time for assembling in the spring, I began to descend the Be-gwi-o-nush-ko to go to the traders on Red River. Most of the Indians had left their camps, and gone on before me. As I was one morning passing a deserted camping place, I saw on shore a little stick standing in the bank, and attached to the top of it a piece of birch bark. On examination I found the mark of a rattlesnake, made with a knife, the handle touching the snake, and the point sticking into a bear, the head of the latter being down. Near the rattlesnake was the mark or totem of a beaver, one of its teats, showing it to be a female, touching the snake. This was left for my information, and I learned from it that Wa-me-gon-a-biew, whose totem was the rattlesnake, had killed a man whose totem was the bear. The murderer could be no other than Wa-me-gon-a-biew, as it was specified that he was the son of a woman whose totem was the beaver, and this I knew must be Net-no-kwa. As there were but few of the bear totem in our band, I was confident that the man killed was a young man named Ke-zha-zhoons; that he was dead and not wounded merely, was indicated by the drooping down of the head of the bear.

I was not deterred by this information from continuing my journey, although I could not tell whether my brother left it in order to warn me or to hasten my coming to him. I went on as quickly as I could, and arrived in time to witness the interment of the young man my brother had killed. Wa-me-gon-a-biew had gone by himself to dig the grave, and he dug it wide enough for two men. When the friends of Ke-zha-zhoons brought his body, Wa-me-gon-a-biew stripped himself except his loin cloth, and sat down thus almost naked at the head of the grave. He then handed his knife to the nearest male relative of the deceased. "My friend," he said, "I have killed your brother when I was in a passion. You see I have made a grave

wide enough for both of us, and I am now ready and willing
to sleep with him." The first, then the second, and eventually
all the friends of the murdered young man, refused the knife
offered to each in succession. The relations of Wa-me-gon-a-
biew were many and powerful, and the fear of them I believe
it was which saved his life. At all events it was a politic thing
for my brother to act as he did, even if he felt no generous
compunction for his deed of blood. When he saw that none of
the male relations of the deceased were willing to avenge
their comrade's death, or at least publicly to undertake his
punishment, Wa-me-gon-a-biew said to them, "Trouble me no
more, now or hereafter, about this affair; I shall do again as I
now have done if any of you venture to give me similar provocation." It seems the quarrel began by the murdered man rid-
iculing my brother's disfigured face, and calling him cut-
nose.

Indian graves and mourners.

The method by which information of this affair was communicated to me at a distance, is one in common use among
the Indians, and in most cases it is perfectly clear and intelli-
gible. The men of the same tribe are generally well
acquainted with the mark, or totem, belonging to each. If on

any record of this kind the figure of a man appears without any designatory mark, it is understood immediately that he is a stranger, or not known. But in most hieroglyphic letters of this sort, there is no figure, but only the totem or surname given. If the information is to be communicated that a band or a person is starving, the mouth of the figure, or of the totem of the tribe or person, is smeared with white paint.

After visiting the trader on Red River I started with the intention of again trying to come to the States, but at Lake Winnipeg I heard that the war still continued, with such disturbances on the frontier as would render it difficult for me to pass with safety. I was, therefore, compelled to stop by myself at that place, where I was, after some time, joined by Pe-shaw-ba and others, to the extent of three lodges. I was sorry to see Pe-shaw-ba now in an enfeebled state of health. His old friend and companion, Waus-so had been accidentally killed by an Assineboin, and this preyed much on his spirit. It will be remembered that I first knew Pe-shaw-ba when I was comparatively young, and he was then advanced in years, but a fine and noble-looking man. He and Waus-so, with two or three other Ottawwaws, had then come from the neighbourhood of Lake Huron, where they had lived for some time, because they had heard of distress among some of the people of their race, and they came to help them in hunting. He was related to Net-no-kwa, and I have formerly described my first interview with him. He had then become my friend and protector, and I always retained much regard for him. I was glad now to be able to help and to comfort him in his old age, for we were living in plenty and contentment. But he grew feeble, and soon was conscious that his end was drawing near. He told us he could not live long. He spoke with much reverence of the Great Spirit, and he said that he had tried to do what was just and right. "I have not," he said, "struck my friends in their lodge. I have disregarded the foolishness of young men who would have offended me, but have always been ready to lead our brave men against the Sioux. To you, my son, I have been a protector, and you will grieve when I leave you; but be not like a woman, you will soon follow in my path." Soon after this the old man walked out of the lodge, looked at the sky, the sun, the lake, and the distant hills; then came in, and lay down composedly in his place in the lodge, and in a few minutes ceased to breathe.

After the death of Pe-shaw-ba the friends who had come with him remained with us till winter was over, and in the spring went to Dead River, where we planted corn, and spent the summer. In the fall, after the corn was gathered, we went to the hunting-grounds. When the hunting season was over, and many had gathered at the trading station at Pembinah, the chiefs built a great lodge, and called all the men together to receive some information concerning a new revelation from the Great Spirit. The bearer of this revelation was Manito-o-gheezik, a man of no great fame, but well known to most of the Ojibbeways of that country. He had disappeared for about a year, and in that time he pretended to have visited the abode of the Great Spirit, and to have listened to his instructions. Some of the traders informed me that he had only been to St. Louis, on the Mississippi. He may have there picked up some knowledge not possessed by the Indians among whom he alone had lived previously.

When the assembly met, the Little Clam undertook to explain the object of the meeting, and described some of the leading features of the revelation brought by Manito-o-gheezik. The Indians were no more to go to war; they were no more to steal, defraud, or lie, or get drunk. There was no unnatural and foolish precept, like that of the Shawnee emissary, who forbade fires to be lighted, and ordered the dogs to be slain. Most of the maxims and directions communicated to the Indians at this assembly were of a kind to be permanently useful to them; and the effect of their influence was for a time manifest in their more orderly and peaceable conduct, and somewhat improved condition.

When we were ready to separate from the trading post, Aisainse (the Little Clam) invited several of us, myself in particular, to accompany him to his home at Spirit Lake. But I declined, as I wished to go to a woody country for the purpose of hunting the fur-bearing animals. Ten men, among whom were Wa-ge-tote and Gi-ah-ge-git, with some women and their families, accepted his invitation, and set out with him. A young man, a friend of Aisainse, before they separated from us at Pembinah, predicted that he would be killed at Spirit Lake. Having obtained much credit among the Indians, his admonition of impending danger to those who would go with Little Clam began to be so much regarded that Wa-me-gon-a-biew and many others became uneasy and returned. Last of all came Match-e-toons, a foolish and lying young man, who reported that the indications of danger were thickening round Little Clam and his band, and that he had heard the firing of the Sioux at the camp he had left. We did not immediately believe this report, but having waited anxiously for several days, we sent out twenty men to ascertain whether there was any foundation for his statement. This party, when they arrived at the place where the Little Clam had been encamped, found that the whole band had been cut off. First of all, and in advance of all the camp, lay the body of Se-gwu-noons, the young man who had predicted the attack before he left Pembinah. Near him lay some men of his own age, and farther back the body of Little Clam. In the camp the ground was strewed with the bodies of the women and children. At some distance was the body of one of the Sioux, in a sitting posture, and covered with the puk-kwi, or mats, which had belonged to the Ojibbeway lodges. Not one escaped except Match-e-toons, but some doubted whether he had not fled in the time of the fight, instead of the evening before, as he had stated. Thus died Little Clam, one of the last of the considerable men of his time, belonging to the Ojibbeways of Red River.

We then went down to Dead River, planted corn, and spent the summer there, Sha-gwa-koo-sink, an Ottawwaw, an old man, first introduced the cultivation of corn among the Ojibbeways of the Red River country.

Chapter XI.

***PEMBINAH TRADING STATION—THE RIVAL
TRADERS: THE HUDSON BAY COMPANY AND
THE NORTHWEST COMPANY—A CHURLISH
AGENT—ATTEMPT TO OVERREACH ME AND TO
SEIZE MY PROPERTY—SUCCESSFUL RESIS-
TANCE—NIGHT ATTACK ON A FORTIFIED STA-
TION—ALARMS FROM THE SIOUX—MY
MEDICINE BAG—JOIN THE BAND OF AN OLD
HUNTER, SHA-GWAW-KO-SINK—HIS DEATH—
APPEARANCE OF A NEW PROPHET—TROUBLES
CAUSED BY MY DENOUNCING HIM AS A ROGUE
AND IMPOSTOR—INTRIGUES OF THE
PROPHET—ENMITY IN MY TRIBE AND FAMILY
INDUCED BY HIM—I AM COMPELLED TO LEAVE
MY LODGE AND PEOPLE.***

Pembinah was the trading station to which I had always
chiefly resorted, and where I was well known. There were
agents there of the North-West Company and the Hudson's
Bay Company, but the latter had recently left the place to their
rivals. Some incidents occurred at this time, which show the
selfish rapacity too often characteristic of the fur traders. A
Mr. Henry had for ten years managed the trade for the North-
West Company. He was succeeded by a Mr. McKenzie, who
remained only a short time, and after him came Mr. Wells,
whom the Indians called Gah-se-moan (a sail), from the
roundness and fulness of his person. He built a strong fort on
Red River, near the mouth of the Assineboin. The Hudson's

Bay Company had now no post in that part of the country, and the Indians were soon made conscious of the advantage which had formerly resulted to them from the competition between rival trading companies.

At the commencement of winter, Mr. Wells called us all together, giving rum and tobacco to those who assembled, and at the same time told them that he would not credit one of them to the value of a single needle. When they brought skins he would take them in exchange for such articles as were required for their use and comfort. I was not present when this talk was made. When it was reported to me, and a share of the presents offered me, I not only refused to accept anything, but reproached the Indians for submitting to such terms. They had long been accustomed to receive credits in the fall; and they were accordingly now entirely destitute not only of clothing, but of ammunition, and most of them of guns and traps. It might be proper, after due notice, to establish the proposed system, but how were they, without the credit that had always been given by the traders, to support themselves and their families during the ensuing winter?

Fur company's fort and trading station.

I went to Mr. Wells a few days afterwards, and told him that I was poor, with a family to support by my own exertions, and that I must unavoidably suffer, and perhaps perish, unless he would give me such a credit as I had always, in the fall, been accustomed to receive. He would not listen to my representations, and told me, roughly, to be gone from his house. I then brought eight silver beavers, such as are worn by the women as ornaments on their dress, and which I had purchased the year before at just twice the price that was commonly given for a capote. I laid them before him on the table, and asked him to retain them as a pledge for the payment of the price of the garment, as soon as I could procure the peltries. He took up the ornaments, threw them in my face, and told me never to come inside of his house again. The cold weather had not yet set in, and I went immediately to my hunting ground, killed a number of moose, and set my wife to make the skins into such garments as were best adapted for the winter season, and which I now saw we should be compelled to substitute for the blankets and woollen rugs we had been accustomed to receive from the traders.

I may here remark that, at the trading stations, the skin of the beaver was the standard of value by which all other peltries were regulated. In obtaining stores or ammunition, or other articles, for services rendered or labour executed, the payment is reckoned by skins, that of the beaver being the unit of computation. Thus, for instance, supposing that four beaver skins are equal in value to a silver fox skin, two martens or sables are equal to a beaver, twenty musk rats to a marten, and so on. If an Indian wishes to buy a blanket or a gun, he will have to account to the trader of the Company so many beaver skins, so many martens, or other furs. The Company usually gives in advance blankets or ammunition or other necessaries, when the summer supplies arrive at the posts or trading stations, these advances being paid for at the close of the hunting season. At this time the traders used to supply rum and other intoxicating spirits to the Indians, who often wasted in this way the whole of their earnings, to the benefit of the traders, and had to go without necessary or useful articles of winter supply. Many of them thus continued in a state of constant poverty and dependence. Not having taste for drinking, I was usually less pressed than most of my people, but the churlishness of Mr. Wells put me to much inconvenience.

I continued my hunting with good success, but the winter had not half passed when I heard that Mr. Hanie, a trader for the Hudson's Bay Company, had arrived at Pembinah. To him I immediately went, and he gave me all the credit I asked, which was to the amount of seventy skins. Then I went to Musk-rat River, where I hunted the remainder of the winter, killing great numbers of beavers, martens, otters, and other game.

Early in the spring I sent a message by some Indians to Mr. Hanie that I would go to the mouth of the Assineboin River, and meet him there, in order to pay my credit, as I had skins more than enough for this purpose. When I arrived at the Assineboin, Mr. Hanie had not yet passed, and I stopped to wait for him opposite Mr. Hanie's trading-house. An old French trapper offered me a lodging in his house, and I went and deposited my peltries under the place he gave me to sleep in. Mr. Wells having heard of my arrival, sent three times, urging me to come and see him. I took no notice at first, but yielded to the solicitations of my brother-in-law, and crossed over with him. Mr. Wells professed to be glad to see me, and treated me with much politeness; he offered me wine and provisions, and whatever his house afforded. I had taken nothing except a little tobacco, when I saw his Frenchman come in with my packs. They carried them past where we were sitting, into an inner room, locking the door and taking out the key. I said nothing, but felt not the less anxious and uneasy, as I was unwilling to be deprived of the means of paying Mr. Hanie his credit; still more indignant was I at what seemed an attempt to deprive me of my property by compulsion and without my consent. Whether he intended to make me any offer I cannot say, but it would probably have been far below the real value of the peltries of which he had the actual possession. I watched for some time, and presently Mr. Wells had occasion to go to the inner room to take something from a trunk. I rose and followed him into the room. He told me to go out, and then seized me in order to push me out, but I was too strong for him. After he had proceeded to this violence, I did not hesitate to take up my packs, but he snatched them from me. Again I seized them, and in the struggle that ensued the thongs that bound them gave way, and the skins were strewed about the floor. As I went to gather them up, he drew a pistol, cocked it, and presented it to my breast. For a moment I stood motionless, making sure he would fire, for he was terribly enraged. But as he continued with the pistol pointed at me, I seized his hand, and turned it aside, at the same time drawing from my belt a large knife, which I grasped firmly in my right hand, still holding him by my left. Seeing himself thus suddenly and entirely in my power, he called out to his interpreter who was in the next room to come and put me out of the house. To this he replied, "You are as able to put him out as I am." Some Frenchmen were in the house, and came on hearing the noise, but they declined to give him any assistance.

Finding he was not likely to intimidate me nor to overcome me by violence, he had recourse once more to milder measures. He offered to divide with me, and to allow me to retain half my peltries for the Hudson's Bay people. "You have always," said he, "belonged to the North-West, why should you now desert us for the Hudson's Bay?" He then began to count the skins, dividing them into two parcels; but I told him he need not do that, as I was determined he should not have one of them. "I went to you," I said, "last fall, when I was hungry and destitute, and you drove me, like a dog, from your door. The ammunition with which I killed these animals was credited to me by Mr. Hanie, and the skins belong to him; but even if this were not the case, you shall not have one of them. You have acted in a violent and at the same time cowardly way. You pointed your pistol at my breast, and yet did not shoot me. My life was in your power, and there was nothing to prevent your taking it, not even the fear of my friends, for you know I am alone and a stranger here, and not one of the Indians would raise his hand to avenge my death. You lacked the spirit to kill me, although you were base enough to try and rob me." He said, "Have you a knife in your hand?" I showed him that I had one at hand, and told him to beware how he provoked me to use it. He went and sat down opposite me in the great room, evidently in great agitation. After sitting awhile, he rose and walked backward and forward, and went out into the yard. I collected all my skins together, and the interpreter helped me to tie them up; then taking them on my back, I walked out, passed close by him, put them into my canoe, and returned to the old Frenchman's house across the river.

Next morning, it appeared, Mr. Wells had thought better of the subject, whether from feeling he acted wrongly, or from motives of policy. He sent his interpreter to offer me his horse, which was a valuable one, if I would think and say no more of what he had done. "Tell Mr. Wells," I said to the interpreter, "he is like a child, and wishes to quarrel and to forget his quarrel in one day. I do not want his horse, I have one of my own. I will keep my packs; nor can I forget his treatment of me, especially his pointing his pistol at my breast."

On the following morning, one of the clerks of the North-West Company arrived from the trading-house at Mouse River, and having seen Mr. Wells, and heard from him what had passed, said he would take the packs from me. Mr. Wells, it seems, cautioned him against it, but he determined to make the attempt. It was near noon, when the old Frenchman, after looking out of his house, said to me, "My friend, I believe you will lose your packs now; four men are coming this way, all well armed; their visit, I am sure, is for no good or friendly purpose." Hearing this, I placed my packs in the middle of the floor, and taking a beaver trap in my hand, sat down upon them.

When the clerk came in, accompanied by three young men, he asked me for my packs. "What right have you," said I, "to demand them?" "You are indebted to me," he said. "When did I owe the North-West anything that was not paid at the time agreed on?" "Ten years ago," he said, "your brother, Wa-me-gon-a-biew, had a credit from us, which he paid all but ten skins; these are still due, and I wish you to pay them." "Very well," said I; "I will pay your demand, but you must at the same time pay me for those four packs of beaver we sent to you from the Grand Portage. Your due bill was, as you know, burned with my lodge, and taking advantage of this, you have never paid me, nor any member of my family, the value of a single needle for those one hundred and sixty beaver skins." Finding this method would not succeed, and knowing, no doubt, the justice of my reply, the circumstance being thus suddenly recalled to his memory, he urged no farther the demand for my brother's alleged debt. I thought he might then resort to violent measures, like those used on the previous day by Mr. Wells, but I showed no sign of fear, and after some threatening words he and his young men walked off, without having touched the skins.

Having ascertained that it would be some time before Mr. Hanie would arrive, I went down to Dead River, and while there killed many musk rats. At last Mr. Hanie arrived at the place where I, with another man, had been awaiting him. He told me he had passed Mr. Wells's trading-house, at the mouth of the Assineboin, in the middle of the day, his crew singing as they passed. Mr. Wells, on seeing him, had immediately started after him with a canoe strongly manned and armed. Perceiving this pursuit, Mr. Hanie went on shore, leaving his men in the canoe, and went up about twenty yards into an open smooth prairie. Hither Mr. Wells followed him, attended by several armed men; but Mr. Hanie made him stop at the distance of ten or twelve yards. A long dispute followed, but after a time Mr. Hanie was permitted to go back to his canoe. I told him my story of the way I had been treated, and I paid him my debt. I traded with him for the remainder of my peltries; and after we had finished, he gave me some handsome presents, among which was a valuable gun, and then went on his way.

After the death of Mr. Wells, which was about three years later, I returned to the North-West Company, and traded with them as I had formerly done, but never while he lived. I have related what to some may appear of little consequence, but the narrative throws light upon the conduct of the traders towards Indians, and also shows the spirit induced by keenness in trading. The rivalry between the two companies often gave rise to personal animosity, not only among the traders, but among the hunters and others dependent upon them.

When I was camping at the Be-gwi-o-nush-ko River, a favourite hunting-place of mine, I was invited to come to near Pembinah, where many had assembled to hear a chief from Leech Lake give an account of the revelation made by the Great Spirit to Manito-o-gheezik. Of this I have already spoken, and told my views on the matter. But I was glad to hear more on a subject then exciting so much attention.

One night, while we were all assembled in a long lodge, erected for the purpose, to dance and feast, and listen to the discourse of the chief, suddenly we heard the report of two guns in the direction of the North-West Company's trading-house, which was now unoccupied, except by two Frenchmen who had that day arrived. The old men looked at each other as if in surprise and alarm. One said, "The Frenchmen are driving off wolves." Another said, "I know the sound of the guns of the Sioux." The night was very dark, but all the young men took their arms, and started immediately. Many of them, getting entangled among logs and stumps, did not make much progress. I kept the path and was the very foremost, when a dark figure shot past me, and I heard the voice of the Black Duck saying, "I am the man." I had often heard of the prowess of this warrior, and in one instance, at the Chief Mountain, I saw him take the lead in what we all supposed would be a dangerous assault, but the Sioux had abandoned the fort before we came up. Now I determined to keep near him. We had advanced within about gunshot of the fort, when he began to leap, first to one side and then to the other, in a zigzag line, yet advancing rapidly. I followed his example, supposing it to be to lessen the chance of being hit when moving forward in a straight line. On reaching the fort he leapt in at the open gate, and I was the only one close after him. We saw within the fort a house, from the window and door of which a bright light shone. The Black Duck had a buffalo robe over his shoulders, the dark colour of which enabled him to pass the window unobserved by the man who was watching within; but my light-coloured blanket betraying me, the muzzle of a gun was instantly presented to my head, but not discharged, for the Black Duck at that moment caught in his arms the astonished Frenchman, who had taken me for one of the Sioux, and was just going to fire at me. The second Frenchman was with the women and children, who were lying in a heap in a corner of the room, crying through fear.

It appeared that the one who was watching by the window, who was the more courageous of the two, had, a few minutes before, been leading his horse out of the fort to give him water, when his horse was shot in the gate by some men concealed near at hand. At first he thought we must have shot his horse, but he soon was convinced of his error, as we did not even know the body of his horse was at the gate, having leapt clean over It when we entered. This Frenchman would not leave the fort; but the Black Duck, who was a relation of one of the women, insisted that they should be taken for protection to the Indian camp. By this time others of the young men had come up, and we determined to watch in the fort all night. Next morning we found the trail of two men who had crossed the Pembinah River, a considerable party having been concealed on the other side. The two men, we afterwards heard, were Wah-ne-tow, a celebrated warrior chief, and a relative of his; they had concealed themselves near the fort, resolved to fire at whatever passed in or out. The first that passed was the Frenchman's horse, which was shot down, and the two men, probably without knowing whether they had killed man or beast, fled back across the river.

Many of our people were disposed to go out after the Sioux, but the chief said: "Not so, my brothers; Manito-o-gheezik, whose messenger and representative I am to you, tells us we are not to go out against our enemies. Do you not see in this instance that the Great Spirit has protected us? Had the Sioux attacked our lodge while we were feasting and in security, without our arms, they might have slain us all; but they were misled, and mistook a Frenchman's horse for an Ojibbeway. So will it be always, if we are obedient to the injunctions we have received."

I was somewhat affected by the words of this chief, of whose sincerity I had no doubt, and for whom I had a much higher regard than for the medicine men and prophets who usually give such addresses. I took an opportunity of speaking to him of my own anxiety about my family, whom I had left at home, and feared that the Sioux might visit them on their way back to their own country. "Go," he said, "if you cannot rest here without apprehension, but do not fear that the Sioux will hurt your wife or children, if you reverence the message of the Great Spirit. But I wish you would go, that on your return you may bring back with you your medicine bag, and I will show you what to do with it."

Accordingly I went to the Be-gwi-o-nush-ko River, and found that nothing had been heard of any enemies in that direction. The wish of the chief, along with my own curiosity to know what he intended to do led me to take the medicine bag, and bring it to the lodge at Pembinah. When I handed the bag to him, he ordered all the contents, except the medicines for hunting, to be thrown into the fire. He said that if any one was sick, if able to walk he must go to the nearest running water with a little tobacco and a birch bowl. The tobacco is to be offered to the stream, and then some of the water to be drunk, the bowl being dipped in the same direction as the stream runs. If any one is too ill to go and do this, the nearest relative must do it for him, carrying home the water for the sick person to drink.

He then gave me a small hoop of wood to wear on my head, not on ordinary occasions, but only in case I should go to bring water for any of my family or friends who might be sick. This wooden band or fillet was marked on one side with the figure of a snake, whose office, he said, was to take charge of the water; on the other half was the figure of a man. I thought inwardly that this was folly and superstition, and I felt vexed at the loss of the contents of my medicine bag, some of which were roots and herbs, the usefulness of which I had myself tested in various disorders, and the use of which henceforth, according to this new authority, was to be debarred. However, as all the Indians present seemed to be persuaded, or at least none of them professed disbelief, and all were in the same position as myself in having allowed our medicines to be destroyed, I was content to submit in silence.

When the spring came on, I went to fulfil an appointment I had made the preceding fall to meet an old hunter, Sha-gwaw-ko-sink, at a certain place. I arrived at the place at the time appointed, and shortly afterwards the old man came on foot and alone, to search for me. He had encamped along with some young hunters, about two miles distant, where they had been for two days, and they had some fresh meat, which I enjoyed. I lived with them during the summer. The old man was too feeble to hunt, but he had some young men who kept him supplied, while game was to be had; but late in summer, towards the fall, the hunting-grounds about us became poor. The weather was very cold, and the ground frozen hard, but no snow had fallen; so that it was difficult to follow the tracks of the moose. The noise of our walking on hard ground gave the animals notice of our approach. So quick is their hearing, and their caution so great, that treading on the smallest dry twig or leaves gave them the alarm. This state of things continuing for some time, we were reduced nearly to starvation.

Sha-gwaw-ko-sink was a very religious man, after the Indian fashion. He attributed our want of success to the neglect of "medicine hunting," especially in not having prepared muz-zin-ne-neen. One night I drew on wood figures of several animals, according to the method in common use. I had been accustomed to do this, like other Indians, although I had never any belief in their efficacy. The ceremony could do no harm if it did little good, although a certain effect might possibly be produced by its causing the hunters to go out with greater spirit and confidence to the chase. In this way even a false and superstitious ceremony may produce favourable effect. I showed my charm to the old man, who was much pleased. At the earliest dawn I started from the lodge in a heavy fall of snow, and before noon I fell on the track of two moose, and killed them both, a male and a female, both in very good condition and extremely fat. The success was chiefly owing to the snow, previous to which it was almost impossible to approach the game, but the old man attributed it to the preparation of the muz-zin-ne-neen, and there was no use contradicting him, or showing incredulity. I have already spoken of the frequent use of these charms, not only in regard to success in hunting, but as commonly employed for many purposes among the Indians. If the image of any person is pricked or cut, pain or disease is invoked in the corresponding part of the person represented. Sometimes the face is blackened, and the effect intended is the change which marks the near approach of death. In other cases the object is to attain some desired end. Many a simple girl gives to some cunning old squaw her most valued ornaments, in order that by preparing a muz-zin-ne-neen, she may influence the affections or favour of some friend or lover. The influence of these superstitious ceremonies is boundless, and there are few who venture to neglect them, still less to ridicule them. Any misfortune that happens to such a one would be sure to be ascribed to the irreverent disregard of the sacred rites. Some of those who practise them are only crafty tricksters, but many of the men who are regarded as wise and sagacious, are equally credulous as to these observances. Old Sha-gwaw-ko-sink had firm faith in them, although his religious feeling was also manifested in his many songs and prayers to the Great Spirit. The old man died not long after, and I was glad that I had been able to help him in his last days by my hunting.

Soon after this, the pretensions to supernatural knowledge and power appeared in a manner and in a person quite unexpected. This affair came to affect my future life in so remarkable a way, that I must narrate the circumstances at some length.

About a year previous to this time, a man of our band, called Ais-kaw-ba-bis, a very ordinary person, and a poor hunter, had lost his wife by death, and his children began even more than formerly to suffer from hunger. The death of his wife had been attended with peculiar circumstances, and this may have caused her loss the more to prey upon his mind. He was very melancholy and depressed, though some of us thought that his indolent and sluggish disposition arose from laziness more than from grief. The Indians are very kind generally to those who are bereaved, and without grudge continued to support the children of Ais-kaw-ba-bis.

At length one day he called the old men and the chiefs together, and with much solemnity announced to them that he had been favoured with a new revelation from heaven. He showed them a round ball of clay, about four or five inches in diameter, rather more than half the size of a man's head, round and smooth, and smeared with red paint. "The Great Spirit," said he, "as I sat day by day crying, and singing, and praying in my lodge, at last called to me and said, 'Ais-kaw-ba-bis, I have heard your prayers, I have seen the mats in your lodge wet with tears, and have listened to your desires. I give you this ball, and as you see it is clean and new and well shaped, I give it to you for your business to make the whole earth like it, even as it was when Na-na-bush first made it. All old things must be destroyed and bad things made good; everything must be made anew, and to you, Ais-kaw-ba-bis, I commit this great work.'"

I was among those whom he had summoned to hear this announcement, and I heard the words which I have recorded. He dismissed the assembly at once, so that no questions were asked, and no remarks made at the time. But in conversation with my companions I soon evinced my total disbelief of his pretensions. "It is well," I said, "that we may be made acquainted with the whole mind and will of the Great Spirit at so cheap a rate. We have now these divinely taught instructors springing up among ourselves; and, fortunately, such men as are worth little or nothing for any other purpose. The Shawnee prophet was far off. Manito-o-gheezik was not with us, though sprung from our own tribe; these were also men; but here we have one too poor, too feeble, too spiritless, to be able to feed his own family, yet professing to be made the instrument, in the hand of the Great Spirit, to renovate the whole earth, as he would have us believe!"

I had always entertained an unfavourable opinion of this man, as I knew him to be a worthless fellow, and I now felt indignant at his attempt to pass himself upon us as a chosen messenger of the Great Spirit. I took no pains to conceal my contempt for him, and I ridiculed his pretensions wherever I went. Nevertheless I had the mortification to find that my opposition was set down to some personal malice, and I saw him gradually acquiring a powerful ascendency over the minds of the Indians. They are so prone to superstition that the most unlikely influences work on their credulity. The more he saw this effect produced, the greater his pretensions were made, and his effrontery displayed. In many ways he contrived to maintain and increase the mystery which gathered about himself and his doings. Sometimes he went out alone in the dead of night, and he was heard far off beating his drum, a noise which, whatever effect it had on others, I thought of only as likely to scare away the game from our neighbourhood. By his proceedings he had found the way of controlling and ruling the minds of most of the people, and all my efforts in opposition to him were in vain. I knew he must hate me heartily, but as I was in good esteem with most of our people, he probably thought it prudent to dissemble his dislike, and treated me with apparent courtesy.

On one occasion I went out to hunt, and wounded a moose. On my return I related this, and said I believed the moose was so badly wounded that he must die. Early next morning Ais-kaw-ba-bis came to my lodge, and with the utmost seriousness in his manner, said to me that the Great Spirit had told him of the moose I had wounded. He had no doubt heard it in some of the lodges, as I had mentioned it to several people the night before. "The moose is now dead," said he, "and you will find him in such a direction. It is the will of the Great Spirit that he should be brought here and cooked for a sacrifice." I thought it not improbable that the moose was killed, and went in search of him accordingly; but I found he was not dead. The seer's vision was at fault. I took care to report this mistake, and to ridicule again the pretensions of the man; but this in no way lessened the confidence of his dupes. Perhaps he told them I had not gone to the place where I would have found the moose dead. Shortly afterwards I went out, and it happened that I again wounded a moose and went home without getting it. "This," said the seer, "is the moose the Great Spirit showed me." So I went and brought him in, and as I knew many of the Indians were in want of food I was willing to make a feast, though not out of deference to Ais-kaw-ba-bis. As we did not consume the whole of the meat, we cut it off the bones, and these were laid before Ais-kaw-ba-bis for the sacrifice, taking care that not one of the bones should be broken. They were afterwards carried to a safe place, and hung up out of the reach of the dogs or wolves, this too being done to avoid injury to the bones, which must never be broken when offered in sacrifice. On the following day I killed another fat moose, on which occasion Ais-kaw-ba-bis made a long address to the Great Spirit, and afterwards said to me, "You see, my son, how your goodness is rewarded; you gave the first you killed to the Great Spirit; he will take care that you never want." Next day I went with my brother-in-law, and we killed each one, and this caused great exultation in Ais-kaw-ba-bis, who announced everywhere that this success was due to the efficacy of the sacrifice he had made, and thus his ascendency was increased.

When the snow began to get hard at top, on the approach of spring, the men of our band, Gish-kaw-ko, Ba-po-wash, and some others, with myself, went to make a hunting camp at some distance for the purpose of making dry meat. Ais-kaw-ba-bis stayed at home with the women and children. We killed much game, as it is easy to take moose and elk at that season; the crust on the snow supports a man even when without snow shoes, but the legs of the moose sink down, so that they are almost deprived of motion. At length Gish-kaw-ko went home to see his family. On his return he brought me a little tobacco from Ais-kaw-ba-bis with this message, "Your life is in danger." "My life," said I, "belongs neither to Ais-kaw-ba-bis nor to myself; it is In the hands of the Great Spirit, and when he sees fit to place it in danger, or bring it to an end, I shall have no cause to complain; but I cannot believe that he has revealed any part of his intentions to so worthless a man as Ais-kaw-ba-bis.

However, the message was much talked about, and the whole of the band determined to return to the camp where their families had been left. I did not accompany them, wishing to visit some of my traps. Having caught an otter, I took him on my back and arrived at the camp alone, not long after the others. I beheld a strange scene. All the separate lodges had been taken down and the poles taken for the erection of one large lodge. The men who had arrived and the women and children were all sitting in the open air round a fire. When I asked what all this meant, they told me that Ais-kaw-ba-bis was preparing for some important communication to be given him from the Great Spirit. He had for some time been preparing the large lodge, during which time no one was allowed to enter, except one or two young men at hand for following his directions. There was to be a dance, as all assemblies have when addresses are to be delivered. It was arranged that at a certain signal Ba-po-wash, who was to lead the dance, should enter, and the others were to follow him, and after having danced four times round the lodge, to sit down, each in his place. On hearing this, as I stood among the others, I immediately went to the large lodge, and entering it with the otter on my back as I had arrived, I threw it down and seated myself by the fire. Ais-kaw-ba-bis gave me an angry and malicious look, then closed his eyes, and pretended to be going on with a prayer that I had interrupted. After some time he began to drum and sing aloud, and at the third interval of silence, which was the signal agreed upon with Ba-po-wash, he came dancing in, followed by men, women and children, and after circling the lodge four times they all sat down in their places.

For a few moments all was silence, while Ais-kaw-ba-bis continued sitting with his eyes closed, in the middle of the lodge, by a spot of smooth and soft ground which he had prepared, like that used by the chiefs on encamping during a war expedition, when they seek by divination to learn something concerning the enemy. Then he began to call the men, one by one, to come and sit down near him. Last of all he called me, and I went and sat down as he directed. Then he spoke thus:—" The Great Spirit has, as you know, my friends, in former times favoured me with free communication of his mind and will; lately he has been pleased to show me what is to happen to each in future. For you, my friends, (addressing the other Indians) who have been careful to regard and obey the injunctions of the Great Spirit as communicated by me, to each of you he has given to live to the full age of man; this long, straight mark is the image of your several lives." Here he pointed to a straight line which he had marked right across the oblong space on the ground. "As for you, (turning to me) Mah-nah Be-na-sa, (evil bird) who have gone from the right way, and despised the admonitions you have received, this short and crooked line represents your life. You are to attain to only half of the full age of man. This line, turning off to the other side, is that which shows what is determined in relation to the young wife of Ba-po-wash."

As he said this he pointed to the marks he had made on the ground; the long line, he said, representing the life of the Indians who followed his precepts, the short, crooked line the continuance of mine, and the abruptly terminating one show-ing the life of Ba-po-wash's wife.

It so happened that Ba-po-wash had dried the choice parts of a fat bear, intending to make a feast to his medicine in the spring. A few days before this meeting, when we were absent at the hunting camp, he had said to the mother of Ba-po-wash's wife, "The Great Spirit has signified to me that some-thing is wrong with the dried bear which your son has hung up; see if it is ail where it was left." She went out and found that the feet of the bear were gone, the rascal, who was a great glutton, having himself stolen them. Ba-po-wash was so alarmed by the evil threatened for his wife that he gave to the lying prophet the whole of the remainder of the bear and other valuable presents. I mention this to show the contemptible character of the man, who made his authority descend to a small affair like this, at the same time that he was solemnly announcing the termination of my life, and the continuance of that of his dupes.

I will not enter into further details as to the proceedings of this man, but only say that he gradually acquired such author-ity that he prejudiced the whole of the band against me, and especially the relatives of my wife. She herself was in some way turned completely to be my enemy, and I became as a stranger and alien in my own home. Old Net-no-kwa had been dead for some time, whose influence might perhaps have kept the younger women from submitting themselves so completely to this man. I felt my position so uncomfortable that I was compelled to leave the place, and returned to Red River, hoping that the spell of this false prophet would be broken, and the delusion pass away from the people among whom I had been living.

Chapter XII.

*ARRIVAL OF SCOTCH SETTLERS AT RED
RIVER—EMPLOYED AS HUNTER BY MR. HANIE,
OF THE HUDSON BAY COMPANY—JOIN AN
INDIAN BAND—QUARRELS OF THE RIVAL FUR
COMPANIES—MEET LORD SELKIRK—OFFER OF
PERMANENT EMPLOYMENT, BUT RESOLVE TO
RETURN WHEN PRACTICABLE TO THE STATES—I
JOIN IN AN ATTACK ON THE NORTH-WEST COM-
PANY'S FORT ON RED RIVER—I GO TO FORT
MACKINAC—THE UNITED STATES AGENT
THERE FORWARDS ME TO DETROIT—MEET
WITH THE SON OF THE INDIAN BY WHOM I WAS
CAPTURED IN BOYHOOD—INTERVIEW WITH
GOVERNOR CASS—GO TO A COUNCIL HELD AT
ST. MARY'S ON THE MIAMI—HOSPITALITY OF
AN OLD INDIAN FARMER.*

It was about this time that a number of Scotch people,
above a hundred, arrived to settle at Red River, under the protection, and by the advice of, the Hudson's Bay Company.
Among them I saw, for the first time for many years, in fact
since I had grown to manhood, a white woman. Soon after my
arrival I was taken into the employment of the Hudson's Bay
Company by Mr. Hanie, the agent who had before befriended
me. He sent me, accompanied by Mr. Hess, an interpreter, to
kill buffalo. The buffaloes were at that time at a great distance, and the newly arrived Scotch people were in much distress for want of provisions. I happened to find and kill two

bulls near home, and after sending back the meat, went on to the herds.

I had hunted here a few days, when our number was increased by the arrival of four clerks and about twenty men, the latter employed in bringing in the meat killed by us to the lodge, whence it was carried in carts to the settlement. With one of these clerks, Mr. M'Kenzie, I became very friendly, and at the end of four months when most of the band were called in to the settlement, he solicited and obtained the permission from Mr. Hanie to remain longer with me, to improve himself in the Ojibbeway language, and he did not leave me until after the sugar season.

I killed, in the four months that I hunted for the Hudson's Bay Company, about one hundred buffaloes; but as part or the whole of many of them was used by the hunters and in my own lodge, I delivered only forty entire and fat ones to the Company's people, for which Mr. Hanie paid me, in the spring, three hundred and ten dollars. The Scotch labourers who were with me were more rough and savage in their manners than any people I had seen before, far more so than the Indians among whom I had lived. Even when they had plenty they often quarreled over their meat, and were like ravenous animals. They must have been of the wildest class of their country, for the clerks were also Scotch, some of them, and frequently punished them for their conduct, but still they continued rough and quarrelsome.

Mr. Hanie, the agent, and the governor for the Hudson's Bay Company, proposed to me to build me a house, and to engage me permanently in their employment, but I hesitated to accept the offer, as I thought it doubtful whether their attempt at settling that part of the country would finally succeed. Some of the Indians whom I had left at the Lake of the Woods had followed me out, spent the winter with me, and returned. I was still remaining by myself at Red River, when Wa-ge-tote came from my father-in-law and mother-in-law with a message. They had lost several of their children by death, and, and, feeling lonely, sent for me to come to them. This message Wa-ge-tote delivered to me in the presence of the traders and some other persons; but afterwards he called me out by myself, and said to me, "Do not believe that your father-in-law sends for you with a good motive. When the children were sick, they called Ais-kaw-ba-bis to do something for them, and he having made a sacred enclosure said he had called you into it, and made you confess that you had pointed at the children, and shot bad medicine at them, though you were at the time at Red River. He made your father-in-law believe that you had the power of life and death over his children, and he continues to believe, as most of the Indians of the band do, that it was your medicine which killed them. I think they send for you with the design of killing you."

Notwithstanding this friendly warning I resolved to go back, because my staying away would confirm the Indians in their belief that I was guilty of what I had been accused of. I had no fear of Ais-kaw-ba-bis, although he had made my position unendurable by his malicious hostility. Illness, however, prevented my starting immediately, and then I went for a short time up the Be-gwi-o-nush-ko River, to a lake of the same name, where I stopped to hunt, and killed plenty of meat. While I remained here, there came to my lodge one day four men from our village at Me-nau-zhe-tau-nang. In one of them, who was painted black, as is usual when prepared for war, I recognised my brother-in-law. The three other children of the family being dead, grief and a feeling of loneliness influenced him to leave his father, and to go in search of some war party, that he might join them against their enemies, and thus have an opportunity of sacrificing, honourably, a life that had become to him irksome. Three young men, his companions, being unwilling to see him depart alone, had voluntarily accompanied him. They did not wish to go to fight, but hoped that the young man's mind would become more cairn and settled after a change of scene. I gave him my horse, and I then went up to the Lake of the Woods to my father-in-law. I remained four days without any unpleasant feeling being manifested on his part, but my wife had left the place, and was with other relatives at a village which Ais-kaw-ba-bis had persuaded them to make at some distance.

After four days I said to the old people "I cannot remain here, while my little brother has gone away in sorrow, with none to protect him. He wishes to join a war-party, and he will be exposed to danger." One or two Indians hearing my determination offered to accompany me, and we went towards Red River. We found that a large number of Crees, Assineboins, and Ojibbeways were preparing to go against the Sioux, and of this the young man had probably heard some rumours before he went out. We found him at one of the encampments. This war excursion was a more futile and feeble affair even than those which I have formerly described. Each day many turned back, as having no heart in the thing. Two or three journeys from Turtle Mountain, it being now late in the fall, a great storm of rain came on, turning to sleet and snow. When we got within two days' march of the nearest Sioux village, there was a mere handful of our band ready to go forward. My young brother-in-law kept with the chief to the last, and the excitement proved of great service to him in diverting his mind from his sorrow. Some of the Sioux came out to watch us, but no attack was made on either side, and the war excursion, for which much preparation seemed to have been made, came to an end. There were six of us to return to the Lake of the Woods, but after going part of the way, I left them, being resolved no longer to return where my relatives were unfriendly and my wife had deserted me. I had three children, the eldest being not four years old. The mother had always shown affection for them, and against me only had her mind been poisoned. So I did not feel any anxiety as to leaving them with her, and I knew the Indians would not suffer them ever to want food or protection. Although they make the women work hard they always support them, and hunt for them and for the children of the lodges.

I went to a chief from whom I had previously received permission to hunt in a place which I had selected; and he said that none of his people should interfere with me there. He endeavoured to dissuade me from going alone and spending the winter by myself. I ought, he said, either to remain near the other Indians of his band, or to take some other woman for a wife. But I would not listen to his advice. At present I had no inclination either to remain with Indians not known to me, or to take another wife. I went to the nearest trading station, and here took credit sufficient for my whole family, not knowing but my wife would rejoin me at some future time. In two or three days I reached my hunting-ground. I had no puk-kwi or mats for a lodge, and therefore had to build one of poles and long grass. Having to make my own moccasins and leggings, after dressing the skins, and also snow shoes, cutting also wood for cooking I was sometimes kept from hunting, and suffered occasionally from hunger; but on the whole I managed pretty well to pass a great part of the winter. Two dogs, which I trained carefully, were very useful in chasing and helping to bring home the game. Several Indians at various times came, sometimes sent I thought by the chief to see how I was getting on, but at other times in such starving condition that they were evidently impelled by hunger, and I was glad to share with them the proceeds of my hunting.

About this time the traders of the North-West Company sent messengers and presents to all the Indians in that part of the country, to call them to join in an attack on the Hudson's Bay establishment at Red River. For my own part I thought these quarrels between white brothers unnatural, both being engaged in the same pursuit, and the field of trade being large enough for both of them. At all events I sought to avoid taking part in the quarrel, though I had long traded with the people of the North-West Company, and considered myself as in some measure belonging to them. Many of the Indians obeyed the call. On the side of the North-West were many half-breeds, sons of Canadian hunters by Indian mothers. One of them, called Grant, distinguished himself as a leader among these men, who were mostly a lawless and evil set. Many cruelties and murders were committed by them at that time. Some of the Hudson's Bay people were killed in open fight, and others were massacred after being taken prisoners. I remember the case of a Mr. Keveny, an agent of the Hudson's Bay Company. He was waylaid and fell into the hands of Mr. Herschel, a clerk of the North-West. This man sent him in a canoe with some Frenchmen (the Canadians were mostly French in those days) and a half-breed, named Maveen, with directions to kill him and throw him into the water. When they had gone some distance, the half-breed wished to have killed him, but the Frenchmen would not consent, whether from humanity, or from his having made promise of reward, I cannot say. They landed him on a small rocky island, from which he had no means of escape, but he was discovered and taken off by some Muskego Indians, who set him at liberty. Mr. Herschel abused and beat the Frenchmen for having neglected to kill the agent when he was in their power, and despatched other men in pursuit of him. The leader of the ba, and white man, had been a soldier, whose well-known cruelty of disposition made him fit to be chosen for such business. With them was the halfbreed Maveen, and by these two the poor man, being retaken, was murdered under circumstances of great atrocity. They then returned with the account of what they had done to Mr. Herschel.

After the settlement at Red River was reduced to ashes, and the Hudson's Bay people driven out of the country, the Indians and half-breeds in the employ of the North-West were stationed at a place called Suh-gi-uk, at the outlet of Lake Winnipeg, to watch for and destroy any of the Hudson's Bay people who should attempt to enter the country in that direction. Ba-po-wash, my brother-in-law, was one of the Indians thus employed. Having grown tired of remaining there, and hearing where I was, and that I had not taken any part in these contests, he came to me. On his way he met Mr. McDonald, a chief man of the Hudson's Bay Company, who with his interpreter, Mr. Brace, was going up to that country. Mr. McDonald was slow to listen to the advice of Mr. Bruce, who being well acquainted with the state of affairs in the country, had many fears on his account. On meeting Ba-po-wash, whom he well knew, Mr. Bruce, who was supposed to be in the interest of the North-West, was able to gain full intelligence of all that had passed. Being convinced of the truth of the information, Mr. McDonald was persuaded to turn back, and probably saved his life by so doing. He went to the Sault de St. Marie, when he met Lord Selkirk, then coming into the country to try to settle the affairs of the two rival companies.

For myself I spent this summer in my usual peaceful occupations; in hunting, fishing, and about the cornfields, or gathering wild rice. In returning from the rice swamps I stopped on one of the small islands in the route towards Rainy Lake to hunt a bear with whose haunt I had been some time acquainted. Late at night, after I had killed my bear, and as I was lying quietly in my lodge, I was surprised to hear a voice, which I soon recognised to be that of Mr. Herschel. I soon also learned that he was on the look-out for some one he had not found. Having descried my light at a distance, he had supposed it to be a light in the camp of Lord Selkirk, and had crept up with the stealthiness of an Indian warrior, or he could not have approached my lodge without my being aware of it. He did not openly avow his intention of killing Lord Selkirk, but I knew him and his companions, some of whom had now come up, and was not at a loss to comprehend his purpose. Nor was I ignorant of the design with which he urged me to accompany him to Rainy Lake. But when he found that his hints and insinuations had no effect, he openly declared that it was his intention to kill Lord Selkirk whenever he found an opportunity, and he then called up his two canoes, that I might see them, each with ten strong, resolute, and well-armed men. He again tried to induce me to join him, but I would not.

After leaving me he went on to Rainy Lake, to the trading-house of Mr. Tace, but he being less inclined to violent measures advised Mr. Herschel to return to his own country. What arguments were used I do not know, but he returned almost immediately towards RedRiver; leaving, however, concealed in the woods near the trading-house the same soldier who had taken part with the half-breed Maveen in the murder of the superintendent the year before. It was not certainly known among us what this man's instructions were, but desperate man though he was, he did not seem to relish his solitary residence in the woods, for after four days he returned to the fort.

In the meantime Lord Selkirk had taken Fort William, which was then held by Mr. Macgillivray for the North-West Company. From Fort William he sent an officer with some troops to take possession of Mr. Tace's trading-house, in which the soldier who had murdered Mr. Keveney was found. He was sent, with some others who had attempted to rise after they had surrendered at Fort William, to Montreal, and I heard that he was there hung for his crimes.

From this time I was more firmly resolved in my own mind to leave this country and return to the States. Not only was I vexed by the ill-will which had been raised against me among the Indians, and particularly in the family of my father-in-law, but I did not like the quarrels and hostilities among the whites, with whom I had relations as a hunter in trading. The war of 1812 was now over, and there was not now the difficulty and risk of journeying on the frontiers. Mr. Bruce, who had always shown friendly feeling to me, and to whom 1 went to tell my purpose, gave me much information and advice, and as he had travelled in many parts his statements encouraged me. But some events occurred which for a time overthrew my plans, and I was soon in the midst of some exciting scenes and adventures which I must relate.

I moved to Rainy Lake where I intended to pass the rest of the winter. I expected to find Mr. Tace at the trading-house, being as yet unaware of the changes that had recently taken place. Instead of him I found the English officer whom I have before mentioned as having been sent by Lord Selkirk to occupy the place. He treated me with much attention, and finding that I knew the country well and that I could speak his language,—for my frequent intercourse with whites had made me able for this,—he had much conversation with me. After some arguments and explanations he succeeded in convincing me that the Hudson's Bay Company, in the present quarrel, was that which had right on its side, or at least was that which was acting with the sanction of the British Government. I did not tell him the whole of my history, which was unnecessary, but I told him that I was a native of the States, and that I had been carried off in early years by the Indians, and had lived among them ever since. He seemed much interested in me, and said he would have great pleasure in aiding me in my design to return to the States. At the same time, by his kind treatment, his presents, and his promises, he induced me to consent to guide him and his party to the North-West Company's house at the mouth of the Assineboin River. I did not without difficulty consent to do this, for I had been employed by the North-West, and had friends among their people; but the captain had persuaded me that they were in the wrong, especially in driving away the Hudson's Bay people from that quarter; and he said I need not take any active part in the quarrel, but only be the guide to his party. The winter was now coming on, and had indeed commenced with some severity. The captain said his men could not live at Rainy Lake, and he wished to go on immediately to Red River.

I started in advance, with twenty men, and went to Rush Lake, whence the horses were sent back, and the captain, with the remaining men, between forty and fifty, came up. At Rush Lake we had snow shoes made, and engaged some Indians to accompany us as hunters. We had a pretty good stock of wild rice, but there were a good many mouths to supply with meat, and we had a long journey to make over the prairie. We sometimes were short of food, and the soldiers grumbled and were almost mutinous, but no serious difficulty occurred. It took a whole month to go from Rainy Lake to Red River. Here we took the fort at the mouth of the Pembinah without any resistance, there being few persons there, except squaws and children, and a few old Frenchmen. From Pembinah we went in four days to the Assineboin, ten miles above the mouth, having crossed Red River a short time before. Here Be-gwais, a principal man among the Ojibbeways, met us with twelve young men. Our captain and governor, who was with the expedition, believed that there were not many men in the North-West Company's fort, but being well armed, and having strengthened the place, he seemed at a loss to know in what manner best to attempt its reduction. Be-gwais advised them to march boldly up, and to show their force, which he thought would suffice to ensure immediate surrender. This advice did not, however, seem good, as the men in the fort were resolute, and a repulse might be disastrous, if a panic followed an over-secure advance.

When the captain had engaged me at Rainy Lake, I had told him that I could make a road from that place to the door of Mr. Herschel's bedroom. He may have thought this to be only idle boasting, but I felt hurt and dissatisfied that they took no notice of me in their consultations, and expected me merely to act as their guide. When we came near the place, and when I heard of their fresh consultations, and the difficulty they seemed to be in, I communicated my dissatisfaction at not being taken into council, to Nowlan, an interpreter, who was well acquainted with the country, and who had a half-brother in the fort, a clerk for Mr. Herschel. We talked the matter over, and one night, after the council had broken up, and no steps seemed to have been resolved upon, while Nowlan and I were sitting by our own fire, we agreed that it would be in the power of us two to surprise the fort, and, if supported promptly, to take it without much risk or loss. So we took into our confidence some soldiers, who followed us at no great distance. There were no knolls, or bushes, or other objects to give any cover for our approach, the surrounding ground being completely cleared; but the night was dark and so extremely cold, that we did not suppose the people within would be very vigilant. We made a scaling ladder, in the way the Indians make them, by cutting the trunk of a young tree with the limbs trimmed long enough to serve to step upon, and placing this against the wall we were soon on the top of the fence, and got down on the inside, on the top of the black-smith's forge, whence we descended silently one by one to the ground. When all were inside, without any alarm having been given, we went to find the people, first cautiously placing two or three armed men at the doors of the houses we saw were occupied, so as to prevent them getting together, or concerting any means of resistance.

The night had been far spent when we got to the fort, and every step had been taken with deliberation as well as with silence, as we did not know the real strength of the people inside, and a premature alarm might have spoiled the whole affair. It was beginning to be daylight before we could discover the sleeping-place of Herschel, whom it was our chief concern to get hold of. When he found we were in the fort, he came out, strongly armed, and attempted to make resistance, but we easily overpowered him. He was at once bound, but as he was loud and abusive, the governor, who had now, with the captain, arrived at the fort, directed us to throw him bound out into the snow; but the weather being so severe that he would have been frozen to death if left there, he was allowed to come in where we had a fire. On recognising me he knew at once that I must have guided the party, and he reproached me loudly with my ingratitude, as he pretended formerly to have done me many favours. Not wishing to have this charge of ingratitude made, and desiring to justify myself before my new friends, I told him, in reply, of the murders he had committed treacherously on his own people, and that on account of these, and his many crimes, I had turned against him. "When you came," I said, "to my lodge last fall, I treated you with friendly hospitality, for I did not then see that your hands were red with the blood of your own people. I did not see the ashes of the houses of your white brothers, which you had caused to be burned down at Red River." But he continued to curse and abuse not only me, but the soldiers, and every one that came near him.

Only three of those captured in this trading-house were kept as prisoners. These were Mr. Herschel, Maveen (or Mainville), the half-breed, who had been concerned in the murder of the Hudson's Bay agent, and one of the clerks. The rest were suffered to go at large. Joseph Cadoth, the half-brother of Nowlan, made a very humble and submissive apology for his conduct, and promised, if they would release him, to go to his hunting, and be no more attached to the traders.

After twenty days I returned to Pembinah, where I met Wa-ge-tote, and with him went to hunt buffalo in the prairie. I heard that not only the Indians but many of the half-breed people in the country were enraged against me for the part I had taken against the North-West Company, and I was told that they were determined to take my life. I told them that they must fall on me as I had fallen on the North-West people, when they were sleeping, or they would not be able to injure me. I thought it best not to seem to be afraid of them; but all this added to my sense of insecurity and discomfort, and I longed the more for the time when I could leave this country and go to the States.

Lord Selkirk was now expecting the arrival of a judge who he heard had been appointed specially to inquire about the preceding disturbances. At length Judge Cottman came, and after he had made his inquiries, and having tried and punished some of the most guilty, matters became more settled. Mr. Herschel and Maveen were loaded with irons, and sent to prison in Montreal. The North-West Company had to pay a fine of some thousand dollars as compensation for the injury done to the property of the Hudson's Bay Company. I need not refer to other proceedings, except such as affected my own case. The governor spoke to Lord Selkirk about me, telling him that I had guided his party from the Lake of the Woods, and performed important services in the capture of the fort. He recommended that a handsome present should be made to me, and this was done. Lord Selkirk used much persuasion to induce me to accompany him and remain in his service. I had some inclination to do so, because I then believed that all my own relatives had been cut off by the Indians; and if they were not, I knew that after so long a lapse of time we must be almost like entire strangers to each other. He even proposed to take me with him to England, but my attachments were to my own country, and it was too late to begin new modes of life, and to form new associations. I could not trust myself to hear further discussion of the matter, and so I left abruptly, and went back to Rainy Lake.

Here, at the trading-house, I found my old trader Mr. Tace. He asked me rather sharply why I came to him, and not to my friends of the Hudson's Bay Company. I told him I wanted to go to the States.

"It would have been well," he replied, "if you had gone long ago." Nevertheless he kept me with him for twenty days, treating me with great kindness. He then took me in his own canoe to Fort William, whence Dr. McLoughlin sent me in one of his boats to the Sault de St. Marie, and thence I went to Mackinac. All the people of the North-West whom I saw on this journey treated me kindly, and no one mentioned a word of my connection with the Hudson's Bay Company.

Major Puthuff, the United States Indian agent at Mackinac, gave me a birch bark canoe, some provisions, and a letter to Governor Cass, at Detroit. My canoe was lashed to the side of the schooner on board which I sailed for Detroit, under the care of a gentleman whose name I do not recollect, but who, as I thought, was sent by Major Puthuff expressly to take charge of me on the way. I think that this was because the agent believed I might, from my experience, be of some service in the Indian affairs, and he may have said this in the letter to Governor Cass. At all events, after our arrival at Detroit, in five days, and seeing the governor, the gentleman left and I heard no more of him.

Next day, when walking up the street in Detroit, and gazing around, I saw an Indian, and going up to him, asked him who he was, and where he belonged. He answered me: "An Ottawwaw, of Sau-ge-nong." "Do you know Kish-kaw-ko?" said I. "He is my father." "And where," said I, "is Manito-o-gheezik, his father, and your grandfather?" "He died last fall." I told him to go and call his father to come, but the old man would not come.

Next day, as I was again in the street, I saw an old Indian, and ran after him. When he heard me coming he turned round, and after looking at me attentively for some moments, he caught me in his arms. It was Kish-kaw-ko; but he looked very unlike the young man who had taken me prisoner so many years before. He asked me, in a hurried manner, many questions; inquired what had happened to me, and where I had been since I left him. I tried to get him to take me to the house of Governor Cass, but he appeared afraid to go. He showed me the direction, and brought me near to it. A soldier sentinel was walking up and down before it, and would not allow me to pass. While waiting at the gate, I saw the governor sitting in the porch of the house inside the court. I held up to him a paper which had been given to me by Major Puthuff, and he then told the soldier to let me pass in. He read the paper, gave me his hand, and asked me several questions. He then sent for Kish-kaw-ko, and an interpreter, by whom my statement was confirmed concerning the circumstances of my capture, and my two years' residence with the Ottawwaws at Sau-ge-nong. After that time his word could not confirm mine, but the governor was perfectly satisfied, and after his leaving continued to talk with me. I found some difficulty in conversation, as he spoke on subjects with which I was not so familiar as those I had been accustomed to speak about at the trading-houses, but I felt that I should soon be able to speak easily the language of my early years.

The governor gave me clothing to the amount of sixty or seventy dollars' value, and sent me to remain for the present at the house of his interpreter, about a mile distant, where he told me I must remain till after a council he had appointed to be held at St. Mary's on the Miami, where he had summoned many Indians and white men to assemble; after which he would send me to my relatives on the Ohio.

Having waited some weeks, without any message from the governor, and being impatient to go on my way, I started with Be-nais-sa, the brother of Kish-kaw-ko, and eight other Indians who were going to the council. I went without the knowledge of Governor Cass, who indeed had already left Detroit, having to make some visits before going to St. Mary's. We suffered much from fatigue and from hunger, especially after passing the rapids of the Miami, where we left our canoe. We met Indians who sometimes gave us a little food, but others refused though they had plenty. The more they are in contact with white men the less are they given to hospitality. We sometimes stopped to rest or to sleep near a white man's corn-field, and though the corn was now fit to roast, and we almost perishing with hunger, we dared not take anything. The Indians said to me, "You have conic far to seek your white relations; now go in and see if they will give you anything to eat! "I went to one house, and stood in the door asking for food, but the people within drove me away, and on my return the Indians laughed at me.

Some time after, when we were in the road close to where we had slept for the night, sonic one came up on horseback, and asked us in the Ottawwaw dialect who we were. On telling him, he said that we should reach his house, if brisk travellers, on the next day after the morrow, at noon, and there we should have plenty to eat. "It is necessary," he added, "that I reach home to-morrow, and I have travelled all night." and thus he left us. On the next day my strength failed so much that I was only able to keep up by being relieved of my load. One took my gun, another my blanket, and we reached that night the forks of the Miami, where was a settlement of Indians, and a trading-house, as well as several families of whites. I applied to the trader, and stated my situation, but we could obtain no relief, and on the next day I felt very weak and little able to travel. We were indebted to the Indians for what little food we obtained, which enabled us the day after to reach the house of the hospitable Indian. This man, named Ah-koo-nah-goo-zik, had two large kettles of corn and venison ready cooked and awaiting our arrival. One he placed before me, and the other before Be-nais-sa, and desired us to help ourselves and our companions, wooden dishes and spoons being before us. After we had eaten, he told us we had better remain with him some days, to rest ourselves after so long a journey, as he had plenty of corn, and fat venison was abundant about him. I told him that we deeply felt his kindness, but that for my own part I had for many years been wishing to make the journey I had in view, and was impatient to see whether any of my own relatives were still alive. The Indians had told him of my having been captured, and this seemed to have caused him to take more interest in me. I said I should be glad to rest with him for two or three days, and afterwards to borrow one of his horses to ride as far as St. Mary's, where I would leave it for him. "I will tell you," said he. Nothing was said till, on the third morning, where we were making up our loads to start, he came to me, leading a fine horse, and putting the halter in my hand, he said, "I give you this for the journey." I did not again tell him I would leave it in charge of some one at St. Mary's, as I had already said this, and I knew that in such cases the Indians do not wish to hear much said.

The kindness of this man impressed me much. He was one of the first Indians I had seen who led a settled instead of a wandering life, and in his house and farm he seemed as prosperous as the white men. He had been, when young, as I afterwards learned, at a missionary's school, and then in the employment of his master, who had been much interested in him, and had taught him many things by which his life was raised above that of the people among whom he was born. I have since seen prosperous Indian settlements in various places, through the same agencies, but at this time I was as yet unaware of the efforts made by good Christians among the whites to improve the condition of the Indians.

Chapter XIII.

AT THE COUNCIL AT ST. MARY—AN EXCITING INCIDENT—HOMICIDE DURING A REVEL—FORBEARANCE OF THE RELATIVES, AND PARDON OF THE CULPRIT—DINING WITH GOVERNOR CASS—BROKEN HEALTH—JOURNEY TO THE STATES—MEETING WITH MY OWN BROTHER—AMONG MY RELATIVES—REVIVAL OF EARLY RECOLLECTIONS—CONVERSATION WITH A CHRISTIAN TEACHER.

In two days I arrived at the place appointed for the council. Governor Cass had not yet come, and there were few people yet there, but a man was stationed to issue provisions to such as should come.

A few days after our arrival an incident occurred which caused a painful excitement at the time, and which is worth narrating as illustrating some traits of Indian life and character.

A young man of the Ottawwaws, Be-nais-sa had given me to cook for me, and to assist me in my sickness, as I was suffering from ague with fever, which, although it did not wholly confine me, was sometimes distressing and enfeebling. This young man went across the creek to a camp of the Po-ta-wa-to-mies, who had just arrived and were drinking. At midnight he was brought into the lodge drunk, and one of the men who came with him, said to me, as he pushed him in, "Take care of your young man, he has been doing mischief."

I called to Be-nais-sa to kindle a fire quickly, and as soon as there was light enough we saw the young man standing with his knife in his hand, and the knife together with his arm and part of his body covered with blood. He stood in a strange absent manner, under the effect of drink, yet not so drunk as to have been unable to direct the men where to take him. The other Indians were all now awake, but they could not make him lie down; he only stood glaring at them. But when I told him, he obeyed immediately, dropping the knife on the ground. I forbade them to make any inquiries about where he had been, or what he had done, and to take no notice of his bloody knife.

In the morning, having slept soundly, he was perfectly unconscious of all that had passed. He believed he had been drunk at the Indian camp, but had no recollection of being brought back. He was astonished and confounded when I told him he had killed a man, and showed him the blood-stained knife. He remembered now that, in his drunkenness, or when nearly overcome by the drink, he had been crying about his father, who had been killed by the whites near that very place where he then was. He expressed the utmost concern about what we told him he had done, and would not rest, till some of us consented to go with him, that he might see the man he had killed.

On going with him to the camp, we learned from the Po-ta-wa-to-mies that he had seen a young man sleeping, or lying in a state of insensibility from drink, and had stabbed him with his knife, without any words having been exchanged, and apparently without knowing who he was. The young man was not dead, but he could not recover, and manifestly was near his end. We had brought with us a very considerable present, made up by one giving a blanket, another some cloth, some one thing and some another. With these, our young man went into the lodge where the dying man lay, and placing them on the ground, he said to the relatives who were standing about, "My friends, I have killed this your brother; but I knew not what I did. I had no ill-will against him. But drunkenness made me a fool, and now my life is forfeited to you. I am poor and among strangers. Some of those who came from my own country with me would take me back to those who know me there; they have, therefore, sent me with this small present. My life is in your hands, and the present is before you; take which you choose, my friends will have no cause to complain."

Having thus spoken he sat down beside the dying man, who was unconscious, his life almost gone; stooping his head, he hid his eyes with his hands, as if waiting for them to strike. There was death-like silence. The Indians, when not excited in war or by drink, do everything in a slow deliberate manner, and apparently impassive spirit. Some of the white people would, under such circumstances, have rushed with wild vengeance upon the manslayer who had placed himself in their power. But they had heard and were now calmly weighing the words he had spoken.

The silence was broken by the mother of the wounded man, an aged woman, who came a little forward, and said, "For myself and my children I can answer, that we wish not to take your life; but I cannot speak for my husband who is not here, nor promise to protect you from his resentment. Nevertheless I will accept your presents, and whatever influence I have with him, I shall not fail to use it in your behalf. I know it was not from design, or from any previous hatred or malice, that you have done this, and why should your mother be made to weep as well as myself?" She accepted the presents, and without molestation from others in the lodge, the young man went out and rejoined our people. We heard that the father returned that evening from hunting, and on the whole affair being told to him, he showed much sorrow, but uttered no threats of vengeance, using only some expressions of submission to untoward fate. The event was reported to Governor Cass, who had arrived a day or two before, and he was satisfied with the course that had been taken, and said he would not appear to know anything about it.

During the night the young man having died, some of our people assisted on the following day in making the grave. When this was completed, the governor gave for the dead man a valuable present of cloth and other things to be buried with him, according to the Indian custom, and these were brought and heaped up on the brink of the grave. The old woman, evidently a shrewd person, and with more sense than sentiment, proposed that these presents, instead of being buried, should be played for, and so made useful. Whatever the older people thought, the proposal pleased the young men, and as the articles were numerous, arrangements were made for various games, on the following day, such as shooting at the mark, leaping, wrestling, and other sports. In these funeral games the handsomest piece of cloth was reserved as the prize for the swiftest in the foot race. The winner of the prize was the young man himself who had killed the other. I feared for the moment that this might have caused some ill-feeling. But again the old woman took the chief part, and in a way that surprised us all. Calling the young man to her she said, "Young man, he who was my son was very dear to me, and I fear I shall weep much and often for him. I would be glad if you would come to be my son in his stead, to love me and take care of me as he did." The young man was struck with confusion at the unexpected offer, but being already deeply grateful for her having saved his life, immediately consented to the arrangement if the father gave his approval. The father was appealed to, and being one who deferred much to the will of his wife, not a thing very usual among the Indians, the adoption was soon agreed to. This old woman reminded me of our Net-no-qua, who till her last days bore rule over all her relatives as well as her husband, in our lodge, in my younger days.

Meanwhile some one told Governor Cass that some friends of the deceased were still determined to avenge his death, and disapproved of the way in which the affair had been passed over, as against all honourable custom. Hearing this he sent his interpreter to the young man to direct him at once to make his escape and flee to his own country. The governor was of course desirous of avoiding any trouble from the event. Knowing the deadliness of such feuds if once the spirit of retaliation is let loose, I, as well as Be-nais-sa, concurred with the governor's advice, and assisted in making preparation for the young man's departure. We sent him off in the night, but instead of making the best of his way homeward, he concealed himself in the woods at no great distance from our lodge.

Very early next morning I saw two of the friends of the slain young man coming towards our lodge. I immediately concluded that the report of intended vengeance was correct, and became alarmed, supposing they were coming with the intention of doing violence. They came into the lodge, and for a long time sat silent. At last one of them said, "Where is our brother? We felt lonely at home, and wish to talk with him." As I saw they were quite unarmed, and spoke with apparent sincerity, I told them he had lately gone out. "Would I fetch him?" I said I did not know where he was or when he would return. As they still remained, I went out on pretence of seeking him, but really to consult with one or two of my friends, and to tell them that the reported threats of violence were unfounded. I had not the slightest expectation of seeing my young servant again. What was my surprise when he stood before me, as I went out of my lodge. He had observed, from his hiding place, the visit of the two young men to our lodge, and judging as I had done, from their manner and from their being unarmed, that they came with no unfriendly design, he discovered himself, and we re-entered the lodge together. They shook hands with him in a friendly way, and carried back a message that, as soon as I could arrange for other help in my lodge, he should go to comfort the parents for their lost son. We afterwards ascertained that all the rumours of their wishing to kill him were false, and that he was quite at home in his new position. Certainly, if forgiveness has any influence he would prove a most faithful servant and loving son.

Before these Po-ta-wa-to-mies left the neighbourhood they gave us a good deal of trouble. Some of them had actually the daring to steal the horse that had been lent to me on the road by the friendly old man, Ah-koo-nah-goozik. As he was expected at the council, I lost no time in going to the camp across the creek, and with the help of some of Be-nais-sa's young men I fortunately recovered the horse, with which no doubt the thieves would have shortly decamped. I restored him to the owner, who knew nothing of the fright I had got. Governor Cass, having heard how kind this man had been to me and my fellow-travellers, and especially in lending me the horse, directed that a very handsome and valuable saddle should be given to him. For some time the old man persisted in declining this present; but at last, when prevailed on to receive it, being told that his refusal displeased the governor, he expressed much gratitude. "This," he said, "is what was told me by the men who gave me instruction many years ago, when I was young. They told me that because the Great Spirit was good, and had been good to me, I must be kind and do good to all men, and chiefly to all who were poor and afflicted, and to the stranger who should come from a far country; saying, if I did so, I would be like my Heavenly Father, who would also remember me to do good to me, and to reward me for what I had done. Now, although I have done so little for this man, see how amply and honourably I am rewarded." This he said to Governor Cass through the interpreter. He would have persuaded me to take his horse as a present, saying he had others, and the saddle was more valuable than the horse he had lent me. Of course I declined his offer, but he still insisted, till I consented that he should consider it as belonging to me, and that he would take care of it until I returned and called for it. I was full of affection for the old man, and as he hoped I should come to see him again, I said I would return now to his house for a short visit, which was less than two days distant. He was leaving the council, which would continue some days longer, so I returned with him.

I had much conversation with him at his house, and heard from him many things that my heart felt to be good. We spoke once about the Shawnee prophet, and about others who pretended to have received revelations from the Great Spirit. He told me that there had been a revelation given, and written in a book from which his teachers had instructed him, but he was unable to read, and only remembered some truths which had been impressed on his memory in early years, and which he had always endeavoured to carry out through life. He believed in the presence of the Great Spirit always and everywhere near him. But he also believed that the Great Spirit had sent to this world one who was the friend and protector of men, who came in the likeness of man, who taught men the will of the Great Spirit, and set them an example. This was long ago, and in a far-off land, the people of which slew this good prophet, because he said he was from the Great Spirit, and because he opposed their evil ways. Bat after he was dead he rose again and he told his followers to go to all lands, and tell of his life and his death, and to make them better. These were among the things he had learned from the white men who were his teachers in his early years. As he was speaking, there came to my memory thoughts that had long been buried in my mind, and dim recollections of things I too had been taught in my childhood. I had sometimes, as I have said, been with white men since my captivity, but had never met with teachers like those whom my old friend remembered with gratitude. I felt now the more desirous to return among my people, where I could learn more about the Maker and the Friend of men. Full of these desires, and with warm feeling of regard and love for the old man, I returned to the place of the council.

The governor, before the conclusion of the council, called me to dine with him. I put on the clothes which he had given to me at Detroit, which I had laid aside carefully, while I was in the lodge with the Indians. I had seen enough of the habits and usages of white men at the trading-houses, and was able sufficiently to speak with them on some subjects. The governor had evidently told them about my history, and several gentlemen were very attentive, and asked me to take wine with them at table. I was careful to avoid taking much, for I had never acquired the same fondness the Indians usually have for intoxicating liquors. Among the guests were two men from Kentucky, one of whom seemed to be strangely interested in me, and after asking various questions, to my astonishment, and to the great delight of the governor, he said he knew something of my relations, and that he often had visited at the family of one of my sisters. As they were going back after the council, I determined to start along with these two men.

A day or two after this I had a fresh attack of fever and ague. Governor Cass had given to me goods and money to the amount of one hundred and twenty dollars. I think some of the gentlemen who met me at his house contributed towards this handsome present. I purchased a horse for eighty dollars, as I had the long journey before me. When we were to start I was so feeble and unwell as scarcely to be able to stand, yet I could not lose this opportunity of going with those who knew the road, and who could guide me to my relatives. I set out with them, but after two days I had become so ill that I could not sit on my horse. They concluded to purchase a skiff, and one of them to take me down by water, while the other went with the horses by the usual route, hiring a man to take charge of them. We went down the Big Miami River, but there were many mill weirs and other obstructions, which rendered even this method not only slow and laborious, but extremely trying to me in my condition. At last I was reduced to such a state of weakness as to be quite unable to move. My companion grew anxious and alarmed. We stopped at a house on the bank of the river, the owner of which, though a poor man, seemed greatly to pity me, and disposed to do all he could for my relief. I determined, therefore, to ask permission to stay here, my friend arranging for my being taken care of, till he went to the Ohio, and either came back himself, or sent some one for me. The man with whom I stopped could speak a little of the Ottawwaw language, and spoke to me, thinking from my dress that I was an Indian. He was surprised when I also spoke in his own tongue, and he did everything in his power to make me comfortable, until my nephew, a son of one of my sisters, sent by my relatives in Kentucky, came for me. By him I learned about the death of my father, and also some particulars about others of my family. Before I saw Kish-kaw-ko, at Detroit, I had always supposed that the greater part, if not all, of my father's family had been killed by Manito-o-gheezik and his band, the year subsequent to my capture.

Our journey was very tedious and difficult to Cincinnati, where we rested a little. Thence we descended the Ohio in a skiff. My fever continued, with attacks daily, and when the chill commenced we were compelled to stop for some time, so that our progress was not rapid. We were accompanied by one man, who assisted my nephew to put me in and take me out of the skiff, for I was now reduced to a mere skeleton, and had not strength enough to walk and stand by myself.

As the night was corning on we arrived at a large farm, with a nice-looking house. Leaving the skiff, they raised me by the arms, and partly led, partly lifted me towards the house, where my nephew asked shelter for the night. He said I was so unwell that it might endanger my life to go farther. But the owner told us we could not stay there, and on my nephew persisting in his request, drove us roughly away. The night was now upon us, but we had to return to the boat. The next place where we saw lights on shore was more than a mile further, and the house being far back from the river, we could not approach in the skiff. They accordingly again supported me, till we arrived at a large brick house. The people within had just gone to bed, but on my nephew knocking at the door, after a little a man came out. When he heard what we asked, and saw me, he took hold of me and assisted me into the house; then called his wife and daughters, who prepared some supper for my companions. For me he got some medicine, and made me go to bed, and I slept soundly. At this house we remained the next day and night, and were treated with the utmost kindness. From that time I began to get a little better, and without much more difficulty I reached the place where some of my sister's children were living. She had been dead some years. I went to the house of another nephew, where I lay sick for some weeks. While there a letter arrived, but I was too ill at the time to be told about it. After recovering somewhat, and being able to move about, they told me it was from my brother Edward, whose name I had never forgotten. He had gone to Red River to search for me. I was also told that one of my relatives, who lived about one hundred miles distant, had wished to come to him.

The thought of my brother Edward being still alive, and in quest of me, dwelt on my mind so much that I declared my intention of taking my horse, which I had now begun to use, and returning towards Red River. My relatives and neighbours tried to dissuade me, but when they found me determined to go, they made preparation for my journey. One of them went with me as far as Cincinnati. When he left me I went on alone. It was a painful and disagreeable journey for me. From day to day I travelled, weak and lonely, and sometimes hungry, meeting more frequently with suspicious looks and rough words than with kind treatment. Although I had enough to pay for corn for my horse, more than once I was refused, and cursed for an Indian. There were occasionally better-hearted people, as one old man who was standing at his door as I passed. He called to me to stop, took my horse and gave him plenty of corn, and leading me into the house placed food before me. I could not eat at the time, upon which he gave me some nuts, some of which I ate. When he saw that my horse had eaten, and that I was impatient to start, he put on the saddle and brought the horse. I offered him money, but he would not take it. At night I did not go to a house, preferring greatly to sleep in the woods, as I found I could sleep there far better. In fact I had been so accustomed to sleep in the open air in the fine season, that I felt oppressed in a house, and my strength was being restored by adopting my old habits of life. When I got near the upper part of the Big Miami the settlements were few and far apart. One day seeing a number of hogs in the woods, I shot one, skinned him, and hung the meat to my saddle, so that I was for some time well supplied. At the forks of the Miami of Lake Erie was a trader whom I knew, and who spoke Ottawwaw as well as I did. He might have been expected to be friendly, but he was a selfish, disagreeable man. When I asked him for something for my horse, he told me to be gone, as he would give nothing; but offered to sell me some corn for my bear meat, as he called the pork he saw hanging at my saddle. But I disliked him, and leaving him, slept that night in the woods. The next day I had the good fortune to come to a house where the woman treated me kindly. She fed my horse and gave me a piece of dried venison, which I cooked and enjoyed at the next place in the woods where I halted.

When within one hundred miles of Detroit, I was again taken very sick, and had to remain in a lodge I constructed, at first almost without hope of recovery. But at length I was again able to resume my journey.

Two days from Detroit I met a man, having a Sioux pipe in his hand, who merely gave me a look as he passed. It struck me as I went on that this man had a strong resemblance to my father, whose appearance was thereby recalled to my memory. On arriving on the second day at Detroit, I learned that this man on the road was really my brother. I was about to return after him, but Governor Cass, to whom I went to announce my arrival, would not let me go. He said that my having passed towards Detroit would be known at the houses on the way; and as he would be sure to inquire at each of these, he would soon hear of me and come back. His opinion appeared to have been well founded, for in three days my brother arrived. He would not have known me, but the affection of a brother was warm in his heart, and he held me a long time in his arms in silence. We were soon able to hear what each was anxious to know, but of this I need not give details. He persuaded me to cut my long hair, which I still wore in Indian style, and also to lay aside the Indian dress. But the dress of a white man was uncomfortable to me, and I was compelled from time to time, as will appear in the sequel, to resume my old dress for work and for comfort.

My brother insisted that I should go with him to his house, beyond the Mississippi, where he had long been settled. We set off thither together. At Fort Wayne we received kind attention from the military commandant, and the journey was, on the whole, pleasant and without incident. Forty days we took to get to the Mississippi, fifteen miles above New Madrid, where my brother lived. Thence we went to Jackson, fifteen miles from Cape Girardeau, where two of my sisters lived. From this place we started to go to Kentucky. Crossing the Mississippi, a little above Cape Girardeau, we went by way of Golconda, on the Ohio, to Kentucky, where several relatives lived, near villages called Salem and Princeton. Here my sister Lucy, married to a Mr. Rukken, lived. She had dreamed, the night before I arrived, that she saw me coming through the corn-field that surrounded the house. I had been too much accustomed to hear of dreams and presentiments, and to believe in them, to express any surprise at what she told me. She had a large family of children, all of whom, with the friends and neighbours, crowded around to witness the lost brother's meeting with his sister. It was a wonderful event in the quiet place. Next Sabbath day there was a great assemblage at the house, and a thanksgiving service was held.

My brother-in-law was exceedingly kind, and he took much trouble, by writing letters and making inquiries, to see if in my father's will any provision had been made for me. Nothing came of this at the time, but he interested so many people that a handsome sum was collected, and I never was so rich before or since. I had five hundred silver dollars when I went back to New Madrid to my brother Edward. I was going thence to my sister's at Jackson, but he would not allow me to go alone, no doubt thinking that the possession of this money might be the means of exposing me to danger or bringing me into difficulty.

I was very glad to remain some time at Jackson with my sister there. She was a truly good woman, and from her I learned much about the religion of which I knew so little. I had met people who called themselves Christians, but who in their lives and ways were not much better than the Indians among whom I was, except in things in which white men had the advantage of more knowledge. I had never happened to meet with any of the Christian missionaries or teachers, of whom I now heard as labouring among the Indians to teach them true religion. The old man, Ah-koo-nah-goo-zik, was the only one who had told me of such teachers. While my sister talked with me there came back to my memory some of the long-forgotten things I had been taught in my childhood, and which I now heard with very different feelings, and which I was able now to understand and assent to. The Indians were not without religious feeling, and some of them were devout as far as their superstitions went. They prayed to the Great Spirit, and made offerings to propitiate his favour. They had ideas of right and wrong, but they regarded things as good or bad only according to the customs of their people. A good minister, whom my sister brought to see me, inquired much about the beliefs and practices of the Indians, and asked my opinion as to the usefulness of sending missionaries to teach them. I told him that there were some who would be grateful to be taught, and that they were ever too ready to listen to any who professed to bring revelations from the Great Spirit. I told him how the pretended prophets and seers had sometimes been obeyed, when they gave precepts, which perhaps they had heard from white men, against lying and stealing and drunkenness and other evils, though they mixed these good precepts with foolish and crafty superstitions. I told him also that the Indians would not be altogether unprepared to receive the teaching about Jesus Christ, the Saviour and Friend of man. They had in their religion not only reverence for the Great Spirit, but their legends also spoke of one whom they called Na-na-bush, who was the creator of men and their patron and protector, and who had sometimes appeared upon the earth as the messenger and representative of the Great Spirit. They believe also in an evil spirit, or devil, called Matche-Manito, of whom they rarely speak, but of whose power and malice they have fear. Their ideas are confused, and may differ in various tribes, but in all there is a sense of some kind of religion, and I thought there was good hope in taking better teaching to them, which would find response both in their understanding and their conscience.

The good minister one day brought a book which he said was the Life of David Brainerd, a missionary among the Indians in times long past, written by Jonathan Edwards, of Princeton College. He read to me something which agreed with what I had told him. It was about a poor Indian who once came to him. He had never had any communication with Christian people, and yet unaided by any written revelation he possessed some just ideas of his own relation and duty to the Great Spirit. Here is the missionary's story:—

"I discoursed with him about Christianity. Some of my discourse he seemed to like, but some of it he disliked extremely. He told me that God had taught him his religion, and that he never would turn from it: but wanted to find some who would join heartily with him in it. For the Indians, he said, were grown very degenerate and corrupt. He had thoughts, he said, of leaving all his friends and travelling abroad in order to find some who would join with him; for he believed that God had some good people somewhere, who felt as he did. He had not always, he said, felt as he now did, but had formerly been like the rest of the Indians, until about four or five years before that time. Then, he said, his heart was very much distressed, so that he could not live among the Indians, but got away into the woods and lived alone for some months. At length he says, God comforted his heart, and showed him what he should do; and since that time he had known God, and tried to serve Him, and loved all men, be they who they would, so as he never did before. He treated me with uncommon courtesy, and seemed to be hearty in it. I was told by the Indians that he opposed their drinking strong liquor, with all his power, and that if at any time he could not dissuade them from it by all he could say, he would leave them and go crying into the woods. It was manifest that he had a set of religious notions, which he had examined for himself, and not taken for granted upon bare tradition, and he relished or disrelished whatever was spoken of a religious nature, as it either agreed or disagreed with his standard. While I was discoursing he would sometimes say, 'Now that I like, so God has taught me,' etc., and some of his sentiments seemed very just. He seemed to be sincere, honest, and conscientious in his own way, and according to his own religious notions, which was more than I ever saw in any other pagan. I perceived that he was looked upon and derided among most of the Indians as a precise zealot, who made a needless noise about religious matters, but I must say there was something in his temper and disposition which looked more like true religion than anything I ever observed among other heathens."

Whether this Indian's religion was "true" or not, it was certainly better than that of many who call themselves Christians. The minister said that this man was one among a thousand, and that there were very few who would thus separate themselves from their fellows and strive to be good as he did. The indulgence of natural desires and passions prevents self-denial. He explained to me that the excellence of the Christian religion appeared most in this, that it gives motive powerful enough to overcome natural desire and evil ways. Out of love and gratitude to the Saviour who died for us, obedience and self-denial become easy, just as we will do and suffer much for a friend or for one loved by us. I have said more than I intended about this, but it may interest those who have read or heard about missions to the Indians. But now to resume my narrative.

Chapter XIV.

*JOURNEY TO ST. LOUIS ON THE MISSISSIPPI—
TO CHICAGO—TO THE SAULT DE ST. MARIE—
HEAR OF MY INDIAN WIFE AND CHILDREN—
RETURN TO MY RELATIVES IN KENTUCKY—DIS-
TASTE FOR CIVILISED LIFE—WANDERINGS
RESUMED—TO CHICAGO AND FORT CLARK—
ADVENTURE AT A FERRY—TO MACKINAC—
COLONEL BOYD AND MR. H. SCHOOLCRAFT—
ENGAGED AS A TRADER—A STRUGGLE WITH
FAMINE—SECOND AND LAST EXPERIMENT AT
TRADING—WITH THE AMERICAN FUR COM-
PANY—INTERVIEW WITH MY CHILDREN AT THE
LAKE OF THE WOODS—THEIR REMOVAL BY THE
INDIANS—ENGAGEMENT AS INTERPRETER TO
MR. SCHOOLCRAFT.*

From Jackson my brother and I went to St. Louis on the
Mississippi, where we saw Governor Clark, who had already
given much assistance to my brother in his journeys in search
of me. He received us with great kindness, and offered us
whatever assistance we might think necessary in accomplish-
ing the object I now had in view, which was to faring my family from the Indian country. My wife I had little hope of
recovering, but I felt unwilling to leave my children among
the people where they were. My brother wished to accompany me, and take a considerable number of men, to aid, if
necessary, in taking my children by force. But I went one day
to Governor Clark and told him not to listen to my brother,

who knew little of the country or people I was going to visit, or of what was needful to my success in the attempt to bring out my family. In truth, I did not wish my brother, or any other white man, to accompany me, as I knew he could not submit to all the hardships of the journey, and live, as I should be compelled to live, in an Indian lodge all winter. Furthermore, I was aware that he would be rather an encumbrance than any help to me; and I persuaded him to return.

Governor Clark wished to send me by the way of the upper Mississippi, but I was unwilling to go that way, on account of the Sioux, through whose country I must pass. He gave me a Mackinac boat, large enough to carry fifty men, with provisions, axes, tents, and other stores. The current of the Mississippi, below the Missouri, soon convinced me that this large boat was not adapted for my journey, and at Portage de Sioux, I disposed of it, and of such of the goods as I could not stow away in a small canoe, in which, with two men, I proceeded to the head of the Illinois River, and thence to Chicago.

I had a letter from Governor Clark to Mr. M'Kenzie, the Indian agent at that place, and as there was no vessel about to sail for Mackinac, he fitted out a bark canoe, with a crew of Indians, to take me on my journey. But the Indians stopped for some days drinking, and a vessel meanwhile arrived, in which I sailed on her return voyage. At Mackinac I waited ten days, when Captain Knapp, of the revenue cutter, offered me a passage to Drummond's Island. Here Dr. Mitchell and the Indian agent, Colonel Anderson, treated me in a very friendly manner, until the latter had an opportunity to send me to the Sault de St. Marie.

At the Sault I remained two or three months, as Colonel Dickson, who was there, would not allow me to go up Lake Superior in the North-West Company's trading vessel, which went and returned three times while I was detained, waiting for him. He was going by boat, and I was to go with him. At last he was ready to start. We were no sooner out from shore than he told me to take an oar, and although I was then in feeble health, he compelled me to row as long as I was able to sit up. Being at last disabled, he set me on shore, at a spot twenty miles above Fort William, where I found Mr. Giarson, who was in charge of some property for the Hudson's Bay Company. I do not know why Colonel Dickson treated me as he had done, except he had been told something against me by the North-West people. When he set me on shore I told him I should be at the other side of the lake before him. Leaving my baggage under the charge of Mr. Giarson, I hired a canoe, with an old Frenchman, and having good luck in crossing I was there before him. He went on by the Indians' road to the Red River. We heard he had a journey of extreme difficulty, and suffered from fatigue and hunger. The Indians greatly disliked this "red-headed" Englishman, as they called him. He was an ill-tempered, rough man. On his way to Red River he passed an enclosed Indian burying-ground, where some of the people known to me were buried. Colonel Dickson and his people broke down the palings, and destroyed the little sheds that had been built over the graves. The Indians were deeply offended by this, and threatened to take his life, which they might probably have done, had an opportunity offered. He went to Pembinah, thence to Lake Naverse, and returned no more into the country of the Ojibbeways.

The village or settlement where I had lived with my family was in an island in the Lake of the Woods. I made inquiries, and learned that my wife and two of her children had left for some distant place. Her conduct, I heard, was such that I lost all wish to see her, though I still retained some feeling towards the children. Being much unsettled, and not resolved as to what I should do, I went to Mackinac. Mr. Boyd, the Indian agent there, wished to hire me as a striker in his smith's shop, but not liking the employment, I did not wish to remain. There was a vessel going to Chicago, and I was willing to pay for a passage, but was refused permission to be a passenger. I was therefore obliged to purchase a canoe, in

which I started, with only one man to assist me. Colonel Boyd
gave me a letter to Dr. Wolcott, who was now Indian agent
there. On arriving after rather a difficult voyage, I was ill with
fever, and my money being now spent I was in great distress.
As soon as I was able I went to Dr. Wolcott to present the letter; but he would not receive it, or take any notice of me. He
knew well who I was, as he had seen me before when I passed
Chicago, and I could not tell why he refused me assistance. I
might have perished but for the kindness of a Frenchman,
who had been to carry some boats across the Portage. His
wife was an Ojibbeway woman, and commonly accompanied
him when he went to take any boats across the Portage.
Though his horses were much tired with the long journey
from which he had returned, he agreed to take me and my
canoe sixty miles. He lent me also one of the horses to ride, as
I was too weak to walk, and he thought that riding would be
less fatiguing than jolting in the cart with the canoe. Before
we got to the end of the sixty miles, as there was now a little
water in the river, I concluded to put my canoe in, and try to
descend in it. My Frenchman, whom I had brought from
Mackinac, had deserted at Chicago, and I now obtained the
help of an old Indian, called the Smoker. We continued our
laborious and difficult route along the bed of the Illinois.
Beyond the Yellow Ochre River there was more water, and in
due time we went down to Fort Clark, which is on a narrow
neck of land between two lakes. Here I met some acquaintan-
ces, or rather some who claimed relationship in consequence
of being in some degree connected with the family I had first
belonged to among the Indians. One of them was a son of the
husband of Net-no-kwa. An old woman gave me a sack of
wiskobimmenuk, as they call corn when plucked green,
boiled, and then dried. Another gave me some venison, the
larger part of a deer he had just killed. He refused any compensation, and when I gave him a little powder and shot, and
some flints, he appeared very thankful. We passed great numbers of Po-ta-wa-to-mies, their lodges standing many together

at every bend of the river. Some of them started out in their canoes occasionally, and accompanied me some distance, asking who I was, and where I was going. They seemed very friendly, and I felt no alarm, having nothing that could induce them to attack me, had they any idea of plunder. In this manner I descended the Illinois River, killing sufficient game when it was wanted, and my health gradually mending, until I came to St. Louis.

Here Governor Clark showed his wonted kindness not only to me, but to the old Smoker, who had been faithful and serviceable to me on the journey. After giving the old man a handsome present, he provided for his return to his own country, and dismissed him.

After staying some time at St. Louis, I went to Cape Girardeau in my birch bark canoe, having a letter from Governor Clark to the Indian agent at that place. At Cape Girardeau, where I left my canoe, and where I remained only a short time, I saw some of Major Long's exploring party, then on their return from the Rocky Mountains. This was in the fall of the year 1820, about a year after my first return to the Ohio. From the time of my capture just thirty years had then elapsed, so that it must have been in the spring of 1789 I was taken prisoner.

From Cape Girardeau it was only about fifteen miles to Jackson, where I remained several months with my sister. Thence I went to Kentucky, and next fall to St. Louis, to see Governor Clark; but he was not at home, and as many people were dying there of fevers, I made but a short stay. On returning to Jackson, I found that there was also much illness there, and several of my relatives, with whom I then lived, died that year.

In the spring of 1822 I started to go again to the north, not finding that I was content among my friends in Kentucky. I had lived so long an active wandering life, that not only my health but my mind would give way if I continued in the uneventful, passive existence I had lately been leading. I went by the way of the Grand Prairie; and having given my canoe to my brother, I procured a horse, and rode to St. Louis, and thence proceeded by way of the Illinois towards Chicago.

The Indian agent for Fort Clark lived at this time at a place called Elk Heart, some distance below. He, as well as most of the people on this route, had been kind, and had shown a disposition to assist me whenever I had need of anything. On this journey I stopped at Elk Heart, at the house of the agent; and though he was not at home, I had my horse fed, and obtained all I required free of expense. On the following day I met the agent on his way home from Fort Clark, and told him of the hospitable reception I had met at his house in his absence. He was glad to hear of this, and he told me I should soon come to a bad river to cross; "but," he said, "there is a boat now on this side, in which I have just crossed. The man to whom it belongs lives on the other side. You must use the boat to cross, and then tell him to take it around to the other river, which is beyond his house, and cross that, and I will pay him for his trouble."

I crossed accordingly, and found the man at his house. He seemed very much struck by my horse, and offered to buy it from me. I told him the horse was necessary for my journey, and I could by no means part with it. Still he insisted, and as much as said he was determined to have it from me. He offered a larger price, and said unless I would let him have the horse, I should not have his boat to cross the river. He then began to bully and abuse me; but all he could say or do would not induce me to consent. The boat had been taken round to the river I had to cross for the use of some other person, and I started off, expecting to find it there.

On my way to the ferry I met the man on horseback. He had gone quickly by another way, and now, on meeting me, said, "I have taken away the canoe, and you cannot cross." Without regarding this, I went on, and when I arrived I found that the canoe was indeed gone, and there were no logs or other materials to construct a raft, which I was ready to do rather than go back. At last I reflected that if he had hidden the canoe, as was most probably the case, his track would lead me to the place. Then going back to the road, at some distance from the river, 1 found his track corning to it. This I followed until I found the canoe, a considerable distance below the ferry. Taking it to the crossing place, I went over, and when the canoe had served its purpose, I pushed it into the stream, and said to it, "Now go, and stay where your covetous, ill-conditioned master hides you." On reaching Chicago, I had to sell the horse for much less than its value, being told I could not take it to Mackinac except at great expense, so I had to make my way there on foot.

A principal part of my design in now going to Mackinac was to engage myself to Colonel Boyd, the Indian agent there, as an interpreter, he having formerly expressed a wish that I should do so, whenever I had recovered and acquired such a knowledge of English as would qualify me to discharge the duties of that office. This I had done in much less time than I had expected, while among my relatives and friends. It was, therefore, a great disappointment when Colonel Boyd told me that I was a little too late, as he had then only recently engaged a man to fill the place. He informed me, however, that an agent to be stationed at Sault de St. Marie was expected immediately, and thought that I might obtain the situation of interpreter for him. Mr. Schoolcraft, the gentleman referred to, arrived shortly after at Mackinac, and he readily entertained my proposal. But he said he could not fix until he knew what arrangements had been made at Sault de St. Marie. He told me to follow him in three or four days, he himself staying only a few hours at Mackinac. I made some preparations, and was nearly ready to start, when a letter came from Mr. Schoolcraft, saying that he found an interpreter at the Sault, and therefore did not require my services. It was a great disappointment, but could not be helped. This was the first time I saw a man whose name has since become known everywhere as a friend to the Indians, and whom afterwards I served for many years as interpreter. But I had some trials and adventures to pass through before obtaining the employment on which I had set my mind.

Being now without employment, I engaged to Mr. Stewart, agent of the American Fur Company, to go with the traders into the Indian country. This I preferred to remaining with the agent at Mackinac, though he proposed, as he had once before done, to hire me for a striker at his smith's shop. My health was now restored, and an active life was more in accordance with my present feelings. For my services with the people of the American Fur Company I was to receive two hundred and twenty-live dollars a year.

I went to the Sault de St. Marie with Mr. Morrison, one of the company's principal clerks. Thence they sent me in a boat with some Frenchmen to Fond du Lac. I was unacquainted with the usages of these people, and should have suffered, and perhaps perished, for want of provisions, not knowing I had to provide them, had I not purchased some occasionally from the boat's crew. From Fond du Lac I went to Rainy Lake with Mr. Cote; but my ignorance of the business to which I had engaged myself exposed me to much inconvenience. I had some traps with me, with which I took a considerable number of musk-rats; but I was not less surprised than displeased when told that what I had taken with my own traps did not belong to me. I was not only compelled to give these up, but I was made to paddle by myself a canoe heavily laden with wild rice, and to submit to various other laborious employments, which I did very reluctantly, supposing that I had been engaged only as a hunter.

When we arrived at Rainy Lake, I went to hunt, but killed nothing, finding no game there at the time. Soon afterwards they sent me to Lake River, and before the ice had formed so as to put an end to fishing, I had taken a large number of sturgeons. When winter commenced, Mr. Cote sent me, along with one clerk and four Frenchmen, with a small outfit of goods, in value about a hundred, and sixty dollars, to trade among the Indians. We were furnished with no other food than wild rice, at the rate of eighteen quarts per man, and instructed not to return till we had exchanged all our goods for peltries. As I knew we should have to travel far before we found the Indians, I requested of Mr. Cote permission to remain while I could prepare a train and harness for two dogs which I had procured, and also snow-shoes for ourselves, but he would not hear of a moment's delay in our departure.

Four days after we started a heavy snow fell, and our wild rice being nearly all expended, the clerk and three of the Frenchmen left me, and returned to the fort. There was now only myself and one Frenchman named Veiage, who, however, was a hardy, patient, and most excellent man, and we struggled on through the snow with our heavy loads as best we could.

After some days, and when we were extremely reduced through want of provision, we found some lodges of Indians, but they were poor; and having only a small supply of dried food, were in an almost starving condition. I left Veiage with them, and with a small portion of the goods I pushed forward in quest of another encampment, which they told me was at no great distance. I found the Indians here in no better condition. On my return to the place where I had left my companion, I found the lodges had been removed, and no person was to be seen. My strength was exhausted, and I sat down in a state of great depression. The night was coming on, and I was afraid I should perish with cold and hunger, when one of the Indians appeared, who had come to the place of the camp to look at some traps he had set. He lighted a fire, and, having raised me up, he assisted me to the place where they had made their encampment. He had taken one beaver, and this was now to be divided among about twenty persons, all of whom were in a nearly starving condition. I found that the Indians had been joined by two other lodges, one of which was that of one who knew me well. His wife began to cry when she saw the extreme misery of my condition on arrival, so much was I reduced and changed by hunger and fatigue. I heard from them something about my Indian family, at least about my son and one of my daughters, who were with a band near the Red River.

The following day six Frenchmen came upon us, having been sent forward by Mr. Cote, who no doubt supposed that I had found buffalo, and must by this time have meat in abundance. The clerk and the three others had not arrived before they left. We were now in a starving condition. One of my dogs died and was eaten. A day or two after we killed and ate my second dog. With bones, old moccasins, and pieces of leather, we had a struggle to sustain life. It was necessary to make some move promptly, and I resolved to push on towards the buffalo region. As we had a considerable distance to travel before we could reach it, we consulted together, and determined to kill one of the Fur Company's dogs of the goods train. We did this, and were enabled, on the strength of it, to reach the buffalo ground, where our distress soon was ended. I killed several, and we laid up a good supply of meat in our camp. The Frenchmen, however, after their pressure was relieved, became lazy and insolent, and refused to go to bring in the meat, to carry packs, or render me as a hunter any assistance whatever. When we were about to return to the trading-house, every one of these men refused to take any load beyond his own blanket and provisions, except Veiage, and with him I divided the peltries which we had obtained gradually for our goods. They weighed in all six hundred pounds. We were delayed a good while in carrying this heavy load to the fort.

When I arrived I accounted for my whole outfit and advances, having peltries in exchange for every article I had taken, except some powder and shot, which we had ourselves expended in hunting. The price of this was deducted from my pay, in my final settlement with the agent of the American Fur Company. Ten dollars also were deducted for the dog we had killed in the extremity of our hunger, although it had been the means of saving not my life only, but that of the Frenchmen who were with me. But Mr. Cote did not consider my return a good one, and complained of me for having refused to take whisky with my outfit. I told him that if I had taken whisky I could certainly have obtained a greater quantity of peltries, but I was averse to trading with the Indians when under the influence of drink, and did not wish to be one, on any occasion, or for any profit, to introduce what was so hurtful amongst them. He was determined, however, to send me out again, and in deference to his very urgent appeals I agreed to conform only for this once to his instructions, which were, "to use every method to procure the greatest possible quantity of skins at the lowest price." He said that his own position, as well as the prosperity of the company, depended on a good return at this time. He insisted therefore that I should take whisky, and I did so, although reluctantly.

This time I went to the country about the Lake of the Woods, and with an outfit valued at two hundred dollars I purchased, through whisky, more than double the number of peltries I had brought in before. Mr. Cote expressed the highest satisfaction at my success; but I told him if he wished his goods sold in that way he must employ some other person, as I could never again consent to take part in such fraud and wrong. I had been so long among the Indians that many of them were personally my friends, and having seen the extent of the mischiefs occasioned by the introduction of intoxicating liquors, I had become desirous to prevent it as far as in my power; at least I was not willing to be myself an instrument in spreading such poison among them. I could not use the advantage to be gained by their unconquerable appetite for drink in bargaining with them; and I knew that though they might be easily defrauded, the fraud thus practised was soon known to them, and would be followed by resentment and dislike in proportion as they were made to suffer; more particularly against me, whom they looked upon as one of their own number. Mr. Cote seemed annoyed, but he saw that I was in earnest in what I said.

I remained altogether fifteen months in the employ of the American Fur Company, during all which time I did not sleep twenty times in the house, so active and laborious were my duties. It had been an item in my agreement with Mr. Stewart that I should be allowed to go to Red River to see my children, and make an attempt to bring them out with me. Accordingly, when the traders were about to make their yearly visit to Mackinac, I was allowed to go by myself; but having been disappointed of moccasins and other articles that had been promised me by Mr. Cote, I suffered much inconvenience, travelling as I did in a small canoe by myself.

Mr. Clark, of the Hudson's Bay Company, who was now stationed at Red River, and to whom I had a letter, refused to give me any assistance in recovering my children. He told me what I knew very well, that Indians whose wives had left them take no thought about the children. This is true in general, but I had now a higher motive in wishing to get my children, so as to bring them under better influences than they were exposed to among those who were untaught and without any restraint on their evil passions. I did not expect Mr. Clark to have any of this feeling, so I said nothing to him about it. In the morning when I arrived there I had left my blanket in his house, expecting at least that I might sleep there; but when at the approach of night I was about to go in, he sent the blanket out to me. From the manner in which this was done I knew if I went in again it would only be to be driven out, and I went immediately to select a place to sleep in the woods at a little distance. But Mr. Bruce, the interpreter whom I have before mentioned, saw me, and calling me into his lodge invited me to remain, and while I did so treated me in the most friendly and hospitable manner. Knowing that I had no reason to expect any assistance from Mr. Clark, who was soon to leave the country, I went to Captain Bulger, the military commandant, to state my business, and received from him a most attentive and friendly hearing. He first asked me where I had slept, as he knew I had arrived the day before. When he heard that I had been refused a lodging in the trading-house, he invited me to come and live with him as long as I remained there. He knew also of my business to the country, and asked me if I could tell where my children were. I had ascertained that they were now with some Indians about the Prairie Portage, and told him so. I did not, however, tell him what some of the Indians about the fort had made known to me, that those of the band with whom my children were had heard of my arrival, and were determined to kill me if I should attempt to take my children from them.

Notwithstanding this information I visited that band as soon as I could make the journey, and went straight to the lodge of the chief, who received me kindly. He did not appear to know anything about what had brought me. When I discovered the lodge where my children were they appeared at first pleased to see me, but I soon perceived that they had no real feeling towards me, and also that the Indians had no intention of allowing me to take them away. There was one man there with whom I had a quarrel long before, and who now treated me with some insolence, and even used threatening language. After having been hospitably received by the chief of the band, they probably were afraid to carry out their hostile purposes, but I did not put myself too much in their power. Being alone I could accomplish no more at present that induce the chief to remove his camp nearer to the fort at Red River.

After they were encamped here, thinking that it was likely that violence would be attempted by them, I asked to be allowed to take the children, but they at once refused to give them up. The same man, along with a younger one, who I afterwards found was attached to my daughter, were the most forward in opposing me. The dispute rose to such a height that it was with the utmost difficulty I restrained myself from striking one of these men, although my own death would have followed had I killed one of them. I thought it best to report to

Captain Bulger the state of matters. He sent Mr. Bruce to call my children into the fort. They came accordingly, and stood before his house, but with ten or twelve Indians accompanying them, who were careful to stand near on each side of them. The captain ordered my children to have some food brought for them, he himself having just then eaten. The Indians snatched the food away, leaving them not a mouthful. A loaf of bread was brought, but went in the same way. Captain Bulger saw this second act of rapacity, and made the children be taken to a store-house where they were made to sit down and get some food. The Indians said again that the children could not be taken from them, and they returned to the camp.

Next day Captain Bulger called the chief to come to have a council in the fort on this matter. He came, and the other principal men of the band, including my two enemies. The chief himself had evidently no feeling in the case, and when we all went into the council room, he came and sat with Captain Bulger and myself, thereby placing the men who were principally active in detaining them as if separate from himself in the dispute.

Presents of considerable value were brought in and placed on the floor between the two parties, and then Captain Bulger said to the Indians that he desired to speak what was just and reasonable, and the pipe full of tobacco between them was to show that he had friendly feeling, as long as they listened to his words. Then he appealed to them, saying that I asked in the name of the Great Spirit, who gave these children to me, that they should deliver them up, and take the presents now before them as a memorial of the good-will subsisting between him and them. The Indians began to deliberate, and perceiving apparently that the commandant had a considerable armed force at hand, they were prudent in their reply, and accepted the presents, promising to surrender the children.

Next morning all the Indians had disappeared from the neighbourhood. I saw it was useless to make any further attempts at that time. Not long after I was engaged by Colonel

Boyd as interpreter at Mackinac, where I remained till the summer of 1828, when I paid a visit to the States. On returning to the north in the following year I was employed by Mr. Schoolcraft, Indian Agent at the Sault de St. Marie, and continued with him for some years as his interpreter.

Chapter XV.

H. L. Schoolcraft, Indian Agent at Sault de St. Marie—His Indian Researches and Books—Changed Condition of Indian Tribes—Progress in Education and Civilization—Their Relation to the American and Canadian People—The Province of Manitoba, and the Great North-West—Testimony and Report of a Scottish Colonist and Banker at Winnipeg.

Here ends the narrative of Grey Hawk's life as a hunter. In the duties of an interpreter there is little scope for incident or adventure. How long he resided at the Sault de St. Marie; when he returned to the south; and the date or circumstances of his death, we have been unable to learn. Only a few things are mentioned about him after entering on the new employment which he had long desired to obtain. He made some further effort to induce his daughters to come to him, but without result. His son, as he grew older, remained attached to the life in which he had been trained as a hunter. The family associations of Grey Hawk may therefore pass out of notice, but many readers may like to be told something about the people and the places most prominent in the latter part of the narrative.

Let us begin with Henry L. Schoolcraft, in whose employment we have left Grey Hawk at the close of his personal narrative. Born in 1793, a son of Colonel Lawrence Schoolcraft, of the army of the Revolution, he early showed a taste for geographical exploration and archaeological research. In 1822 his services were engaged as Government agent for Indian affairs on the north-west frontiers. For twenty years he resided at Michitirnackinac and at Sault de St. Marie, and in all spent thirty years among the Indians; making many journeys also, in which he had abundant opportunity for studying the history, traditions, languages, and customs of various tribes. He published many treatises and volumes, a full list of which occupies above two pages of Allibone's "Dictionary of Authors." The most important works are "Personal Memoirs of a Residence of Thirty Years with the Indian Tribes," published in 1851, a large volume of 700 pages; and "Historical and Statistical Collections," on the same subject, published in five quarto volumes at the expense of the American Government, 1857-8. The Chevalier Bunsen praises this work highly, but Baron Humboldt thought it a crude and not very useful compilation. The truth is that Mr. Schoolcraft gathered very many and varied materials, but did not show much skill in arranging them, or in drawing general conclusions from the miscellaneous facts recorded by him. The poet Longfellow speaks of "The various and valuable writings of Mr. Schoolcraft, to whom we are much indebted for the indefatigable zeal shown in rescuing from oblivion so much of the legendary lore of the Indians."

Mr. Schoolcraft was twice married, his first wife, Miss Johnston, being the granddaughter of Waboojing, a well known chief of Lake Superior.

The tone of Mr. Schoolcraft's works may be gathered from the following brief extracts: "My earliest impressions of the Indian race," he says, "were drawn from the fireside rehearsals of incidents which had happened during the perilous times of the American Revolution, and were all inseparably connected with the fearful ideas of the Indian yell, the tomahawk, the scalping knife, and the fire-brand. In these recitals the Indian was depicted as the very impersonation of evil, a sort of wild demon who delighted in nothing so much as blood and murder. Whether he had mind, was governed by any reason, or even had any soul, nobody inquired and nobody cared. It was always represented as a meritorious act, in old revolutionary reminiscences, to have killed one of them in the border wars, and thus aided in ridding the land of a cruel and unnatural race, in whom all feelings of pity, justice, and mercy were supposed to be obliterated. Those early ideas were sustained by printed narratives of captivity and hairbreadth escapes of men and women from their clutches, so that I had early a most definite and terrific idea impressed on my imagination of the Indian race.

"Fortunately I was still young when my sphere of observation was enlarged by my obtaining a situation as Government agent to one of the leading tribes, at an age when opinions are not too firmly rooted to permit change. At first I still looked upon them as dangerous and bloodthirsty people, who were only waiting a good opportunity to knock one on the head. But I soon had good reason to change my opinions. I need not here detail the steps by which I arrived at conclusions directly adverse to those I formerly held, and which are still commonly received. Having been placed in varied scenes and circumstances, during four and twenty years' residence and travel among these people, I became familiar with their life and character. With numbers of them I have formed an intimate acquaintance, and with not a few I have contracted a lasting friendship. Connected with them by the exercise of official duties, and by closer relationship, I came to be regarded by them as one identified with their history, and received many marks of their confidence. If what I have written about them shall afford the public any means of judging of the Red Race with greater accuracy, I hope it may lead to their being treated with greater kindness, and a more enlarged spirit of justice. The change which has been wrought in my own mind by the facts I have witnessed, has been accompanied by a still more important one, as to their intellectual capacities and moral susceptibilities, and their consequent claims on the philanthropy of the age."

The generous appeal thus made has been since amply responded to, both by the conduct of the American and British Governments toward the Indians, and by the beneficent labours of the Christian churches. Mr. Schoolcraft himself lived to see remarkable changes in the condition of almost all the principal tribes. Here is what he records as to the state of the Choctaws even forty years ago: "The Choctaws," he says, "occupy the country above the State of Arkansas, extending from the Arkansas to the Red River, following up the Canadian branch of the former, comprising an area of about 150 miles in breadth by 200 in length. They are bounded by Texas south-west. The country is well adapted for grain and the raising of stock in its middle and northern parts, and for cotton on the south. Many of the natives have large fields, where but a few years since the forest was untouched. Saw mills, grist mills, and cotton gins are erected or being erected throughout the country.

"The tribe is governed by a written constitution and laws. Their territory is divided into three districts, each of which elects, once in four years, a ruling chief, and ten representatives. The general council, thus constituted, consisting of thirty councillors, meets annually. Voters must be Choctaws of age, and residents of the district. The three chiefs have a joint veto power on all laws passed; but two-thirds of the council may repass them after such rejection. The councillors elect their own speaker and clerk, and keep a journal. They meet in a large and commodious council-house, fixed up with seats for members and spectators, and committee rooms. In addition to this evidence of capacity for self-government, there are judicial districts established, the trial by jury is secured, and there is an appeal to the highest tribunal. The council has passed many good and wholesome laws; among them one against intemperance and the sale of ardent spirits.

"The Choctaws have twelve public schools, an academy, and other educational appliances. There are several missionaries and ministers settled among them.

Similar reports have been given of other tribes, and the progress, since Mr. Schoolcraft's time, is such as would rejoice so warm a friend of the race. In Canada the condition of the settled tribes is even more satisfactory than in the United States. The large body of the Red Men have long since been within the pale of civilization, and even among the nomadic and remote tribes there has been great progress in moral and social state, even where they still adhere to their old occupations and modes of life. The wars of other times are no more heard of, and the young men employ themselves in hunting and trading. At the trading stations intoxicating drink is no longer allowed, and the violence and crimes formerly due to this source are now rarer than in lands that boast of their civilization.

The regions which were the chief scenes of Indian life in the story of "Grey Hawk," are those now included in the rising province of Manitoba. The country round the great lakes of British North America, Winnipeg, and the Lake of the Woods, is now passing from a desert condition, the resort only of wandering hunters, to be the home of emigrant settlers, and the starting-place for a new imperial dominion. In the immediate neighbourhood of these lakes there are districts of rock and forest and swamp, but beyond this, from the Lake of the Woods west to the foot of the Rocky Mountains, there is a land of spreading prairies and fertile plains, a land equal in extent to the United States west of the Mississippi. The fertile belt of the North Saskatchewan, reaching from the Red River to the Rocky Mountains, is estimated to embrace 250,000,000 acres of rich agricultural land, capable of sustaining millions of people, and destined to help the supply of food for older countries. It is a well-known fact that wheat is produced in the greatest abundance and perfection in the highest latitudes that permit it to come to maturity, and in accordance with this, samples have been shown equal in appearance to Minnesota hard, esteemed a champion grain, and weighing sixty-eight pounds to the bushel, raised at Fort Vermilion on the Peace River, at nearly 60° north latitude, 1500 miles north-west from Fort Garry. From Fort Vermilion south to Emerson, on the boundary line of the United States, the distance is as great as from Chicago to Florida. These North-West Provinces, with many other resources and capabilities, will prove above all a great cereal growing region. The wheat of Manitoba is the best in the American market, and the average yield is nearer forty than thirty bushels per acre.

This is the country which the Canadian Pacific Railway is opening up to the world. At the time when Irish famine and distress attracted great notice, thousands and thousands of cultivators vainly trying to live upon patches of ground of a few acres, unfit to support a family, even if there were no rent or other outlay, the president of this railway wrote a letter In the *Times*, saying that if 10,000 of these poor Irish farmers, with their families, 50,000 in all, could be sent out in summer at the expense of Government, every family could be provided with 160 acres of the very best quality of farming land free of cost! Arrangements could be made with the railway, land, and colonization companies interested in the settlement of the country, by winch each of these men would be advanced the capital necessary to build a small house, and to give him a new start in life. All this is mentioned now because in a few years the country will doubtless be densely settled, and we are pointing out the contrast from the time of our story, when there were only Indians wandering over these wide regions, and no fixed settlements existed except the trading post of the Fur Companies. These companies occupy a large place in the history of Canada, as they do in the present tale. A few words may be introduced about them.

The Hudson Bay Company was organized in 1670, under a royal charter given by Charles II., granting it all the lands drained by streams flowing into Hudson Bay, for the purpose of trading with the Indians. Gradually the power of the company grew till it exercised a right of almost dominion over nearly half the North American continent. In the last half of the eighteenth century, many French Canadian traders occupied portions of the territory, especially about Lake Winnipeg and the Lake of the Woods. In 1783, the North-West Company was formed, and in these districts proved a formidable rival to the Hudson Bay Company, though possessing no territorial or chartered rights. The servants of the rival traders were in constant opposition, breaking out from time to time in violent conflicts, in which the Indians sometimes became involved. This state of affairs is referred to in our story. The Earl of Selkirk, a director of the Hudson Bay Company went out, in 1811, to examine the country, and to endeavour to arrange the disputes that were then disturbing the traders. He failed to effect this, but he thought that the Red River would be a suitable place for emigrants. Obtaining a grant of land he brought out a colony of Scottish highlanders, who settled near the present site of Winnipeg. It was a good idea, but apparently before the time, for the settlement was never a thriving one, partly from the hostility of the traders, and partly from unsuccessful farming. Some of them, however, held their ground, and in 1821 the worst of their troubles were over, through the amalgamation of the North-West and Hudson Bay Companies. In that year they finally "buried the hatchet," as the Indians expressed it, and the old company resumed undisputed jurisdiction over the whole north-west, establishing posts from Lake Superior to the Arctic Ocean, and from the Red River to the Pacific shores; exercising through its great army of clerks and officials all the civil, military, and judicial rights of an independent government.

The Red River settlement from this time became a mixed community of Scotch and French and Indians, raising crops and trading by barter, under the sufferance of the commercial lords of the country. So it continued until the progress of emigration brought large increase of people in all parts of the Dominion, and the foundation was laid of the Canadian Confederation. In 1868, negotiations were begun for the extinction of the Hudson Bay Company's title to the lands, which were concluded a year or two later. The company received a money payment, and one-twentieth of the public lands. In remote territories the company still exercises its former rights, but abdicates them as soon as settlements are made and local governments formed.

The annexation of Manitoba to the Dominion was not effected without some trouble, the French Canadians and half-breeds, under Louis Riel, raising the standard of revolt, and forming a provisional government. The presence of British troops, under Colonel now Lord Wolseley, put an end to this rebellion, and in 1871 Manitoba became a province of Canada, and began the career of prosperity which bids fair to be lasting and conspicuous.

The testimony of a Scottish resident, who has witnessed the changes in the North-West, and has strong faith in its progress, will be read with interest. It is one of the clearest and most recent voices from the far country, and may well tempt many of the Scotchman's compatriots to go to such a land of promise. Here is the report, quoted in an Inverness newspaper:—

Speaking at a banquet recently given to him by the citizens of Winnipeg, Mr. Duncan MacArthur, a native of Nairn, who has been a successful banker in Winnipeg, referred as follows to the future of Manitoba:

"And now a few words about the future of Manitoba and the North-West. It is difficult to believe that the North-West territory should have remained, so far as people generally were concerned, a terra incognita until within the last twelve or fifteen years. Yet such is actually the case, and had it not been for the consolidating impulse that accompanied and followed the con-

federation of the British North American Provinces it might have remained a terra incognita to this day. Our statesmen never dreamt, during the earlier stage of their efforts to bring about confederation, that there was an unborn and a greater dominion in the North-West, stretching from Lake Superior to the Rocky Mountains on the one hand, and from the International boundary to the Arctic Sea on the other, containing agricultural, manufacturing, and mining resources sufficient to supply the wants of one hundred millions of human beings—a territory worth more in point of material value than all the other provinces put together.

The country is vast, and its resources are so rich and varied that it is impossible to grasp the extent of the former or to estimate the value of the latter; and very few, even of those who have lived longest and who have travelled most in the interior of the country, possess an adequate idea of the real value of Canada's heritage in the North-West. Confining our view of it to that portion that is suitable for agricultural purposes, we can see, standing as we do on the eastern confines of the fertile belt, an immense tract of country extending from Winnipeg to the Rocky Mountains on the one hand, and from Winnipeg to the fertile valleys of the Peace River country on the other—a tract of country which contains hundreds of millions of acres suitable for farming and grazing purposes, and which is sufficient to afford homes and independence and comfort to the surplus population of Europe for centuries to come; and owing to the exigencies arising from too large populations in many European countries, our North-West is destined to be speedily peopled.

The country is, moreover, accessible to Europe, and apart altogether from the special immigration which has been induced of late years to come here from the other Provinces and from Great Britain, we may expect that the great wave of emigration from Northern Europe, which during the last twenty years has been slowly but surely filling up Minnesota, Dakota, and other United States territories, will reach us and conduce greatly to the rapid settlement of the country.

It requires an ardent imagination to picture the change which awaits the North-West during the next twenty years. Long before that time the face of the country will be covered by a network of railways. Our prairies, that now appear so bleak and boundless, will be cultivated and planted and dotted over with the comfortable homes of an intelligent, a prosperous, and a contented people. We shall be able to grow and to export a sufficient quantity of grain to justify us in calling our country the granary of the world. Many cities and towns of great importance will spring up, and Winnipeg will not only retain her present position and prestige, but will in all probability be the largest and most important city in Canada.

Those who know little or nothing about the North-West and its resources may think these statements are either gross exaggerations or the utterances of a sanguine and partial individual, but the time is not far distant when this great country will be sufficiently well-known to receive the recognition to which it is entitled. With such a future before us we may well work and hope and wait. Unlike many of the older nations of the world who are limited by space, fettered by poverty, and crushed by the exactions of injustice and tyranny, whose greatness and opportunities are in the past, we stand on the threshold of a new land of promise—a land which constitutes one of the fairest portions of the New World—a land on

*which millions of our race are destined to act out the
great drama of life, and which is to witness new and tri-
umphal marches in literature, science, and art, and in
many other forms of national progress and develop-
ment.*

   'We live in the light of the dawning day,
   With our future wide and free;
·   *We wait God's time for out noontide glow*
   And our heroes yet to be.'

*And it behooves us, at this early but critical stage of our
history, to lay well the foundations of our political and
of our educational institutions."*

Mr. MacArthur refers only to the vast future of the province as the home of a great nation of European origin and civilization. He does not in this speech refer to the Red Men who
once were the owners and sole inhabitants of these regions.
We must not forget them, and we conclude with a sentence
concerning them.

From Selkirk as far as habitable land extends the banks of
the river are occupied by an Indian reservation, and are par-
tially under cultivation. The author of a handbook of the
Canadian Pacific Railway, speaking of Winnipeg in July,
says, "At this season of the year the Indian agent makes his
annual visit, and his wards were flocking in great numbers to
receive their annuity. On our return a few days later they were
assembled in form about the chief's house, and their teepees,
canoes, dogs, and children added a picturesqueness to the
scene. The Indians on the lake are chiefly Ojibbeways and
Crees, and they are so mixed that there is little tribal individu-
ality left in any of the settlements. They have made some
progress in civilization, and now constitute the chief reliance

of the Hudson Bay people for labourers, having replaced the French Canadians of other days."

When these regions have become the seat of a busy and prosperous agricultural and commercial community, we hope that some will still continue to read with interest Grey Hawk's story of his adventures in times when Indian hunters and fur company's traders alone were seen in the great North-West of America.

The Sun Dance Of The Sioux Indians.

[OF THE INDIAN NATIONS AND TRIBES REFERRED TO IN THIS STORY, THE SIOUX APPEAR TO BE LESS CHANGED THAN ANY OTHER, AND TO HAVE BEEN LEAST INFLUENCED BY CONTACT WITH THE WHITE MEN. FROM THE LEISURE HOUR OF 1879 WE GIVE THE ACCOUNT OF A VISIT TO A SIOUX CAMP, COMMUNICATED TO THAT JOURNAL BY AN OFFICER OF THE UNITED STATES ARMY.]

AT full moon in the month of June each year, a grand festival is held by the Sioux Indians in honour of, and as a propitiation to the sun, to them the visible embodiment of the Great Spirit. If the hunter desires special good fortune in the chase, if the warrior hopes for revenge, if a relative is sick, if any favour is wished by an Indian from the Supreme Power which he recognises and appeals to after his own barbarous fashion, he vows if the boon is granted to take part in the next Sun Dance. Many, indeed, participate from religious fanaticism alone, without any view to their own advantage, except in a general way.

In the year 1878 the Sun Dance of the Sioux nation was held about twelve miles from Fort R———. A small party of officers stationed there determined to see if it was possible to gain admission to the ceremonies. In the early morning a light wagon, drawn by four stout little ponies, climbed the steep hills behind the garrison, and gaining the flat table-land of the upper prairie, halted, after a rapid drive, at Seven Mile Spring, a little oasis, known far and wide to frontier travellers as the spot where weary man and beast can find shady trees and cool fresh water. Again on the road, the gay party dashed down into deep ravines, climbed steep bluffs, pushed down into a ravine again, then on between high hills. All the surface of the country gave proof that in past ages it had been the scene of tremendous upheavals and outbursts of volcanic energy.

At last, on one of the huge mounds, appeared the form of a horseman waving a scarlet blanket, whilst his pony executed curvets and caracoles which testified to the rider's skilful horsemanship. One of the military scouts went forward to the Indian to discover the meaning of this demonstration, and found the man had been sent out four miles to direct the "pale faces" to the camp, the Sioux having learned of the intended visit by means of the perfect system of espionage exercised over the whites all through the Indian country. Guided by this warrior, decked out in paint and feathers, the travellers soon reached a point from which they beheld a wild and picturesque scene.

Sioux encampment

The valley far below, or as these wide open spaces between hills are called, "the bottom," was covered for miles with lines of teepees, or wigwams. The central point of the camp was the vast empty amphitheatre where the Sun Dance was to be performed. Five or six chiefs, elaborately costumed, approached the wagon as it entered the camp, and shook hands with their guests with great dignity, uttering the peculiar guttural "how," the all-expressive word of salute and welcome. Two white tents were pitched, buffalo robes, blankets,

"Red Shirt" with war hood.

and provisions sheltered therein, and half a dozen white men found themselves "at home" in a camp of six thousand Sioux Indians. As they stood gazing at the village which placidly basked in the fierce summer sun, groups of fantastic figures continually passed to and from the open area, which the next day was to be at once the place of worship and the scene of torture.

The tents of those who were to take part in the dance were ranged in a circle. For three days each man must be secluded in his little hut, without food or water, and subjected to a continual steam bath. This is prepared by immersing large stones in boiling water, and permitting the steam to evaporate in the closed hut, the occupant being rolled in heavy buffalo robes to facilitate perspiration.

The first day of the festival is devoted to the "cutting of the pole." Certain Indians, deputed for the purpose, take charge of the ceremony, which is preceded by "making medicine," a sacred mystery which no white man is allowed to witness. After this observance is concluded, all the men of the tribe assist in collecting the logs and brushwood which form the outer wall of the arena. The active ponies dart hither and thither in the bushes, the riders cutting branches with their belt knives, and fastening them in some way to their person, until they resemble a moving forest on their return to camp. Stakes are driven into the ground describing a large circle, an opening being left at one side; and the brushwood is woven in between these stakes so as to form a dense wall around the enclosure. The pole, forty feet high, is selected from a number of others by certain Indians, and then cut down and transported to the grounds by two maidens. After the top has been gaily trimmed with feathers, greens, and flowers, four ropes are attached a little more than half way up, which, when stretched out, reach the ground about twenty-eight feet from the base of the pole.

Before the dance begins criers go throughout the camp, summoning all the people to come to look at the "holy thing, the beautiful thing." Then the dancers are led from their huts, covered from head to foot with buffalo robes to look at the scene of their trial on the next day.

Before the true Sun Dance commences the Indians engage in many wild and curious ceremonies which are preliminary to the main performance, and work themselves into a state of the fiercest fanaticism. These exercises consist in the main of dancing, beating the tomtom, singing, and grotesque physical contortions.

Early on the morning of the second day the camp was astir, and the amphitheatre crowded with eager spectators. The white visitors were presented to the great chief, Spotted Tail, who had not shown himself before. He received them with dignity, and ordered seats to be prepared for the accommodation of the strangers. Many times they wished themselves far distant from those comfortable blanket-cushions before the cruel scenes of the day were over.

Chief's squaw and papoose.

The ceremonies were opened by twenty-five warriors on their horses, gorgeous in finery and war-paint, filing into the arena, bringing with them a child. The little one was seated on a pony, led by its father; following it came the mother. The father informed the master of the ceremonies that he would give the pony the child was riding, and the mother would give the blanket she wore, to the Indian who would cut holes in the child's ears. This offer was made known to the audience by the master of ceremonies. At once some Indian, only too delighted at the chance of cutting anything, although not indifferent to the pony and blanket, stepped forward, and with his sharp knife cut a hole in each of the child's ears. After the ears had been slit, a piece of cloth, twisted into round cord-like shape, was thrust through the wound to ensure an opening for ornaments after it should have healed. Of course, during this painful and barbarous performance the poor papoose screamed with pain and fright, but its cries were drowned by the hooting, yelling, and singing of surrounding braves and squaws. This was continued until all the youngsters present had undergone the operation.

Following this came a grand drill and review, in which four hundred warriors, distinguished for bravery or cruelty, took part. These men were magnificently dressed; they were divided into squads, stationed at different points of the arena; but instead of the ordinary evolutions of a military drill, the performance consisted of singing and dancing to monotonous music made by measured strokes upon a drum, and the beating with sticks upon a dry beef hide stretched on the ground.

At a given signal Chief Spotted Tail arose with as much dignity as any feudal lord among his vassals, walked slowly round the circle and inspected the men, carrying in his hand a stick three or four feet long, on the end of which was fastened a scalp of long auburn hair, evidently taken from some white woman. As he passed round the circle he used the scalp and stick as a *baton,* and as he moved it to and fro the line of braves would advance or retreat, dancing, singing, and hooting incessantly. It may be here remarked that Spotted Tail, who presided over this orgie, and directed the movements of his warriors by waving a white woman's scalp, holds the commission of lieutenant in the United States army, and every month draws from the people's treasury the sum of 150 dollars.

At another signal the braves suddenly broke their lines, rushed to their ponies picketed near by, and in an incredibly short time they came tearing up the valley, formed in solid column, the thundering of hoofs shaking the earth beneath them. As they approached the wide entrance to the arena, the column separated into two parts; these again into two, and again and again, until the eye failed to follow the intricate convolutions, and the moving mass resembled a gaudy kaleidoscope. Upon the conclusion of this cavalry review, during which the braves performed the most difficult feats of horsemanship, the Sun Dance proper began.

Forty-seven Indians had volunteered to submit themselves to this inhuman rite. The dancers were brought into the arena one at a time, each attended by his relatives. As he entered he raised his hand in adoration of the sun before he advanced to and embraced the sacred pole. Their only clothing was a breech-cloth. One fine stalwart youth was so overcome by the prospect of his approaching torture, that, as he embraced the pole and leaned his head upon his folded arms, his whole frame trembled and heaved with emotion. Instantly he recovered his stoicism, and took his place in the row of dancers with an unmoved countenance. At a sign from Spotted Tail the dancer lay down on his back, his head touching the foot of the pole. Two slits, about four inches long and half an inch apart, were then cut in each breast; the skin between the wounds was torn from the flesh, and a strong, hard wood stick thrust in; and to the ends of this stick the ropes fastened to the poles were securely tied. When thus prepared, the dancer sprang to his feet, the blood streaming down from his wounds; slits were also made under the shoulder-blades, and in the backs of the hands, and sticks thrust through. In this condition, with a whistle between his teeth, upon which he blew unceasingly, the victim, or rather the fanatic, began to dance, amid the most unearthly din; drums beating, whistles screaming, six thousand throats hooting, yelling, and singing, and he keeping his eyes fixed upon the sun during the whole time of his ordeal. If he lowered his eyes, or turned them aside from the dazzling blaze, some Indians reflected the rays into his face from small looking-glasses. While he dances, his hands are outstretched, and at intervals he rushes backwards, and throws his whole weight upon the rope which is fastened to his breast. This he must continue until the skin gives way, and the sticks are torn from the wounds. Before this is accomplished the skin is raised from the flesh over the entire breast, and the blood flows freely from the ugly wounds. In some instances nine hours have passed before the dancer could tear himself loose, but on this occasion the longest time of endurance was two hours and a half.

One rather slender youth gave tokens of exhaustion in a short time after being fastened to the pole. He tottered from side to side, and was in such a state of nervous excitement that the pulsations of his heart could be distinctly seen at a distance of several feet. His mother, an old squaw, shrivelled and wrinkled, came forward and took her place beside him; she began to sing first a war song, then praises of her son's bravery, and exhortations to fortitude, finally promises of gifts and honours if he came triumphantly forth from the ordeal. The young man persevered for a time, but it was a most painful exhibition.

Many of the dancers became faint before their vow was fulfilled, and could not throw themselves against the rope with sufficient force to break away. But to fail is lifelong disgrace; the brave who succumbs to physical anguish must have his hair cut close to his head, and must be banished and disowned by his tribe; so the dancers persist, stimulated now and again by a looker-on stepping up and spitting on them.

When it became apparent that a dancer would not by his own efforts succeed in breaking loose, one of his friends clasped him around the waist and dragged him backward, until the thongs burst from his flesh and he fell exhausted on the earth. Then the ragged skin was trimmed off and his wounds dressed with pieces of charcoal. After a short rest he would join in the dance around the outer circle, which is continued until all who have volunteered have undergone the torture.

The dance is continued from two to three days. During this time the dancers are kept entirely without food or drink; but as the conclusion of the ceremonies a grand feast is celebrated. Ponies, blankets, and skins are then given to the dancers, and they are treated with all imaginable honours.

As an exhibition of human fortitude under privation and intense physical agony, the Sun Dance of the Sioux is perhaps unequalled in this age of the world. But it is very sad to have to record the continuance of ceremonies so barbarous and repulsive, in connection with religious belief or social life. Let us hope that these poor Sioux may come under the better teaching which has exerted a civilizing influence on other Indian nations.

The Hudson's Bay Fur-Hunters.

[OF LIFE AMONG THE FUR-HUNTERS OF THE NORTH-WEST, SOME INTERESTING GLIMPSES ARE AFFORDED IN THE FOLLOWING NARRATIVE OF AN ADVENTURE, IN TIMES BEFORE THE TIDE OF EMI-GRATION HAD SET TOWARDS LAKE WINNIPEG AND THE SASKATCHEWAN RIVER.]

OUR brigade of four boats lay moored on the banks of the great Saskatchewan; which river, taking its rise amid the rugged steeps of the Rocky Mountains, flows through the great prairies and woodlands of the interior of Rupert's Land, and discharges into Lake Winnipeg.

The men were ashore at breakfast. On a low gravelly point that jutted out into the stream, smoked three large fires, over which stood three rudely-constructed tripods, from which depended three enormous tin kettles. Robbiboo was the delectable substance contained in these kettles. Pemmican is a compound of dried buffalo meat, melted fat, and hair—the latter being an accidental ingredient. Mix pemmican with flour and water, boil and stir till it thickens, and the result will be "robbiboo."

Around these kettles stood, and sat, and reclined, and smoked, about thirty of the wildest and heartiest fellows that ever trod the wilderness. Most of them were French Canadians; many were half-breeds; some were Orkneymen, and one or two were the copper-coloured natives of the soil. But Canadians, Scotch, and Indians alike were servants of the Hudson's Bay Fur Company; they were all burned to the same degree of brownness by the summer sun; they all laughed and talked, and ate robbiboo more or less—generally more; and they were all clad in the picturesque habiliments of the north-west *voyageur*. A loose-fitting capote, with a hood

A bivouac on the Saskatchewan

hanging down the back; a broad scarlet or parti-coloured wor-sted sash round the waist; a pair of cloth leggings, sometimes blue, sometimes scarlet, occasionally ornamented with bright silk or bead-work, and gartered at the knees; a pair of chamois-lcather-like moccasins made of deer skin; a round bonnet, or a red nightcap, or a nondescript hat, or nothing: such is the outward man of the *voyageur.*

"Ho! ho!" shouted the gruff voice of the guide, as the men, having emptied the kettles, were hastily filling and lighting their pipes—"embark, my lads, embark."

In five minutes the boats were afloat, and the crews were about to shove off, when the cry was raised, "Mr. Berry! hold on; where's Mr. Berry?"

Poor Berry! he was always late, always missing, always in the wrong place at the right time and in the right place at the wrong time. His companions—of whom there were two in charge of the boats along with himself—called him an "old wife," but qualified the title with the remark that he was a "good soul," nevertheless. And so he was—a beardless youth of twenty-two summers, with a strong tendency to scientific pursuits, but woefully incompetent to use his muscles aright. He was for ever falling into the water, constantly cutting his fingers with his knife, and frequently breaking the trigger of his fowling-piece in his attempts to discharge it at half-cock. Yet he was incomparably superior to his more "knowing" comrades in all the higher qualities of intellect. At the moment his name was called, he sprang from the bushes, laden with botanical specimens, and, crying "Stop! stop! I'm coming," he rushed down to the boat of which he had the special charge, and leaped in. Five minutes more, and the brigade was sweeping down the Saskatchewan, while the men bent lustily to their oars, and filled the shrubbery on the river's bank and the wide prairies beyond with the ringing tones of one of their characteristic and beautiful canoe-songs.

The sun was flooding the horizon with gold, as it sank to rest. The chorus of the boatmen had ceased, and the only sound that broke the stillness of the quiet evening was the slow and regular stroke of the heavy oars, which the men plied unceasingly. On turning one of the bends of the river, which disclosed a somewhat extended vista ahead, several black objects were observed near the water's edge.

"Hist!" exclaimed the foremost guide, "they are buffaloes."

"A terre, à terre! "cried the men, in a hoarse whisper.

A powerful sweep of the steering oar sent the boat into a little bay, where it was quickly joined by the others.

"Now, then, let the crack shots be off into the bush," cried the gentleman in charge of the brigade. "Away with you, Gaspard, Antoine, Jacques. Mind you don't waste powder and shot on old bulls. Hallo! Mr. Berry, not so fast; let the hunters to the front."

"Ah! Misser Berry him berry bad shot," remarked a middle-aged Indian, regarding the youth somewhat contemptuously. Berry armed for the chase with frantic haste, dashing about and tumbling over everything in search of his powder-horn and shot-pouch, which were always mislaid, and moving the muzzle of his gun hither and thither in such a way as to place the lives of his men in constant and deadly peril. He started at last, with the speed of a hunted deer, and made a bold sweep into the woods in order to head the buffaloes. Here he squatted down behind a bush, to await their coming.

A short time sufficed to bring the stealthy hunters within range. Three shots were fired, and two animals fell to the ground; while a third staggered with difficulty after its companions, as they bounded through the woods towards the prairies, headed by the patriarchal bull of the herd. This majestic animal had a magnificently shaggy mane and a pair of wild glittering eyes, that would have struck terror into the stoutest heart; but Berry was short-sighted; moreover, he had concealed himself behind a shrub, through which, as he afterwards remarked, he "could see nicely." No doubt of it; but the bush was such a scraggy and ill-conditioned shrub, that the buffalo-bull could see through it just as nicely, and charged, with a hideous bellow, at the unfortunate youth as it came up the hill. Berry prepared to receive him. For once he remembered to cock his piece; for once his aim was true, and he hit the huge animal on the forehead at a distance of ten yards; but he might as well have fired against the side of a house; the thick skull, covered with its dense matting of coarse hair, was thoroughly ball-proof. The bull still came on. Just at this moment another shot was fired, and the animal hurled forward in a complete somersault; the bush was crushed to atoms, and Berry was knocked head-over-heels to the ground, where he lay extended at full length beside his slaughtered foe.

"Ah! pauvre enfant," cried Antoine, running up and lifting Berry's head from the ground. "Is you hurt ver' moch? Dat bull him break de ribs I'fraid."

Antoine's fears were groundless. In half an hour the youth was as well as ever, though somewhat shaken by the fall. The choice morsels of the dead buffaloes were cut off by the men with an adroit celerity that was quite marvellous, and in a very short time the boats were again rapidly descending the stream.

The bivouac that night resounded with more vigorous mirth than usual. The camp fires blazed with unwonted power and brilliancy. The cook's office—no sinecure at any time— became a post of absolute slavery; for there was a glorious feast held beneath the spreading trees of the forest, and the bill of fare was "buffalo-steaks and marrow-bones." But if the feast was noisy, the hours that succeeded it were steeped in profound silence. Each man, having smoked his pipe, selected for his couch the softest spot of ground he could find, and, wrapping himself in his blanket, laid him down to rest. The deep breathing of untroubled slumber was the only sound that floated from the land and mingled with the rippling of the river; and not a hand or foot was moved until, at daybreak, the loud halloo of the guide aroused the sleepers to their daily toil.

A week or two passed, and we had left the lands of the buffalo far behind us, and were sailing over the broad bosom of Lake Winnipeg. It was calm and polished as a sheet of glass when we entered it, but it did not remain long thus. A breeze arose, the sails were hoisted, and away we went out into the wide expanse of fresh water. Lake Winnipeg is a veritable ocean. Its waves rival those of the salt sea in magnitude, and they break upon a shore composed in many places of sand and pebbles. If we sail straight out upon it, the shore behind us sinks in the horizon, but no opposite shore rises to view, and the unbroken circle of sky and water is presented to our gaze, as it appears on the great ocean itself.

The wind rose almost to a gale as we careered over the billows, and the men had to keep up incessant baling. It was almost too much for us; but no one murmured, for, had the wind been ahead, we might have been obliged to put ashore and remain there inactive for many days. As it was, we made a rapid run across the lake and entered the river, or rather the system of lakes and rivers, which convey its waters to the ocean. Hudson's Bay was our goal. To this point we were conveying our furs for shipment to England.

Many days passed, and we were still pushing onwards towards the sea-coast; but not so rapidly now. The character of the navigation had changed very considerably, and our progress was much slower. Now we were sweeping over a small lake, anon dashing down the course of a turbulent stream, and at other times dragging boats and cargoes over the land.

One afternoon we came to a part of the river which presented a very terrible appearance. As far as the eye could reach, the entire stream was a boiling turmoil of rocks and rapids, down which a boat could have gone with as much safety as it could have leaped over the falls of Niagara. Our advance was most effectually stopped, as far as appearance went. But nothing checks the onward progress of a north-west *voyageur* except the want of food. The boats ran successively into a small bay, the men leaped out, the bales of furs were tossed upon the banks of the river, and the boats hauled up.

Then every man produced a long leathern strap, with which he fastened a bale weighing upwards of 90 lbs. to his back; above this he placed a bale of similar weight, and trotted off into the woods as lightly as if he had only been laden with two pillows. The second bale is placed above the first by a sleight-of-hand movement which is difficult to acquire. Poor Berry well-nigh broke his back several times in attempting this feat, and eventually gave it up in-despair.

In an hour the packs were carried over the portage, and deposited beside the still water at the foot of the rapids. Then the men returned for the boats. One was taken in hand at a time. The united crews seized the heavy craft with their strong hands, and shoved against it with their lusty shoulders; a merry song was struck up, and thus the boat was dragged through the forest for nearly a mile. The others quickly followed, and before evening all was carried over, and we were again rowing down stream.

Not long after this, we came to a rapid, in the midst of which was a slight water-fall. The water was deep here, and the rocks not numerous, and it was the custom to run the boats down the rapids and over the fall, in order to save the labour of a portage. Three of the boats ran down in grand style and reached the foot in safety. Berry and I were in the last boat. The steersman stood up in the stern with his hands resting on the long heavy sweep, while his gaze was directed anxiously towards the boiling flood into which we were just entering. The bowman, an immensely powerful man, stood up in front with a long strong pole grasped in both hands, ready to fend off from the sunken rocks. The men sat in their places with their oars ready for action.

"Now, boys, look out," cried the guide, as we plunged into the first billow of the rapids. The boat flew like an arrow straight towards a rock which was crested with white as the water burst against its ragged front. To all appearance our doom was scaled. The bowman regarded it with a complacent smile, and stood quite motionless, merely casting a glance backward. The steersman acknowledged the glance with a nod; one long stroke of the great oar; the boat turned sharply aside and swept past in safety. There was no danger in such a big blustering rock as that!

"Prenez garde," cried the bowman in a warning tone, pointing to a spot where lay a sunken rock. The steersman's quick hand turned the boat aside, but the bowman had to lend his aid, and the strong pole bent like a willow as he forced the boat's head away from the hidden danger. And now the fall appeared. It was not high, perhaps four feet, but there was a mighty gush of water there, and it was a bold leap for a heavy boat.

"Prenez garde, mes ganjons! hurrah! lads, give way! well done." The boat plunged almost bows under, but she rose again like a duck on the foaming water. The worst of it was past now; but there was still a ticklish bit below—a bend in the river, where the sunken rocks were numerous, and the surface of the water so white with foam that it was difficult to detect the channel. The bowman's duty now became more arduous. With knitted brows and compressed lips he stood, every nerve and muscle strung for instant action. The steersman watched his movements with intense earnestness, in order to second them promptly. Ever and anon the stout pole was plunged into the flood, first on one side, then on the other; the two guides acted as if they had been one man, and the obedient craft sprang from surge to surge in safety. Suddenly the bowman uttered a loud shout, as the pole jammed between two rocks and was wrenched from his grasp.

"Another! another! vite! vite!"

One of the crew thrust a fresh pole into his hand. Plunging it into the water, he exerted his giant strength with such violence as nearly to upset the boat, but it was too late. The planks crashed like an eggshell as the boat dashed upon a rock, and the water began to rush in, while the stern was swept round and the blade of the steering oar was smashed to atoms. Almost before we had time to think, we were swept down stern foremost, and floated safely into an eddy at the foot of the rapids. A few strokes of the oars brought us to the land; but short although the interval was between our striking the rock and running ashore, it was sufficient to half fill the boat with water.

The danger was barely past, and the intense feeling of it was still strong upon my mind, yet these light-hearted *voyageurs* were jesting and laughing loudly as they tossed the packs of furs out of the water-logged boat, so little did they realize the imminence of the peril from which they had been delivered—the shortness of the step that had separated them from the immediate presence of God.

The remainder of that day was spent in drying the furs that had been wetted, and in repairing the damaged boat. Afterwards we continued our voyage, which, without further accident, terminated at length on the shores of Hudson's Bay.

THE NARRATIVE PRESS
TRUE FIRST-PERSON HISTORICAL ACCOUNTS

THE HISTORICAL ADVENTURE AND EXPLORATION SERIES

The *Historical Adventure and Exploration Series* from The Narrative Press are all first-hand reports written by the explorers, pioneers, scientists, mountain men, prospectors, spies, lawmen, and fortune hunters themselves.

Most of these adventures are classics, about people and places now long gone. They take place all over the world – in Africa, South America, the Arctic and Antarctic, in America (in the Old West and before), on islands, and on the open seas.

Some of our authors are famous – Ernest Shackleton, Kit Carson, Henry Stanley, David Livingston, William Bligh, John Muir, Richard Burton, Elizabeth Custer, Teddy Roosevelt, Charles Darwin, Osborne Russell, John Fremont, Joshua Slocum, William Manley, Tom Horn, Philip St. George Cooke, Apsley Cherry-Garrard, Richard Henry Dana, Jack London, and Buffalo Bill, to name a few.

One thread binds all of our books: every one is historically important, and every one of them is fascinating.

Visit our website today. You can also call or write to us for a free copy of our printed catalogue.

THE NARRATIVE PRESS
P.O.BOX 2487
SANTA BARBARA, CALIFORNIA 93120 U.S.A.
(800) 315-9005
www.narrativepress.com